DATE DUE

MOTHER EARTH

MOTHER
▴ EARTH ▴

An American Story

SAM D. GILL

The University of Chicago Press
Chicago and London

SAM D. GILL is professor of religious studies at the University of Colorado, Boulder. He is the author of *Native American Religions, Beyond the "Primitive": Religions of Nonliterate Peoples,* and several other books on Native American religions.

The University of Chicago Press, Chicago 60637
The University of Chicago Press, Ltd., London

© 1987 by The University of Chicago
All rights reserved. Published 1987
Printed in the United States of America
96 95 94 93 92 91 90 89 88 87   54321

Library of Congress Cataloging-in-Publication Data
Gill, Sam D., 1943–
  Mother Earth.

  Bibliography: p.
  Includes index.
  1. Mother-goddesses—North America.   2. Earth—
Religious aspects.   3. Indians of North America—
Religion and mythology.   I. Title.
BL325.M6G54   1987   291.2′11   86-30711
ISBN 0-226-29371-8

For my parents
Lelah Grantham Gill
and
Chester Dale Gill
*in celebration of their
fifty years of marriage
commemorated
July 12, 1986*

Contents

Acknowledgments

In one way or another, many people have been involved in my study of Mother Earth, some in ways that they have not known. Years ago when I was a graduate student at the University of Chicago, one of my teachers, Jonathan Z. Smith, briefly mentioned a work of Olof Pettersson that critically evaluated Albrecht Dieterich's study of Mother Earth. Smith said that if Pettersson is correct, the whole Mother Earth concept is in question. That had little impact on me then, but years later when I found myself concerned about the existence of Mother Earth in North America, I read Pettersson's study and it gave me the motivation and courage to pursue research on the subject.

After several years of investigation, I had come to a point of difficulty in seeing how to present all of my findings positively and constructively. At that time I met Professor Wendy D. O'Flaherty and became acquainted with the stories she tells about the stories she studies. Though I discussed my research on Mother Earth with her only briefly, I began to see, in the light of Professor O'Flaherty's work, that the report on my research should tell the story of Mother Earth as she has appeared in North America.

I have presented lectures and papers drawn from this research on several occasions. These were trial balloons set aloft to test the weather. Most did not make it to much height before hitting storms of critical lightning. To those who invited me to make these presentations and for those many who loosed their thunder and lightning (and sometimes the hint that the skies would eventually clear), I express my sincere thanks. I made presentations at Wichita State University, Harvard Divinity School, a plenary session in Seattle of the Northwest Region of the American Academy of Religion, a plenary session in Vancouver of the Canadian Society for the Study of Religion, and Arizona State University.

I would like to thank my former colleagues at Arizona State University, especially Delwin Brown, Richard Martin, and James Foard. Though only the first stages of my research on Mother Earth were done while I was at Arizona State, I was much enriched by these friends who struggled with me through the times when we all were trying to figure out the study of religion and to find our roles in it, a process perhaps without end.

Over the years several of my students have assisted with research or taken a special interest in my research. I would like to thank Roxie McLeod, Frank Korom, and John Minear.

My thanks go also to my friend Thomas Parkhill for reading portions of the manuscript with care and for providing a key reference. The University of Colorado, Boulder, has provided much-appreciated research and typing support. I want to thank Frederick Denny and Rodney Taylor and Dean Everly Fleischer for making this support possible and Gladys Bloedow for typing the manuscript.

▲ 1 ▲

Mother Earth: The Story Begins

Mother Earth is one of the most well-known, firmly established, and emotion-laden figures in Native American religions. Many are familiar with the statement about the earth made a century ago by an Indian named Smohalla: "Shall I take a knife and tear my mother's bosom? . . . Shall I dig under her skin for bones? . . . how dare I cut off my mother's hair?"[1] Navajo tribal chairman Peterson Zah recently said, "The earth is our Mother. When we talk about development of our land which involves mining, we ask ourselves: 'How can we take from her face? . . . Can we do this much to our Mother?' "[2] According to Indian activist Russell Means, "Mother Earth will retaliate, the whole environment will retaliate, and the abusers will be eliminated."[3]

For more than a century scholars have documented Mother Earth as a major Native American goddess. Edward B. Tylor, the father of modern anthropology, wrote, "among the native races of America the Earth-mother is one of the great personages of mythology."[4] Very recently, Åke Hultkrantz, a major Swedish scholar on Native American religions, wrote: "The belief in a goddess, usually identified with Mother Earth, is found almost everywhere in North America."[5] Many other scholars have upheld this view.

Mother Earth is not only a Native American goddess but a goddess of peoples the world over and since great antiquity. Mother Earth's character and existence seem to be common knowledge, for

1

she is referred to casually in the most public of forums. For example, in a *Newsweek* (July 15, 1985) article, "A Scholar's Sacred Quest," an encomium of the remarkable career of Mircea Eliade, attention was drawn to his contribution to our understanding of Mother Earth.

> Particularly impressive is his analysis of how the invention of agriculture some 10,000 years ago was a revelation to man that the cosmos was a living organism, governed by repeated cycles of life and death. To understand and explain their world, those ancients developed images such as Mother Earth that have yet to be dislodged from human consciousness.[6]

Hultkrantz's study of the North American goddess begins with her emergence among hunting peoples at the end of the last Ice Age, some 25,000 years ago. In 1905, Albrecht Dieterich published a book on Mother Earth in which he documented her existence in cultures the world over, though the center of his interest was in the study of her existence in Roman religion.[7]

There has been uncontested agreement among Indians, scholars, and the general American populace that Mother Earth is a goddess widely known since great antiquity, one central especially to the religions of native North American peoples. Knowing this, I found it peculiar that references to Mother Earth, especially references to "our Mother Earth," began some years ago to bother me. It took me quite some time to become fully aware of the fact that I seemed in some way to be questioning the existence of this figure. It took me even longer to evaluate this reaction and to develop my responses positively and constructively.

As I analyzed it, my difficulties with Mother Earth were rooted in my understanding of Native American tribal traditions, whose diversity, complexity, and richness I greatly appreciate, an understanding I knew to be documented in an unmatched and unprecedented ethnographic and historical record as well as an abundance of living resources. My studies and experiences with Native American cultures and peoples had deeply impressed upon me how much more important it is to consider the distinctiveness of specific tribes than to attempt to distill some general commonalities among the hundreds of tribes spread throughout the continent. A simple illustration drawn from the southwestern United States demonstrates this perspective. There are many tribes living within the boundaries of the state of Arizona, but to summarize in terms of only three—Navajo, Hopi, and Yaqui—is sufficient.

The Navajos live widely dispersed, not in villages though sometimes now in towns. About a thousand years ago, along with the Apaches to whom they are related, the Navajos migrated into the region from northwestern Canada, where they were hunters. Their religious traditions center on healing and re-creative ritual processes focused largely on individuals and individually felt needs. Their neighbors, the Hopi, whom they physically surround, live concentrated in village clusters on mesa tops. They are ancient agriculturalists and seasonal hunters, and their religious traditions center on the growing cycle, with major community dances maintained and performed by societies. The Yaqui are recent residents of Arizona, having come northward from Sonora Mexico around the beginning of the century. Their major religious ceremonial performances have every appearance of being Christian, but more careful analysis shows that the Yaqui have skillfully and creatively appropriated Christian trappings to enhance religious beliefs and values that are in continuity with their traditions of many centuries ago.

In just these three among dozens of native cultures in the Southwest, there are two language families represented, three very different histories, three distinct material cultures and subsistence patterns, and three religious traditions whose similarities seem superficial when compared with their differences.

Consequently I have resisted and countered the common tendency to speak of "the Indian religion" (singular) and have stressed the variety, the distinctiveness, the complexity, and the sophistication of each tribal tradition, and often even of subtraditions within a tribe.[8] While there are comparative categories that apply to Native Americans at a level beyond the tribe, and most certainly there are categories in which to consider conjointly Native American religions with other religious traditions throughout the world and history (goddesses, femininity, and women and religion are among them), I have found no basis for conceiving of the religious traditions of the hundreds of tribes native to North America as a single, homogeneous tradition. Navajo, Hopi, and Yaqui religious traditions (and those of all culturally and religiously distinct peoples in the Americas) deserve the same attention, require the same attention to be adequately understood, as that given to other perhaps geographically more widespread religious traditions. While it may be impractical to study every Native American religious tradition (and to do so seriously is presently unlikely), the traditions of any tribe should be approached with the same dedication and seriousness with which any other religious tradition is approached, including the consideration of history, institutions, languages, cultures, practices, and beliefs.

In these views and convictions lies the reason for my experiencing

some discomfort and holding some reservations about statements of
the ubiquity and antiquity of Mother Earth, at least in North America. My studies of Native American tribal traditions made me familiar with a variety of female figures in story and ritual. To briefly
describe these figures for the Navajo, Hopi, and Yaqui will help to
illustrate.

First Woman is a major character in the extensive Navajo story-
tradition telling of the emergence journey of the Navajo's predecessors from below the earth to the present world. First Woman is a
leader, but not a creator. Ultimately she becomes associated with
malevolence, what Navajos call witchcraft, and she still functions in
this negative capacity from her home beneath the earth's surface.
One of the richest and most complex figures in all of Native American religions is the Navajo figure Changing Woman. She is inseparable from the creation of the Navajo world, though she is not a
cosmic creator. She created the first Navajo people from balls
rubbed from her skin which she mixed with corn meal. She established the way of life for Navajos. She undergoes cycles of change, as
her name suggests. She is time, the force of the temporal process.
She is life and the power of life. She is almost wholly benevolent, in
striking contrast with the dozens of other Navajo spiritual figures
who may harm as well as help Navajo people. She is the model for
women, but is not simply the patron of women. Presently she lives in
her home in the ocean to the west of the Navajo world. A full comprehension of Changing Woman would be coincident with comprehending the greatest depths of Navajo religion. The Navajo
Changing Woman is no doubt historically related to the Apache figure White Painted Lady, also known as Changing Woman and
White Beaded Lady. There are certain similarities, particularly in
terms of their roles in girls' puberty rites, although they are as distinct as are Navajos and Apaches.

The female figures of the Hopi are many. Corn girls and women
occupy a variety of roles. Spider Woman and Salt Woman are richly
developed in story tradition. They are the frequent concern of Hopis
throughout their daily lives. There are dozens of the distinct female
kachina figures whose presence at Hopi is familiar, from the powerful Crow Woman to various female clowns.

By the late nineteenth century, the Yaqui had centered one aspect
of their religious traditions upon the Virgin Mary, formally develop-
ing a cult of the Virgin. She is represented by wooden or plaster
images and by a rough cross of mesquite. In the spring these images
are dressed and ornamented in special devotion to her. The roots of
this cult clearly precede the introduction of the Christian elements.

Distinct and complex females can be easily found in many other tribes throughout North America. There are Thought Woman of the Keresan tribes, White Buffalo Calf Woman of the Sioux, Sedna and Selu of the Eskimo, the Woman-who-fell-from-the-sky of the Iroquoian tribes, and the corn women of southeastern tribes who are murdered in fear of their ways of producing corn by defecation. For all of these figures there are rich story-traditions and often significant ritual roles. Some of these figures are associated with the earth, others with the sky, the sea, plants, or animals. All of them are complex, and their characters are as distinctive as are the religious and cultural traditions of which they are a part.

In my attempts to confirm and verify the ubiquity and antiquity of Mother Earth I could call to mind only a few scant bits of possible evidence from tribal traditions. My knowledge of many tribal traditions was and remains superficial, but for all the tribes I knew, I could think of none that considered the earth as a major goddess. The most obvious evidence I could think of to support the existence of Mother Earth was the often-quoted statement of Smohalla, but even that statement was obviously made in response to pressure for change and, when considered carefully, is metaphorical rather than theological.

Systematically, I reviewed the ethnographic and scholarly literature on native North America. The ethnographic literature produced little, and it surprised me to find that, while the scholarly discussions of Mother Earth uniformly considered her to be universal among tribes and to have existed since great antiquity, the majority of the evidence used as the basis for these claims was the statement made by Smohalla, with an occasional reference to a statement made by the Shawnee leader Tecumseh. In fact, I found that both of these statements are frequently used as major references in studies of Mother Earth worldwide. The rare references to tribal traditions I found were largely limited to the Zuni of New Mexico and the Luiseño of southern California. I also began to discern that in the history of scholarship on Mother Earth in North America there is a heavy dependence upon a very few published sources; that is, most scholars who have written of Mother Earth in North America have depended upon other scholars and most of these have relied upon peculiar and highly limited secondary materials. Few of these scholars had actually studied Native American religions either from extensive examination of source materials or by personal research among Native Americans.

These findings were too remarkable for me to easily dismiss, though it seemed folly to question a figure like Mother Earth; her existence is confirmed by one and all without contest or controversy. Furthermore, the statements of contemporary Native Americans and numerous respected scholars, often made to the general public, must be taken with the utmost seriousness. Mother Earth is and has been a figure of much significance to all of these people, if not to the tribal traditions, and her existence must be recognized and comprehended. Yet, I could do so not by accepting the claims about Mother Earth as historically and ethnographically sound but finally only by comprehending how, given the divergence from the ethnographic and historical record, the present widespread views of Mother Earth have come about historically. An exhaustive search for Mother Earth among tribal traditions would offer no resolution. When a review of a score of major tribal traditions revealed numerous yet widely varying female figures but not Mother Earth, to continue searching for her in the ethnographic materials would not be fruitful; it would be simply irrelevant.

What I finally comprehended was that, to know Mother Earth, it is essential to learn and to tell her story. This would require the careful examination of the evidence from history and from the tribal cultures on which the discussion of Mother Earth has centered. To discern the story would require an examination of the interpretations of this evidence made by scholars. To comprehend the fullest extent of the story would require a study of the impact all of this has had on the history of Native American cultures and religions and on the responses and interpretations Native Americans have themselves made.

As I have come to know it, the story of Mother Earth is a distinctively American story. Mother Earth, as she has existed in North America, cannot be adequately understood and appreciated apart from the complex history of the encounter between Native Americans and Americans of European ancestry, nor apart from comprehending that the scholarly enterprise that has sought to describe her has had a hand in bringing her into existence, a hand even in introducing her to Native American peoples.

The American story of Mother Earth has many episodes and these can conveniently be told separately, chapter by chapter, though each builds upon and clarifies those told before.

The story begins with a statement attributed to the Shawnee, Tecumseh, who reportedly said in 1810 during a meeting with William H. Harrison, "The earth is my mother and on her bosom I will repose." This is the earliest statement cited as evidence for the Native American religious belief in Mother Earth, but when it is placed in the broader historical context the statement stands in the midst of a story of imagining America that began as early as 1575 and is still in progress. This story episode overlaps with the story of the famed statement of Smohalla uttered around 1885. The story that turns about Smohalla's statement spans the entire nineteenth century and it too is inseparable from the history of encounter.

Two tribal cultures, the Zuni and Luiseño, are the ones most commonly cited as evidence for the existence of Mother Earth in tribal traditions, though they are by no means the only cultures in which female figures have been identified as Mother Earth. Each of these cultures, and their religious traditions, conjoined with the story of the scholarly interpretations of them that focused upon Mother Earth, become two more episodes of the Mother Earth story.

With these several story episodes told, it becomes clear that Mother Earth has come into existence in America largely during the last one hundred years and that her existence stems primarily from two creative groups: scholars and Indians. These two story episodes, although they clearly interact, are presented separately here.

When her story is told, it becomes clear how all Americans, whatever their heritage, may proclaim Mother Earth to be the mother of us all, but as in any good story there are quite a few surprises and when the telling is complete there is still much to ponder.

▲ 2 ▲

"On her bosom I will repose"

"The earth is my mother—and on her bosom I will repose," is a statement attributed to Tecumseh, spoken during a meeting in 1810 with General William H. Harrison. The meeting was in the Indiana territorial capital, Vincennes, and dealt with the settlement of the lands along the Wabash River.[1] By the end of the nineteenth century this statement became a principal piece of evidence used to document the widespread belief among Native Americans in a goddess named "Mother Earth."

There is much more to the statement than appears on the surface. I have found the statement to be the nexus of a number of interwoven stories, stories that must be told.

The Vincennes Meeting

The treaty negotiated by Harrison with the Indians in a meeting at Fort Wayne in 1809 is a point at which the telling of one of these stories may begin. In 1809, Tecumseh was visiting Iroquois tribes in an attempt to persuade them to join his growing alliance of Indians from many tribes, a coalition to stem the United States program of territorial expansion and thereby to protect coveted native lands. To Fort Wayne Harrison called representatives of a number of tribes then living along the upper Wabash River on lands very desirable for settlement. In their meeting, Harrison gained an agreement in which

8

these tribes would forfeit to the U.S. government the lands along the river—some three million acres—thus opening them to settlement, in exchange for specified goods and annuities in the amount of $10,000.

When Tecumseh learned of the treaty, he was deeply angered, and he threatened to kill the chiefs who had signed the treaty. He immediately set upon a course to seek revocation of the treaty. The importance of the issue was widely felt, and this contributed to a broad development of support for Tecumseh's efforts among members of various tribes in the area—Kickapoo, Potawatomie, Winnebagos, and Shawnee, later to be joined by the Wyandots, Sauk, and Fox. The Wabash River was the last barrier to settlement east of the Mississippi and south of the Great Lakes. These Native Americans perceived that this was their last stand against the United States. It had to be made immediately or all would be lost.

Harrison's sources informed him of the possibility of a general massacre, and he began to take steps to assure compliance with the terms of the treaty and to establish his own military forces to protect settlers and to counter any native military efforts. Harrison and Tecumseh (as well as the latter's brother, Tenskwatawa, the Shawnee Prophet) engaged in an extensive encounter initiated primarily by Harrison. Tecumseh countered Harrison's conciliatory messages with curt or militant responses. Tecumseh forcefully rejected annuities that were to be distributed according to the treaty arrangements. Encouragements to relocate to the west were sent to the Indians along with promises that annuities would follow. These too were ignored. Finally, Harrison tried one other tactic to remove the Shawnee and his followers from the land. He sent a message to the Prophet by Harrison's most trusted interpreter, Joseph Barron, seeking a meeting with the Shawnee leader and requesting that he present any proof that the Shawnee held ownership to the land that had been the subject of the Fort Wayne treaty negotiations. Harrison, of course, knew that they could not possibly present any acceptable documentation or basis for such a claim, and held to the evidence that the aboriginal lands of the Shawnee were in Georgia. He naively hoped this tactic would silence the Shawnee in their claims to the land and that he would finally succeed in the removal of these Indian holdouts.

Barron delivered the message to the Prophet, who reportedly associated Barron with a string of "spies" that had been sent by Harrison and was prepared to kill him. But Tecumseh intervened and received the message himself. He agreed to go to Vincennes to meet with Harrison.

Tecumseh wished to present his understanding of ownership of land to Harrison. In the face of the loss of tribal lands, Tecumseh had come to articulate the philosophy that land was the common property of all the tribes, even though certain tribes lived upon particular land areas. A summary of this point of view can be found in the record that Barron made of his conversations with Tecumseh during the trip on which he arranged the meeting with Harrison. Barron reported to Harrison what Tecumseh had said:

> The Great Spirit said he gave this great island to his red children. He placed the whites on the other side of the big water. They were not contented with their own, but came to take ours from us. They have driven us from the sea to the lakes. We can go no farther. They have taken upon themselves to say this tract belongs to the Miami, this to the Delawares, and so on. But the Great Spirit intended it as the common property of all the tribes, nor can it be sold without the consent of all. Our father tells us we have no business on the Wabash; the land belongs to other tribes. But the Great Spirit ordered us to come here and we shall stay.[2]

The philosophy of land ownership would be the issue central to the meetings at Vincennes. Neither party was prepared to comprehend the position of the other, as is evident in the records of the meetings. And, of course, there was never any real possibility that Tecumseh's efforts would reverse the treaty so that the Indians might remain on the land. Nonetheless, the meetings had major significance. They attest to the courage and character of Tecumseh, who was increasingly to become a heroic figure in the eyes of both Native Americans and European-Americans. Later in the nineteenth and early twentieth centuries the development of pantribal alliances in the movement of Indian resistance to American demands for lands looked to Tecumseh both as a model and for inspiration. Tecumseh's statement also came to play an important role in the development of the broadly held notion that the land is mother to the Indians.

For Harrison the Vincennes meetings crystallized his policy toward the Indians. He put that policy into action in the battle of Tippecanoe, very likely planned to take place while Tecumseh was away. Tippecanoe became the hallmark of Harrison's character and capabilities and contributed to his being elected president of the United States.

It was a great show of courage for Tecumseh to go to Vincennes. He knew that the territorial capital had been secured by a military buildup. Tecumseh, accompanied by at least 300 warriors, arrived in eighty canoes on the Wabash on Saturday, August 11, 1810. They were dressed as warriors and wore vermillion war paint. They set up camp and spent two days preparing for the meetings. There were preliminary negotiations about how many warriors were to accompany Tecumseh to the governor's newly built mansion, Grouseland, and what arms they would bear.

It was not until Tuesday afternoon, August 14, that Tecumseh and his delegation arrived for the first meeting with Harrison. In preparation for the meetings, Harrison had placed a canopy over an arbor that adjoined a small veranda on the southwest side of the mansion. Herein chairs had been arranged for the principals as well as for a number of dignitaries that he had invited to witness the meeting. The first meeting was the setting for the statement Tecumseh is said to have made. At this point we must consider the evidence on which the historical accuracy of this statement may be determined.

No official record was made of the speeches and proceedings at Grouseland, perhaps because this was not an official treaty negotiation but, rather, discussions designed to lead to the accomplishment of the Fort Wayne Treaty already signed. Harrison himself provided documentation of the meetings through a series of letters he wrote during the meetings to the secretary of war, William Eustis.

In a letter dated August 22, 1810, Harrison described the early meetings with Tecumseh. The letter makes no reference to the famed statement, nor even the slightest allusion to the incident. Harrison wrote only that "his [Tecumseh's] speeches the two first days were sufficiently insolent and his pretensions arrogant, but that of Monday I enclose to you entire."[3] Of all the bits of evidence that were written at the time of the meetings to document what happened, this reference by Harrison to Tecumseh's insolence and arrogance is as close to firm historical documentation of the statement as exists.

Surprisingly, the first written source for the statement is an account published on May 12, 1821, in the *National Recorder*. Many others soon followed. But much happened in the period between 1810 and 1821. That segment of the story needs to be told before these many accounts are considered.

Tippecanoe, the War of 1812, and the Aftermath

The failure of the 1810 meetings became evident by the following spring, as Tecumseh and his followers, encouraged by the British in Canada, plundered the houses of settlers and were a menacing pres-

ence throughout the area. War with the Indians seemed inevitable to
Harrison, so in the early summer of 1811 he sent a message to
Tecumseh and Tenskwatawa warning them of the outcome if they
did not cease their warlike actions. Tecumseh agreed to again visit
Harrison at Vincennes and did so in late July. After a repeat performance of the previous summer's meetings, Tecumseh left, heading
south to visit the Creeks, Choctaws, and Chickasaws in an effort to
win them to his alliance.

With Tecumseh away, Harrison took a stronger stand with the
tribes in the region of the Wabash River, and this led to the battle of
Tippecanoe which Harrison used effectively to demonstrate the
firmness and decisiveness with which he acted not only toward Indians but toward any obstacles in the advancement of the American
destiny.

When Tecumseh returned, the situation he found forced him to
abandon his policy of neutrality between American and British interests in the region. He joined forces with the British, who held out
the promise that, with the help of his Indian alliance, they might
recover the region from the Americans. The British indicated that,
upon their success, they would return portions of the land to the
Indians.

Without recounting the history of Tecumseh's relationships with
the British, especially the military leaders, it is sufficient to say that
Tecumseh distinguished himself as a leader, warrior, statesman, and
orator. Many are the stories of his courage, leadership (especially
noticeable compared with the failure of certain British leaders), and
his humanity.

The British-Indian alliance was not adequate to overcome the
American forces, and finally Harrison's troops decided the issue in a
battle fought on October 5, 1813, along the Thames River north of
Lake Erie. The British commander, Henry Procter, reportedly failed
to show any leadership or military knowledge in preparing for Harrison's attack. The result of his ineffectiveness was the flight of many
British soldiers at Harrison's attack, leaving Tecumseh and his band
of Indians to fight the battle. Many are the accounts of Tecumseh's
bravery and leadership during this battle that lasted throughout the
night. By morning Tecumseh was nowhere to be found. It is likely
that he was killed in battle and his body removed by Indians, but
mystery has surrounded his death ever since.[4]

The heroism, bravery, and humanity of Tecumseh were quickly
appreciated by Americans. After the War of 1812, Indians in the
region ceased to be a problem to settlement. A new mood evolved in

which the passing Indian and Indian way of life were lauded and highly romanticized. Being a figure of such stature, mystery, and color, Tecumseh became a focal point for the expression of these new American sympathies. Many cities were quickly proclaimed as the birthplace of Tecumseh. It was suggested that the capital city of the new state of Indiana be named after Tecumseh. A letter to the *Indiana Centinel* at Vincennes published December 2, 1820, supported this action, noting that "every schoolboy in the Union now knows that Tecumseh was a great man. He was truly great—and his greatness was his own, unassisted by science or the aids of education. As a statesman, a warrior and a patriot, take him all in all, we shall not look upon his like again."[5] Sherman, the great Civil War general, was born in Lancaster, Ohio, on February 8, 1820, whereupon he was named "William Tecumseh" by his father Charles, who greatly admired the Indian.[6]

The period of time between the 1810 meeting and the first published appearance of Tecumseh's statement that was attributed to that meeting was a period of many changes and transformations. In 1816, Indiana had become a state, partly due to the outcome of the War of 1812. The Indians had been removed from the land so that settlement was well in progress. In the eyes of the Americans, Tecumseh had been transformed from the obstacle to land settlement and the thorn in Harrison's side into a widely known heroic figure. Tecumseh was nothing short of being a folk hero.[7] It is essential that these transformations be fully understood as the historical context in which we must examine the many documents that report Tecumseh saying to Harrison, "The earth is my mother and on her bosom I will repose."

Documentary Evidence for the Statement

The documentary evidence that emerges, beginning in the 1820s, is of primarily two types, although these soon become interwoven. One important type is histories for this area written during the period. Most include an account of the Harrison-Tecumseh meeting of 1810. The first such account was written by Moses Dawson and was published in 1824. Many more soon followed. The other major type of documentation comprises journalistic, literary, and other more or less popular publications. These references to Tecumseh's statement invariably use it to attest to the character and stature of Tecumseh the folk hero. A chronological examination of these accounts, especially the first several, is revealing. In total, I have found twenty-

seven accounts of this meeting that present or allude to Tecumseh's
"the earth is my mother" statement.

The *National Recorder* account, published on May 12, 1821, is
but a short filler piece set near the back of the magazine. It is entitled
"Tecumseh." The bulk of the piece is the story of the Tecumseh-
Harrison meeting. It attributes the statement to the 1811 meetings
rather than the 1810 meetings. The description of the exchange is as
follows:

> It was in the progress of the long *talks* which took place in the con-
> ference, that Tecumseh having finished one of his speeches, looked
> round, and seeing everyone seated, while no seat was prepared for
> him, a momentary frown passed over his countenance. Instantly, gen-
> eral Harrison ordered that a chair should be given him. Some person
> presented one, and bowing, said to him—"Warrior, your father, gen-
> eral Harrison offers you a seat." Tecumseh's dark eye flashed. "My
> father!" he exclaimed, indignantly, extending his arm toward the
> heavens; "the sun is my father, and the earth is my mother; she gives
> me nourishment, and I repose upon her bosom." As he ended, he sat
> down suddenly on the ground.[8]

In 1821, Henry Rowe Schoolcraft traveled through Indiana collecting information about a variety of things, from mineral resources
to aboriginal peoples. In his account of these travels, published in
1825, Schoolcraft presents a biographical account of Tecumseh in a
section entitled "Observations at Tippecanoe." This biography concludes with some anecdotes to illustrate the character of Tecumseh.
Schoolcraft writes,

> The spirit and fearless energy of this man's character shone through-
> out all his actions. In one of the councils held by Gen. Harrison with
> the Indians at Vincennes, previous to the commencement of hostili-
> ties in 1811, in which Tecumseh was present, this chief, on conclud-
> ing a long and animated speech, found himself unprovided with a
> seat. When this neglect was observed, Gen. Harrison directed a chair
> to be placed for him, and requested him to sit down. "Your father,"
> said the Interpreter, "requests you to take a chair." "*My* father!" re-
> plied the haughty chief, "the *Sun* is my father, and the *Earth* is my
> mother, and on *her* bosom I will repose." So saying he sat down
> suddenly, in the Indian manner.[9]

These two accounts are remarkably similar, so much so as to suggest that one is dependent upon the other. Schoolcraft dates the
meetings as "previous to the commencement of hostilities in 1811,"
a vague reference referring either to the spring hostilities of 1811,

that is, the talks of 1810, or to the battle of Tippecanoe in November 1811, which would be the 1811 talks. The *National Recorder,* however, dates the talks as taking place in 1811. While the *National Recorder* account was published prior to Schoolcraft's account, it was not published prior to Schoolcraft's travels through the Indiana Territory in 1821. This suggests that Schoolcraft was perhaps the author of the *National Recorder* piece or that Schoolcraft's manuscript descriptions of Tecumseh were the source for the *National Recorder* account.

Whatever the case, what first emerges in print regarding Tecumseh's statement is clearly not a historical document but a legend told of a folk hero enormously popular at the time. Neither account is concerned about the actual meeting between Harrison and Tecumseh. They are interested in attesting to the remarkable character of Tecumseh, to what Schoolcraft called "the spirit and fearless energy" of the man. Tecumseh's alleged statement is the more powerful when addressed to Harrison.

The version of the legend demonstrated in these accounts is distinguished by its attribution of the motivation for Tecumseh's speech to the oversight of not providing him with a chair. This is conjoined with the use of the term "your father" to describe the relationship of Harrison to Tecumseh. Such a term was commonly used in United States negotiations with Indians. It reflects the paternalistic attitude the government assumed toward Native Americans.

Moses Dawson's book, published in 1824, provides a careful historical examination of Harrison and the nature of his relationship with Tecumseh and his brother. Dawson was the editor of the *Cincinnati Advertiser.* The book's title reflects the sympathies and intentions of the author as standing with Harrison and defending him against the shadows falling upon him from the heroic heights being then attained by Tecumseh. Dawson claimed to have worked personally with Harrison in the preparation of the book and to have used "original and authentic documents furnished by many of the most respectable characters in the United States." The full title of Dawson's book is *Historical Narrative of the Civil and Military Services of Major-General William H. Harrison, and a Vindication of his Character and Conduct as a Statesman, a Citizen, and a Soldier, with a Detail of his Negotiations and Wars with the Indians, until the Final Overthrow of the Celebrated Chief Tecumseh, and his Brother The Prophet.*

Dawson's intent was to vindicate Harrison, but he attempted to do so by the method of history. His book provides extensive details of the historical events. While his commentary needs to be viewed in the light of his intentions, the historical details of his account are perhaps as nearly based on eyewitnesses and participants as any that exist. He describes the Vincennes meeting as occurring in an atmosphere of considerable tension. Tecumseh came to Vincennes with hundreds of painted warriors. Dawson indicates that much discussion took place about what arms were to be acceptable, and it appears that neither party trusted the other. This tension and mistrust is apparent in Dawson's description of the setting for the first meetings.

> A general invitation was therefore given to all those who chose to attend. The judges, of the supreme court, the secretary of the territory, many officers of the army, and a large number of the citizens, were accordingly present. They were all seated, many of them upon chairs and benches, around the Governor, and Tecumseh, with the Indians upon the grass, immediately before him. At a small distance to the left the Potawatamie chief, Winemack, lay extended on the grass with one of his young men near him. To this chief the Governor had a few days before presented a pair of pistols, which he had asked for, to defend himself, as he said, against the assassination which was meditated upon him by Tecumseh and his followers.[10]

According to Dawson, Tecumseh made an opening speech in which he dwelt upon the injustice of Harrison's land policies and treaty negotiations. When Harrison began his speech in response, "Tecumseh arose, and began to speak with great vehemence." This aroused the governor and his party who apparently feared that Tecumseh was about to do violence on them. The Potawatamie chief Winemack was observed preparing his pistols, and one of Harrison's generals called up the guard for protection. "The Governor then addressing Tecumseh, told him that he was a bad man and that he would hold no further communication with him—that, as he had come there under the protection of the council fire, he might go in safety, but he must immediately leave the neighborhood."[11]

Dawson comments on this situation after describing how Tecumseh apologized to Harrison and assured him he would act more properly thereafter:

> It is very difficult to determine, whether it was really the intention of Tecumseh to commit any violence upon the Governor. There are certainly some circumstances tending to show that he had meditated some improper act. He had violated his positive promise, made to captain Wilson, to bring but a small number of warriors with him to

the council, and it was remarked that all those he did bring with him, were uncommonly well armed. His refusal to hold the council in the portico of the Governor's house, which had been prepared for the occasion, was evidence that he either meditated or feared some fraud or treachery. He said, indeed, that the earth was the most proper place for the Indians, as they liked to repose upon the bosom of their mother; but no such objection had ever been made before, nor did he make it upon a subsequent occasion, but used the benches which had been provided for them. It is probably that some mistake had been made, in giving the signal for the rising of his men; or, that they had been intimidated after rising, but seeing the guard at a short distance, which they could not see before they rose.[12]

Dawson's comments are illuminating. He describes the common difficulties of any negotiations in which the setting and rules reflect the relationships of power between the negotiating parties. There is also evidence of a mutual concern about security. Even Dawson's comments about where Tecumseh preferred to sit are significant. The phrase "to repose upon the bosom of their mother," as describing, in Tecumseh's terms, where he wished to sit, seems to puzzle Dawson, since apparently the balance of his sources indicated that Tecumseh sat upon benches at all of the other meetings. Since it was Dawson's intention to vindicate Harrison's character against the popular views of the day, it seems quite likely that he is not reporting an eyewitness acount by including Tecumseh's alleged statement, but rather is calling into question the statements so common in the popular lore of the day with the contrary evidence of his historical sources.

Dawson, by giving close attention to the historical documents of the Tecumseh-Harrison meeting, was drawn to comment upon the strategies and dynamics of negotiations and to attempt to explain the failures of the first meetings. In this focus, Tecumseh's "the earth is my mother" statement is seen not as religious, or as evidence of Tecumseh's character, but simply as a hitch in the negotiations. Dawson considered the statement only in terms of the physical setting for the negotiations and saw it as an infelicity, for he knew that on no other occasion did Tecumseh refuse to sit on the benches provided. Others at this time understood Tecumseh's statement in very different terms, as is evident from the appearance of the statement in literary works beginning in the mid-1820s.

From the early 1790s well into the nineteenth century poetry and drama about Indians were very popular.[13] As early as 1766 Indians had been portrayed in American drama, but the period from the

mid-1820s until shorty after 1840 was an especially enthusiastic one
in terms of the theatrical portrayal of Indians.

The first American drama depicting primarily Indians was written
by Major Robert Rogers in 1766. It was *Ponteach, or the Savages of
America.* This play was not highly regarded for its dramatic art, but it
is of interest as a literary precedent for a play written in 1826 by
Alexander Malcomb, dedicated to the governor of the Michigan Territory, that centered on the 1763 siege of Detroit by Pontiac. The
play, called *Pontiac; or the Siege of Detroit,* was based on historical
accounts of the event with the exception, acknowledged by the author, of the final scene depicting the capture and death of Pontiac.
The play was published finally in 1835. The final scene is notable for
our concerns because this fictional conclusion borrows from the
popular legend of Tecumseh's encounter with Harrison. The scene
takes place after the British have overcome the Indians and made
peace with them. Pontiac had earlier been captured and imprisoned.
The Indians, now at peace, have come to ask for Pontiac's release.
This is the scene.

> COL. GLADWIN *(British officer)*: Adjutant! cause Pontiac to
> be released and conducted to this assembly. *(The Adj. rises
> and makes his exit R. H., and returns with Pontiac in chains.
> All the Indians are seated, and there is no place for Pontiac.)*
> OTSCHEO *(an Indian)*: Pontiac! there's your father *(pointing
> to Gladwin)*.
> PONTIAC: My father! I have no father but the Sun—no
> mother but the Earth. She feeds me, she clothes me. I shall
> recline upon her bosom. *(He throws himself at full length on
> the stage.)*

The conclusion is a sad one. Pontiac refuses to sign the peace treaty
and is subsequently murdered by the Indian chiefs as a necessary
sacrifice for peace. Upon stabbing Pontiac, Agushaway proclaims,
"There is a sacrifice, to our country's peace, of one of the bravest
warriors and most consummate Chiefs."[14]

While of no greater literary merit than the earlier play by Rogers,
this play was popular and successful. It ran successfully at the National Theater in Washington in 1838 and included the participation
of the United States Marine Corps.[15]

Other literary works of the period include the Tecumseh statement or they allude to it and attribute it to Tecumseh. In the preface
to James S. French's novel *Elkswatawa or, The Prophet of the West*
(1836), which is about the prophet brother of Tecumseh, French

lauds Indian people generally. He found them eloquent in public speaking, and in testimony wrote, "the answer of Tecumseh to Gen. Harrison, when offered a seat by him at the council, will compare with any reply in ancient or modern history."[16]

Dr. William Emmons published in 1836 a five-act play he described as "a national drama," called *Tecumseh: or the Battle of the Thames.* In 1822 he had written a pamphlet on the subject, and in 1827 a long poem on the War of 1812. In the drama he has Tecumseh respond to an incidental mention of the name of Harrison, "Harrison! I met him once in council. He said—'Tecumseh, sit thou here beside me.' He was my foe. Me scorned his offer,—on my mother's breast—the earth—I rested me my limbs."[17]

We may begin to see the character that distinguishes these more folkloric and literary references to Tecumseh's statement to Harrison. They are placed loosely, if at all, in historical context. The motivating issue is greatly simplified from the concern over council settings to the matter of manners and courtesy. They are invariably dramatic in presentation, with the statement presented as a direct speech or quotation, with stage directions (such as the way Tecumseh looked, held his hand, or sat on the ground), and highly conventionalized in terms of phrasing and even interruptions of the speech to present stage directions and to identify Tecumseh as speaker.

Another biography of Harrison, written by James Hall, was published in Cincinnati in 1836. It includes an account of Harrison's meeting with Tecumseh, but Hall adds a dimension of the Tecumseh legends that was not present in Dawson's earlier account. He describes the setting in which Tecumseh approaches the awaiting governor and says that Tecumseh, upon being asked

> to take a seat, refused, observing that he wished the council to be held under the shade of some trees in front of the house. When it was objected that it would be troublesome to remove the seats, he replied, "that it would only be necessary to remove those intended for the whites—that the red men were accustomed to sit upon the earth, which was their mother, and that they were always happy to recline upon her bosom."[18]

Two things are notable here. First, Hall transforms the motivation for the statement; for the absence of a chair conjoined with the reference to Harrison as his "father," he substitutes the inconvenience of moving chairs from the portico to a grove of trees. This suggests a second version of the legend of Tecumseh's encounter with Harrison, a fuller account of which I will present shortly. The second notable aspect of Hall's statement is his use of quotation marks to set off this portion of the account. Hall precedes the quotation marks with the attribution of a quotation to Tecumseh (indicated by "he replied"), although the wording that follows is not in the style of a direct quotation but rather describes what Tecumseh said. I would submit that this confusion of style directly reflects a confusion between the legendary accounts of Tecumseh and history. Hall is simply so familiar with the story of this encounter and the style in which it is presented that he cannot present it otherwise, even when he is writing not as a dramatist or storyteller but as a historian.

Evidence that a second version of the story was widely known is its appearance in *The Legislator,* a newspaper published at Georgetown, Ohio, in Brown County. On June 12, 1832, the following account appeared.

> The portico of the Governor's house had been selected for the meeting of the council. After the party had appeared, Tecumseh objected to the place, and proposed to adjourn to the yard in front of the house. One of the Governor's aids remarked that it would be troublesome to find seats enough for all the party. Tecumseh replied there would be seats enough for all the whites, and that earth was the most proper place for the Indians, as they liked to repose on the bosom of their mother. The meeting was adjourned to the open air.

This newspaper account was one of the sources for Benjamin Drake's 1841 biography of Tecumseh. Drake wrote many books on Indians, and his work on Tecumseh, entitled *Life of Tecumseh, and His Brother The Prophet,* is a standard biography. A handwritten copy of the account from *The Legislator* is in Drake's papers. Drake's account develops even further along the lines drawn by Dawson and Hall, especially in terms of its literary style.

> At the appointed hour Tecumseh, supported by forty of his principal warriors, made his appearance, the remainder of his followers being encamped in the village and its environs. When the chief had approached within thirty or forty yards of the house, he suddenly stopped, as if awaiting some advances from the governor. An interpreter was sent requesting him and his followers to take seats on the portico. To this Tecumseh objected—he did not think the place a suitable one for holding the conference, but preferred that it should take place in a grove of trees,— to which he pointed,— standing a short distance from the house. The governor said he had no objection to the grove, except that there were no seats in it for their accommodation. Tecumseh replied, that constituted no objection to the

grove, the earth being the most suitable place for the Indians, who loved to repose upon the bosom of their mother. The governor yielded the point, and the benches and chairs having been removed to the spot, the conference was begun, the Indians being seated on the grass.[19]

Drake drops the quotation marks yet retains the conventional introduction "Tecumseh replied," even set off by a comma, and the conventional phrasing "repose upon the bosom of their mother."

Later historians and biographers tended to maintain the line established by the earlier histories and biographies. Their treatment of this incident is characterized by their emphasis upon the logistics of the meetings, most commonly on the arrangement of seating as the motivation for the statement of Tecumseh.[20]

Popular interest in the Tecumseh legend continued throughout the balance of the nineteenth century and on into the present century. For example, in 1840 the story appears in the *Southern Literary Messenger*.[21] It is in Samuel Drake's *The Book of the Indians* (1841), in which Schoolcraft is credited as the source.[22] It is in the *Ladies Wreath* in 1850[23] and in a travel column in the *Chicago Tribune* in 1886.[24] Ethel T. Raymond's biography *Tecumseh: A Chronicle of the Last Great Leader of His People* includes the statement.[25] A book about the Wabash River published in 1940 includes the legend.[26] This is but a small sample of the many appearances of the story in print.

Several other appearances are important and need to be considered in more detail.

One particular account of the Tecumseh statement to General Harrison is distinguished for being one of the principal sources cited by E. B. Tylor in 1873 in support of his contention that "the idea of the Earth as a mother is more simple and obvious, and no doubt for that reason more common in the world, than the idea of Heaven as a father."[27] This is the version appearing in Josiah Gregg's book *Commerce of the Prairies* published in 1844. Gregg was a physician who traveled to the western prairies to seek relief from ill health. His first journey was taken in 1831, and he returned in 1833 and again in 1836. He kept journals of daily occurrences and interests, and these journals were the basis for *Commerce of the Prairies*. The work was republished many times and appeared in a German translation in 1845. It is both as documentation of the extent to which the story was told in the 1830s and as the basis for a fuller appraisal of one of the principal sources for our later concerns with scholarly views that I recount Gregg's version in full. The context for Gregg's account,

interestingly enough, is his discussion of religion among the Indians.
He writes, "there are very few but profess a faith in some sort of First
Cause—a Great Spirit, a Master of Life, who rules the destinies of
the world." Gregg notes that with few exceptions the Indians tend to
identify this figure with the sun. He then moves to a discussion of
the Shawnee:

> But of all the Indian tribes, none appear to have ascribed to the
> "fountain of light" more of the proper attributes of deity than the
> Shawnees. They argue, with some plausibility, that the sun animates
> everything—therefore, he is clearly the Master of Life, or the Great
> Spirit; and that everything is produced originally from the bosom of
> the earth—therefore, she is the mother of creation. The following
> anecdote (as told to me by a gentleman of integrity), which transpired
> upon the occasion of an interview of Tecumseh with Gen. Harrison, is
> as illustrative of the religious opinions of the Shawnees, as it is char-
> acteristic of the hauteur and independent spirit of that celebrated
> Shawnee chief. The General, having called Tecumseh for a "talk,"
> desired him to take a seat, saying, "Come here, Tecumseh, and sit by
> your father." "You my father?" replied the chief, with a stern air—
> "No! yonder sun is my father (pointing towards it), and the earth is
> my mother; so I will rest on her bosom"—and immediately seated
> himself upon the ground, according to Indian custom.[28]

In a footnote Gregg indicated that he had seen the same incident
recounted in Schoolcraft's work.

Of further interest is the fact that Gregg's statement, contrary to
the assessment of it given by Tylor, very clearly indicates a primacy
and superiority to the sun as "the Master of Life." But even more
important is Gregg's comment on and presentation of the statement
of Tecumseh. Up to this time, the statement had been cited as evidence of Tecumseh's character; here, for the first time, it is made to
document the nature of his religion. Gregg's knowledge of the religion of the Shawnee is scant and anecdotally based, being learned,
supposedly, from "a gentleman of integrity." The clear continuity
with the legendary and theatrical versions widely published before
Gregg's account is evident—the direct quotation of Tecumseh's
statement, the interruption for stage direction, and the conventional
wording. The conventional style of presentation casts a shadow
upon Gregg's "gentleman of integrity." The utilization of the story
as evidence of the nature of Shawnee religion, however, appears to
be the invention of Gregg, though it is clearly an incidental, almost
an offhand, remark. That it should serve later as it did for Tylor and
for the many who followed his lead and used his evidence to estab-

lish Mother Earth in North America, is another story and one that I will tell in some detail in a later chapter.

Two other accounts are notable in claiming to be those of eyewitnesses. These must be carefully considered. In the late nineteenth century, Lyman D. Draper was associated with the State Historical Society of Wisconsin. He had a long and tireless interest in Tecumseh and pursued information about him from every source and in every possible regard.[29] Early in 1885 Draper corresponded with Francis V. LeSieur about Tecumseh. Mr. LeSieur indicated that his father-in-law, Augustus Jones, had been in the Indiana territory during the early part of the century and doubtless knew something of Tecumseh. Draper immediately wrote to Jones. Jones's response is dated February 4, 1885. The only information that he advances about Tecumseh is the folkloric version of the story; however, Jones indicates in his introduction of the account that he had personally witnessed the event. He wrote (actually, because of his poor eyesight, his wife wrote for him),

> I once saw the distinguished brave Tecumseh, at a Council in Vincennes. Gen. Harrison presided and as a mark of distinction, he had a seat placed near himself for Tecumseh. When Tecumseh was told that his Father Gen. Harrison, desired him to take the reserved seat near himself, instead of being flattered by the honor, he rose, and standing erect in the native dignity of his race, with his hand pointing upward, he exclaimed, "Gen. Harrison, is not my father—the Great Spirit is my father, (and then pointing down) the Earth is my mother, and I will repose upon her bosom." Seating himself upon the ground, the impression has always been that Tecumseh hated Harrison.[30]

Another item appears in Draper's materials that is of interest and should be considered along with Jones's letter. It is undated but its place in the Draper materials suggests a date around 1885. It is a handwritten scrap of paper, apparently a record by Draper of an interview he had with a Major Jos. McCormick of Wisconsin. My guess is that Draper met and interviewed this old gentleman, who reported his birthdate to be April 18, 1787. McCormick claimed to have been a guard for Harrison and to have been present at the meeting in Vincennes in 1810. The only information recorded on this scrap of paper is the following:

> A large bowery was prepared for the treaty—Tecumseh by agreement left the warriors behind. He marched to the treaty bower at the head of some twelve chiefs—Gen. Harrison met him and offered him a chair—"Your Father invites you to be seated in it." "My father, said

Tecumseh, is above—& the Earth is my Mother, & I will repose on
her bosom, & sat down on the ground."[31]

Since these accounts claim to be based on eyewitness, some, such
as Glenn Tucker, who wrote *Tecumseh: Vision of Glory* (1956), have
cited them as documentation for the historical accuracy of the widely
quoted statement of Tecumseh. There are at least two major reasons
why they cannot be considered as adequate for historical documentation. Most detrimental to their historical accuracy are the dates when
they were written. Both were recorded around 1885, that is, three-
quarters of a century after the event. Both of the authors were very
old men when they provided these accounts. According to his son-
in-law, LeSieur, Augustus Jones was born in February 1796, making him fourteen in the year 1810 and ninety-one at the time he
prepared his recollections of the Tecumseh speech to Harrison. Major McCormick, born apparently in 1787, was in his late nineties
when he told his account to Draper. In itself the ages of these gen-
tlemen need not prejudice their evidence, for certainly some people
have remarkable memories even into advanced age. However, it
seems rather unlikely that they would tell the account in precisely the
style, with the same written form, stage directions, punctuation, and
conventional wording, as dozens of published accounts that had appeared so often in the sixty years before 1885.

Yet another story of the Tecumseh-Harrison meeting must be
considered. I have found only one full telling of the story, though it
is a remarkable one. Interestingly, this story also deals with where
Tecumseh and Harrison *sat* when they met each other. This story
was published in the *Vincennes Commercial* newspaper January 8,
1889. The detail of the account makes it worth quoting in full. It is
entitled "The Red Man's Argument," and was told by Mr. Felix
Bouchie.

> Gen. Harrison had fears that Tecumseh, who was visiting the Indi-
> an tribes along the valleys of the Wabash and Illinois Rivers in 1810,
> was stirring them up to war, and conceived that Vincennes would be
> the first point of attack. Desirous of averting any such danger, Gen.
> Harrison sent a messenger to Tecumseh at Prophet's Town inviting
> him to a council to be held in Vincennes. Fearing treachery, Gen.
> Harrison stationed armed men in close proximity to the Harrison
> mansion, yet standing just north of the O & M Railroad, near the
> bridge. Mr. Bouchie relates this conversation as it has been told in his
> family ever since. He says it is not exactly as the histories relate the
> circumstances, but he says the histories are not exactly right.
> Joseph Barron and Pierre LaPlante, Mr. Bouchie went on to say,

were the interpreters. Tecumseh told Barron to tell his Big Man to bring a bench, that he wanted to talk sitting on it. "What do you want that for!" Gen. Harrison asked him through the interpreter, who understood the Shawnee language quite well. "To sit down by him," answered Tecumseh.

There was no bench accessible save the rude puncheon benches in the Catholic church. One of these was procured, and the men sat down on it. Harrison and all present were not a little curious to know what Tecumseh would do in a treaty with the bench. When they sat down together Tecumseh sat close to Harrison, even crowding him. Harrison moved away a little, but Tecumseh followed him up, and still crowded him. Not a word was said while this was going on. At last Harrison reached the end of the seat, and then he said to the interpreter: "Tell him he is about to crowd me off." This was Tecumseh's opportunity, and he straightened up in his seat, saying to the interpreter: "Eh! ugu? Ask the Big Man how he would like for me to crowd him clear off. Ask how he would like for me to crowd him clear out of the country, as he is crowding me and my people. Tell him that we were once to the sea or the East, but we have been crowded back and off. Tell him that all the earth—the hills, the valleys, the forests and the streams, and all the fullness thereof were ours one time, but now the pale face has crowded us back while only the space toward the setting sun is ours."

The proud and bold warrior had made his point, and it was a forcible argument, such as was felt by all present. It was an impeachment of the methods used by the white people to acquire their lands. Gen. Harrison replied that they had dealt fairly and honestly with them, always having regard for justice and right. To this Tecumseh said: "Tell the Big Man he is a liar." Harrison said: "We bought our lands from the chiefs that occupied them." "Tell him he is a liar," insisted Tecumseh: "I am the chief. No one has a right to dispose of the earth."

This heated controversy broke off the treaty for two or three days. There were some who wanted to kill Tecumseh and end the whole matter, but Harrison threatened to bind the one in chains who would dare do such a deed of violence to his invited guest. The treaty, however, was not accomplished at all, and Tecumseh started South.[32]

According to the editor of the *Commercial,* to whom Lyman Draper wrote inquiring about the teller of this story, Felix Bouchie was seventy years old at that time and told the story in good faith, although the editor noted that some of the local historians doubted it because it had not been previously recorded.

The details of this story, compared with those commonly found in the many folkloric and literary versions of the other Tecumseh speech, appear much more firmly founded in historical detail, and the story is factually corroborated at least in contextual detail by the accounts of historians. Attention to the presence of interpreters, the naming of the interpreters, and the constant noting that Tecumseh and Harrison spoke to each other through interpreters attest to the historical validity of the incident. Further, and most important, the reported exchange accurately presents the fundamental position that was often stated by Tecumseh regarding his views of the sale and ownership of land. Even Harrison, in writing of Tecumseh's early speeches, indicates that Tecumseh complained "that the Americans had driven them from the sea coast, and would shortly, if not stopped, push them into the lakes."[33] While it is not possible to determine the historical authenticity of the bench action Tecumseh is reported to have performed, it appears at least consistent with the concerns Tecumseh had. Notably, Homer J. Webster, who wrote a history of Harrison's administration of the Indiana territory, published in 1907, comments in a footnote that he was aware of the existence of the two stories. He believed that the one (the "sun is my father, the earth is my mother" story) appeared to be "well authenticated; the second, if not true, is certainly a good story."[34]

The extant evidence so far examined leaves us really no basis for holding that the statement attributed to Tecumseh is historically founded. There is no evidence to support this position and much to suggest that he did not make such a statement. But by this time in our investigation this issue of historicity is not really that important or that interesting. Two others issues, however, are. First, it is important to consider Shawnee religion, to ascertain whether or not it was at all consistent with the conclusions drawn by Gregg, Tylor, and many others from the alleged Tecumseh statement. (There are some surprises in this story.) But even more important is a second issue. What in American history, in the American ethos, motivated the strong attachment to the Tecumseh story and to the imagery of a brave Indian chief sitting resolutely on the bosom of his mother, the earth, in defiance of the great white father, General Harrison? To answer this question, a much longer view of American history and the imaging of Indians must be presented.

First, however, let us consider Shawnee religion.

Mother Earth in Shawnee Religious Traditions

Having considered the historical background of the famed statement of Tecumseh that has so often been used as documentation for the

Shawnee belief in Mother Earth, we may now examine other sources in an effort to determine whether or not such a goddess figure existed in Shawnee religion either at the time of Tecumseh or since.

This is a most interesting consideration for several reasons. First, Gregg, certainly no authority on Shawnee religion or Native American religions, used the Tecumseh statement to document his impression that the Shawnee held belief in a major solar deity. Further, in Tecumseh's many recorded speeches he consistently placed authority for the Indian relationship to the land and their defiance of U.S. government claims in "the Great Spirit," apparently a male sky-oriented figure. The earth-as-mother part of Gregg's statement was clearly secondary to his concern, although it led him to recall Tecumseh's statement to Harrison. Further, among all the many deities and spirit beings of the North American tribes, the Shawnee deities are unusual in having received a fair amount of scholarly attention and this from a historical perspective. Finally, the deity that is clearly the most important to the Shawnee of more recent generations is female!

Among the earliest records of Shawnee religion is C. C. Trowbridge's book *Shawnese Traditions*. It is based on interviews of Tenskwatawa, the prophet, brother to Tecumseh, that were probably conducted in 1824. According to Trowbridge, "They [the Shawnee] believe in one Supreme being who has a moral superintendence over the affairs of the world. He is called Muyaataalemeelarkwau (Muyetelemilakwau), or the Finisher, and is served by two subordinate deities, one to take charge of the Indians, and the other of the Whites."[35] The inclusion of a subordinate deity to take care of the whites attests to the awareness by the Shawnee of differences between their religious beliefs and those of the European-Americans and to the Shawnee manner of attempting to accommodate differences within their theological and religious worldview.

Lewis H. Morgan adds to our knowledge of nineteenth-century Shawnee religious beliefs by listing the names of Shawnee deities in his book *The Indian Journals, 1859–62*. He lists the first three as: "1. Great Spirit, Ma-ya-ta-la-ta-ga, the Creator, 2. Great Spirit, Ta-pa-la-ma-la-kwa, the Master, 3. Great Spirit, O-a-si-man-a-too, the good or powerful being."[36] While it is not at all certain, it appears that the early Shawnee conceived of their major deities as male and having residence in the sky realms.

The Shawnee of the twentieth century in Oklahoma identify their major deity as "Our Grandmother" and to her is attributed the role

of creator and overseer of her creation. For C. F. and E. W. Voegelin, who studied the Shawnee in the early 1930s, this presented an
important historical concern. They not only studied the roles and
character of the Shawnee female deity, they attempted to recon-
struct the history of the Shawnee to show how the belief in a male
deity in the early nineteenth century had, by the early twentieth century, become a belief in a major female deity.[37]

It is not important to recount this history here, and the Voegelins
were unable to suggest any very definite explanation for this shift.
What is important for our concerns is that, in the considered opinion
of students of Shawnee religion, opinion supported by abundant
historical documentation, the Shawnee of the early nineteenth century held belief in a major creator deity who was male and who was
associated with celestial realms. Further, the more recent belief in a
female deity Go-gome-tha-na, Our Grandmother, is a belief in an
anthropomorphic female goddess with gray hair living in a spacious
lodge in heaven. I have found no reference to her identification with,
or domicile in, the earth.

These beliefs in major sky-dwelling, world-creator deities, be they
male or female, do not prevent the Shawnee from also holding a
belief that the earth is personified as mother, a spirit-being or deity
in a pantheon of Shawnee deities. In this connection, we need to
consider Shawnee conceptions of the earth. Trowbridge made a
statement on this matter:

> They [the Shawnee] believe that we live upon an island, which is a
> plane of earth, extending to great length from east to west, & of com-
> paratively small width, that underneath this island is a vast body of
> water, and that the earth is supported by a great Turtle, swimming in
> it, and placed there for that purpose by the Great Spirit.[38]

The Voegelins wrote about the domains of deities:

> The Shawnee pantheon includes also deities which dwell on vari-
> ous levels in the universe, which is thought of as an amygdaloid figure
> containing the earth at its broad base and the home of the Creator
> near its apex, just below the sun. There appears to be some feeling for
> a level of heaven above the Creator, but its resident is absent in the
> current mythology. The levels below the Creator (including the ob-
> servable heavenly bodies, invisible regions of the winds, floating is-
> lands, stations for birds, etc., and the earth with regions within the
> earth) are almost densely populated with mythological figures and
> minor deities. These have a certain power of their own but in their
> adventures are never quite free from the controlling influence of the
> Creator.[39]

There is further evidence to suggest that the earth is personified. In a prayer accompanying the Bread Dance, observed by the Voegelins in 1933, "Earth Person" was addressed. The sex of this figure is indeterminate from their documentation. Further, it appears possible that Earth Person and the many others addressed in this prayer, like Corn Person, Pumpkin Person, and North Wind Person, are all facets of the creator, who is the one addressed by the prayer.[40]

Other evidence of the Shawnee personification of the earth is to be found in an analysis of story sticks, or pictographic boards, that Tenskwatawa made and distributed among his followers. The sticks were mnemonic devices that served to recall the cosmological system advanced by the prophet. Of the fourteen figures inscribed on the sticks, one of them, the second from the bottom, is identified as "earth." Still, there is no indication of the sex of this deity. According to W. A. Galloway's interpretation of the pictographic representations, they are deities to be addressed in prayers.[41] Furthermore, it must be remembered that, because Tenskwatawa was a prophet, his cosmology was unlikely to be typical of Shawnee thought.

From an examination of the considerable evidence about Shawnee deities that dates from the early nineteenth century, it is quite clear that the Shawnee did not hold a belief in a creator-goddess named Mother Earth or anything that might translate closely to this. Still, the Shawnee of the time possibly recognized as deities or spiritual entities many dimensions of the natural world. It would have been possible for the Shawnee of Tecumseh's day to have referred to "Earth Person," referring to some spiritual conception of the earth. But this type of conceptualization was extended to forms throughout the natural world.

Something, but not a great deal, is gained by showing that, whatever he said to Harrison, Tecumseh was not attesting to Shawnee and most especially to Native American religious beliefs. In the most generous of interpretations, one could say no more than that Tecumseh was acutely aware of the importance of the setting for negotiations, both for political purposes and for his concern with security. It seems likely that he insisted on meeting some distance from the governor's mansion for a variety of practical concerns. I do not believe that he made a statement even approximating the one so often attributed to him. Belief that he made the statement doubtless emerged in the explosion of legend, lore, and literature that, after his death, transformed Tecumseh from an obstacle to settlement into a heroic figure.

The impact of Tecumseh's statement on history and on scholarship is a story to be told in another chapter. Most fascinating now is an exploration of the power of this statement and of the figure of Tecumseh in nineteenth-century American history. But here too the roots of the story are dense and go deep.

The Triumph of Civilization over Savagism

In the decades following the founding of the United States in 1776 the nation was not only established on the lands of the eastern seaboard but expanded into adjacent lands to the west. In the last quarter of the eighteenth century and the first years of the nineteenth century the presence of Indians was all too real. Not only were Indians fought with and treated with, they were written about and discussed by many Americans. The nature of "the Indians" and their proper treatment became a major arena in which to discuss, theorize, and implement views of the American character.

Several views were voiced, but they often centered around a principal distinction. Indians were seen as hunters and warriors roaming about the land, making few claims upon it, and failing to realize its productive potential. Americans were seen as agriculturalists and builders of cities. They laid claim to the land. By the exertion of their wills upon the land, they transformed it, increased its productivity; in short, they civilized the land. It is essential to note, though it seems almost unnecessary, that this imagery does not reflect reality, especially that of Native Americans, since tribes in the eastern United States practiced agriculture as well as hunting, and certainly tribes in many parts of the areas into which the United States wished to expand had practiced agriculture for millennia. Still, this distinction articulated a key difference between civilization and savagism in American minds, and it was used to justify numerous removals of Native Americans from their ancestral lands in the late eighteenth and early nineteenth centuries. It also articulated a real difference in concepts of the relationship between people and land. Native Americans did not think of land as personal property, though doubtless they held notions of territorial rights. European-Americans saw that civilization was inseparable from personal property.

The imagined savagery of the Indians was contrasted with the civilization of the European-Americans, as the forest land was contrasted with the cultivated field. While certainly the political and economic interests were firmly aligned with the sentiment that required the displacement of the Indians and the destruction of the forests, there were some during the late eighteenth century who utilized the same imagery to support the opposite position, a primitivist position, holding that Indians should not be displaced. Many are the authors that can be aligned with these primitivist and antiprimitivist positions.[42]

Shortly after the beginning of the nineteenth century, as civilization began to triumph, strictly primitivist views ceased to be espoused, doubtless because primitivism was perceived as an obviously lost cause. The United States was expanding its territory rapidly, and the Indians were scarcely to be found outside of literature.

As the primitivist view of the Indians waned, the counterview underwent a transformation. As Indians ceased to be a threatening presence, they could now be granted a native nobility, a dignity based on physical bravery and natural eloquence, although this was a characterization still incompatible with civilization. The Indian, in physical absence, had become a vehicle by which European-Americans sought self-definition. This imagery was explored so extensively during the second quarter of the nineteenth century that Roy Harvey Pearce has described the effort as an obsession.[43] Ample evidence of the motif is to be found in the fiction of such authors as James Fenimore Cooper and William Gilmore Simms, whose Indian characters commonly were marked by the qualities of savage nobility yet were limited by their life of hunting and warfare. (Cooper published *The Pioneers* in 1823, *The Last of the Mohicans* in 1826, and *The Prairie* in 1827.)

If we return now to consider the alleged statement of Tecumseh, it is notable that the appearance of his statement in print correlates closely with the rise in popularity of a view of Indians as noble savages, unfit for or unable to accept civilization. The characterization of Tecumseh illustrated by his statement also correlates strongly with the obsessive characterization of Indians during this part of the nineteenth century, and it contrasts with the way Indians were viewed earlier in that century. Harrison, for example, was not at all interested in or motivated to see Tecumseh as noble and eloquent. In his August 22, 1810, letter to the secretary of war (and it is not coincidental that the letter was to the secretary of *war*) he described Tecumseh as "insolent" and "arrogant," and in his letter of August 28 he wrote that "the mind of the savage is so constructed that he cannot be at rest, he cannot be happy unless it is acted upon by some strong stimulus that which is produced by war is the only one that is sufficiently powerful to fill up the intervals of the chase if he hunts in the winter he must go to war in the summer."[44] In 1810 Tecumseh espoused the view of property that characterized for many Americans the savage hunter/warrior. This was to Harrison, as to most others of the day, simply savagism that had to be swept away so that civilization might triumph.

By the 1820s much had changed. The land was not only won but now occupied. The Indians were either dead or gone. In the face of success, and perhaps not without a twinge of conscience, Americans had new needs, and these were met in part by bestowing upon the victims of civilization an image of nobility and dignity, albeit one tainted by a savagism that made it finally wholly incompatible with civilization. When we think of the statement attributed to Tecumseh, we see this imagery fully present. Tecumseh speaks with dignity, in a physical posture of nobility, asserting his kinship with the earth and sky, his lineage with nature. He is here the consummate hunter/warrior savage. He speaks in defiance of Harrison and all that he represents. One cannot but admire Tecumseh for his courage, his eloquence, his native simplicity and directness. Yet the failure of Tecumseh, and thereby of all Indians, is an aspect of the statement as well. It is Tecumseh, hampered by his savagism, his primitive condition, who can never accede to a state of civilization. It is all too obvious that his savagism and American civilization cannot coexist.

When seen in light of the obsessive motif that characterized the American imagery of Indians in the second quarter of the nineteenth century, the time when the statement attributed to Tecumseh not only appeared but was so often quoted, Tecumseh's statement to Harrison clearly portrays the national sacrifice of the Indians to civilization, a sacrifice that, in American minds, the Indians willingly made by their recognition of the unsuitability of their own primitive nobility to the civilizing processes they encountered. This sacrifice was unmistakably presented in Alexander Malcomb's drama, mentioned above, in which the Tecumseh statement was placed in the mouth of Pontiac. When Pontiac utters the statement he demonstrates his nobility, bravery, and eloquence while he resolutely denies civilization. His fellow chiefs instantly recognize the irreconcilability and act upon it. As Agushaway kills Pontiac in the closing scene, he gives voice to this view: "There is a sacrifice, to our country's peace, of one of the bravest warriors and most consummate Chiefs."

Malcomb's play also shows how easy it was, using the same words, to portray the motif through other characters. Once we recognize that the statement served American needs to utilize Indians as vehicles of self-appraisal, we begin to recognize the imagery in the stories not only of Tecumseh and Pontiac but of others such as Logan[45] and Hiawatha.

A final observation is to be made regarding the story reported to the *Vincennes Commercial* by Felix Bouchie in 1889, in which Tecumseh used a bench to make a point to Harrison regarding the Indians being pushed off their lands by greedy Americans. We can now see why this story would not have satisfied the American imagination during the second quarter of the nineteenth century. While it depicts Tecumseh as clever and cunning and, therefore, admirable, it does not portray him in the state of hopeless savagery, impotent against the tides of civilization. By its portrayal of Tecumseh as the victor both rationally and morally, the story would not have satisfied the needs of Americans during this period, however historically accurate it was.

The imagery of the Indian examined thus far has been primarily masculine. The images have been of savage hunters and warriors—male Indians—as opposed to the images of the civilized American farmers and builders—male Americans of European descent. All of the principals of this story appear to be male, be they Indian or American. But there is a female dimension to the imagery of Indians encountering civilization and it runs deep in American history. This dimension is relevant and complementary to the part of the story we have thus far considered.

During the period in American history preceding the founding of the United States, there was a long sequence of images in which America and the American character were depicted, particularly by Europeans, as feminine and Indian in form. This personification of America as a female Indian can be found especially in graphic and decorative arts. The history of these forms depicts the changing image Europeans had of America, but it also is a measure of the development of the utilization of the Indians as means for American self-definition.

Studies of this iconography have established two dominant images of these early Miss Americas in two major periods. The first period is from 1575 to 1765, when "America" designated the entire Western hemisphere, conceived as the fourth of the four continents of the world. During this period America was depicted as an Indian queen. She was queen of the fourth part of the world, the counterpart to queens reigning over the other three continents. The Indian queen was Amazonian in size, having a swarthy hue, and dressed in a feathered skirt with feathered headdress. Her breasts were uncovered. She sometimes had a feathered cape and jewelled anklets. She was armed with either a club or a bow and quiver of arrows. Animals that served as her mount or on which she stood were first the armadillo and later the alligator. She was also associated with the parrot, monkey, puma, and stag.[46]

This Caribbean-inspired Indian queen slowly gave way to other imagery during the colonial period; it was still a female Indian, but now an Indian princess, younger, less barbarous, and less Caribbean than the Indian queen. The Indian princess is not the creature of an alien race, she is the daughter of Britannia. Her major concern is the attainment of liberty, not the domination of savage enemies. The Indian princess is depicted as a handsome, vigorous, young woman. She has a tawny complexion and long dark hair. She wears a feathered headdress and cape or skirt. E. McClung Fleming's examination of representations of the Indian princess, including many by Americans such as Paul Revere, revealed three overlapping themes in the allegorical situations in which she is depicted. He identifies these as "her mother-daughter relation to Britannia, her pursuit of liberty, and her command of the strategic factor of overseas trade."[47] Fleming's historical study also reveals a marked sequence of transformations of the Indian princess during the late eighteenth and early nineteenth centuries. With the establishment of the United States, the Indian princess was presented in such a fashion as to depict United States sovereignty. She came to hold the flag and, as an expression of the maturing image of the young United States, she gradually began to acquire aspects of a Greek goddess. By the late nineties, according to Fleming's study, "it is often not clear whether a feathered Indian Princess had been changed into a Greek goddess or whether a Greek goddess has placed a few feathers in her hair."[48]

Thus, there is a long history, beginning as early as 1575, in which America, as land and as idea, was depicted and expressed through the imagery of a female Indian. The creation and use of this imagery became distinctly self-conscious by Americans following the establishment of the United States, which was enjoying its most energetic and transformative stage in the late eighteenth and early nineteenth centuries.

A counterpart to the Indian princess can be found in history and was developed in literature in the story of Pocahontas. Philip Young's study, with the significant title "The Mother of Us All: Pocahontas Reconsidered" is revealing for our present concerns.[49]

The basic elements in the story of Pocahontas are well known. The English arrived in Jamestown in 1607, and Captain John Smith was among them. In December of that year Smith was captured by a group of Indians, whose chief was Powhatan. Smith's two companions were killed, but he was spared when the chief's daughter, a young girl called Pocahontas, intervened by stepping forward to the stone onto which they were forcing Smith's head, the better to smash it to bits; taking Smith's head into her arms, she laid her head upon his.

Smith returned to England in 1609, the same year that John Rolfe arrived in Jamestown. Rolfe met Pocahontas in 1613 and fell in love with her. He applied for and received permission to marry Pocahontas, which he did following her conversion, the first effected by the colonists, and her christening as Rebecca. They soon had a son, named Thomas, and in 1616 the family went to visit England so that John could publicize the success of producing tobacco in Jamestown.

In London, Rebecca was the toast of the town. She visited the king and queen and other dignitaries. She saw John Smith in a meeting forever shrouded in mystery. Upon preparing to return to America, she took sick with smallpox and died in London in March 1617. Thomas, her son, grew up in England but returned to America. From him proceeded an important lineage of Virginians. Today some two million Americans trace their ancestry back to Thomas and thus to Pocahontas, including such families as the Jeffersons and Lees, the Randolphs and Marshalls.

The details of the story are scant and based primarily on the account as written by John Smith in his *Generall Histories* (1624). Other hints of the character of Pocahontas can be found, such as the delightful observation included by William Strachey in his *Historie of Travaile into Virginia Britannia,* which was written about 1615 but not published until the middle of the nineteenth century. Strachey describes the youthful Pocahontas as a "well-featured but wanton yong girle" who used to come to the fort and "get the boyes forth with her into the markett place, and make them wheele, falling on their hands, turning their heels upwards, whome she would followe and wheele so herselfe, naked as she was, all the fort over."[50]

So well known is the story of Pocahontas today that one would assume that it has been so since Smith recounted it in 1624, but such is not the case. The enormous popularity of the story can be traced to an English sailor named John Davis who came to the United States in 1798 and spent nearly five years traveling about on foot. In his book about his journey called *Travels of Four Years and a Half in the United States of America* (1803), Davis told the story of Pocahontas, which he claimed to present as history: "I have adhered inviolably to facts; rejecting every circumstance that had not evidence to support it."[51] His telling was, in fact, a highly romanticized presentation, though Davis should be given credit, in Philip Young's view, "for having seen the possibilities of uniting richly embroidered history with a mammary fixation (habitually the bosoms of his Indian women are either 'throbbing' or 'in convulsive throes')."[52] Davis, an insatiable admirer of Pocahontas, also wrote what he called a "historical novel" about her entitled *First Settlers of Virginia* (1806).

Davis's story struck the literary imagination of Americans, who at that time were beginning to exploit the potential the Indian character offered. The country was soon awash with stories of Pocahontas, and the deluge has yet to subside. The first important Pocahontas play appeared in 1808, written by James Nelson Barker, ex-mayor of Philadelphia and future first controller of the Treasury under Van Buren. George Washington Parke Curtis, step-grandson of George Washington, wrote his *Pocahontas* in 1830, Robert Dale Owens wrote his in 1837; Charlotte Barnes Conner came out with *The Forest Princess* in 1844, and John Brougham with another *Pocahontas* in 1855. Literally hundreds have followed, many written in this century. For the 350th anniversary of the founding of Jamestown, celebrated in 1957, Paul Green wrote a "symphonic outdoor drama," performed at Williamsburg, called *The Founders;* the story of Pocahontas was a significant part of this drama. John Barth's version of the story of Pocahontas in his novel *The Sot-Weed Factor* (1960) is among the most imaginative.

Unquestionably, the story of Pocahontas has captured the American imagination since early in the nineteenth century, but what of its historical authenticity? The question was not raised until about 1860, when historians Edward D. Neill and Charles Deane began to state objections. They were joined by Henry Adams and Henry Cabot Lodge. The basis for their objections was that, while Smith had published his *True Relation* in 1608 and his *New England Trials* in 1622, describing in both his capture and release by the Indians, he did not tell of Pocahontas until the publication of his *Generall Histories* in 1624. Philip Young shows that Smith calls suspicion upon the authenticity of his report of his rescue by Pocahontas by boasting in his *Generall Histories* of being "offered rescue and protection in my greatest dangers" by various "honorable and vertuous Ladies." Young also notes that there was historical precedent for the Pocahontas tale. It was the story of Juan Ortiz, a soldier lost on an expedition to Florida in 1528. He was lost for twelve years, until found by De Soto. His story, published in London in 1609, tells of him being captured by Indians and being saved by the chief's daughter, at the last minute, from being burned at the stake. Notably, 1609 was the year Smith returned to London.

Young's great contribution to the reconsideration of the Pocahontas story is to show that both of these stories have a precedent in one of the oldest stories in human history, "the tale of an adventurer who becomes the captive of the king of another country and another faith, and is rescued by his beautiful daughter, a princess who then gives up her land and her religion for his."[53] Young notes many examples of the story type, including the Odysseus and Aeneas stories, and he recalls that the motif was so common in the Middle Ages that medieval scholars coined a name for it, "The Enamoured Moslem Princess."

With an appreciation of the rich literary heritage of the Pocahontas story, Young discerns that "the story will work for any culture, informing us, whoever we are, that we are chosen, or preferred. Our own ways, race, religion must be better—so much better that even an Indian (Magian, Moor, Turk), albeit an unusually fine one (witness her recognition of our superiority), perceived our rectitude." Further, Young observes that "Pocahontas is . . . a 'good' Indian, and by taking her to our national bosom we experience a partial absolution. In the lowering of her head we feel a benediction. We are so wonderful she loved us anyway."[54]

Little wonder, given the needs of the American people in the first half of the nineteenth century, that the story of Pocahontas became so popular. But the richness of the story was not exhausted in that century and has remained fertile ground to be plowed by many twentieth-century writers. Notably in Vachel Lindsay's 1918 poem, "Our Mother Pocahontas," the savior of Smith and Jamestown is elevated to be representative of the American spirit. Lindsay wrote:

> John Rolfe is not our ancestor.
> We rise from out the soul of her
> Held in native wonderland,
> While the sun's rays kissed her hand,
> In the springtime,
> In Virginia,
> Our mother, Pocahontas.[55]

In Hart Crane's poem "The Bridge" (1930), Pocahontas was depicted as "the natural body of American fertility," the land that lay before Columbus "like a woman, ripe, waiting to be taken." Here Pocahontas is none other than the earth itself, "our native clay . . .

red, eternal flesh of Pocahontas . . . . "[56] This image of Pocahontas
as the earth is furthered by Archibald MacLeish, in his *Frescoes for
Mr. Rockefeller's City* (1933), in which he describes the American
landscape as a beautiful naked Indian girl, inviting lovers. Here she is
the counterpart of Ceres, Demeter, and Gaea—a fertility goddess, an
earth mother, a mother of a new race in America. These twentieth-
century literary presentations of Pocahontas strikingly parallel the
early nineteenth century's transformation of the Indian-princess into
a Greek goddess.

While she is mother and goddess, she is all the richer and more
powerful for being the victim of sacrifice. As Young concludes,
"Pocahontas is the archetypal sacrifice to respectability in America—
a victim of what has been from the beginning our overwhelming
anxiety to housebreak all things in nature, until wilderness and wild-
ness be reduced to a few state parks and a few wild oats."[57]

As I have noted, it is surely not accidental that the story of
Pocahontas became so popular in the second quarter of the nine-
teenth century. This story provides a female counterpart to the male
Indian imagery of the same period.

Unlike her male Indian counterparts, Pocahontas, the Indian
princess who is the American earth, gives up her native lineage, even
betraying it, to join in sexual union with the white Americans, notably and obviously male. This act, as Young has interpreted it, is ritu-
alized, with Pocahontas offering herself as bride. It is a marriage that
leads to her respectability—that is, to her acquisition of Christianity
and civilization—but ultimately it leads also to her death. The story
of Pocahontas captures that peculiar ambiguity of the American story: in the acquisition and cultivation of the American soil the land is
conquered and civilized by the white masculine Americans, but in its
domestication and civilization there remains the poignant suggestion of subjugation, destruction, and death.

There is little evidence of a white female counterpart to the predominantly male depiction of Americans, but the few examples that
exist are consistent and one is of particular interest. There is the
novel *Hobomok* (1824), by Lydia Maria Child, that tells the story of
Mary Conant, whose white lover is believed to be dead. In her state
of anxiety she marries the Indian Hobomok, who worships her. Hobomok has the qualities of the noble savage, yet remains childlike,
that is, primitive, in his manners and language. Though Hobomok
truly loves Mary and she knows that he does, she is saved only when
her white lover, alive after all, returns and, in his nobility, Hobomok
divorces her and disappears forever.[58]

Of even greater interest is a story told of a love affair Tecumseh had with a white woman. The woman was Rebecca Galloway, daughter of an Indian fighter who lived in Green County Ohio. Tecumseh, according to the story, met Rebecca on a visit with her family. Becoming enamored of her, he returned at every opportunity to court this "young, golden-haired girl with deep-blue eyes." In love with Rebecca, Tecumseh is depicted as sitting at the feet of his maiden receiving instructions in English and being read passages from the Bible, Shakespeare, and world history. The Galloway family upheld the story, as for example in William Albert Galloway's book *Old Chillicothe* (1934), insisting that Tecumseh asked for Rebecca's hand in marriage. Rebecca is supposed to have agreed, on the condition that Tecumseh give up his Indian ways and adopt the white way of life and dress. Tecumseh, of course, who could never do this, had to refuse and this ended their relationship.[59]

The statement attributed to Tecumseh and the story of Pocahontas are two aspects of the same American story: the story of the sacrifice of the Indian in the triumph of civilization over savagism. This powerful story reveals the sentiments of Americans and their need to conceive the earth as female and as Indian.[60] There is a homology between the conception of the earth as the mother on whose bosom (a term peculiarly prominent in all of these stories) Tecumseh and the Indians would prefer to rest, the sequence of images of America as female Indian, and the stories of Pocahontas who, in laying her bosom upon the head of John Smith, entered into marriage with Europeans and their cultivating ways. Pocahontas, the Indian princess, the earth mother, is mother to us all and sacrificial victim to American respectability. The seeds are thus sown. The conception of Mother Earth in North America has taken place.

▲ 3 ▲

"Shall I tear my mother's bosom?"

My young men shall never work. Men who work can not dream, and wisdom comes to us in dreams. . . . You ask me to plow the ground. Shall I take a knife and tear my mother's bosom? You ask me to dig for stone. Shall I dig under her skin for bones? You ask me to cut grass and make hay and sell it, and be rich like white men. But how dare I cut off my mother's hair?

This statement, attributed to a Wanapum man by the name of Smohalla, is among the most quoted of all Native American statements. It is perhaps the most commonly cited piece of evidence documenting the Native American belief in Mother Earth. It is presented here as it appears in James Mooney's well-known monograph "The Ghost Dance Religion and the Sioux Outbreak of 1890."[1] Mooney was interested in the statement as evidence of what he believed were historical precedents for the Ghost Dance of 1890.

The statement is often quoted in literature about Indians, and these quotations are almost always drawn from this Mooney monograph. They rarely place the statement in the context in which Mooney presented it, that is, the history of millenarian movements spawned in part by the pressures Native Americans felt from the European-Americans' insatiable desire for land. The statement is nearly always used to exemplify or to document the universal belief

40

in a Native American goddess named "Mother Earth" or to attest the Indian ethos toward nature. This usage has occurred despite the fact that a cursory reading of the statement, even out of context and in the highly edited version in Mooney, reveals that it is a direct response to "white" pressures placed on native relationships with the land. The "you" in the statement clearly refers to European-Americans. The earth is spoken of as mother in metaphorical terms. Thus it remains to be determined whether or not the statement is also theological and whether or not it is an adequate basis for documenting the general Indian belief in Mother Earth. Predictably, the more fully we pursue this issue, the more it becomes evident that this is not what is most important or interesting. Yet, as we tell the stories that converge on this statement, we gain insight into Smohalla and other native peoples faced with the radical transformation of their lives, cultures, and the earth; we learn some important things about the interaction between Native Americans and Americans with European ancestry; and we see something of the dynamic interrelationship between history and story.

A History of the Interior Plateau Region of Washington and Oregon

In order to place Smohalla's statement and other earth-as-mother statements made by Native Americans in the interior plateau regions of what are now the states of Washington and Oregon, it is essential to outline the history of the region.

It is difficult to document the first contact in this area between Native Americans and European-Americans. The honor is usually given to Lewis and Clark, who traveled through the area from 1804 to 1806. Prior to first physical contact, there was an extended period when peoples of this area knew of the existence of European-Americans and grew to anticipate, even predict, contact with them. It is impossible directly to document the nature or extent of this precontact knowledge and experience, but that it existed and that there were certain expectations related to it can scarcely be questioned.[2] There was extensive movement among tribal peoples, as the dispersion through trade of material goods shows. This movement especially increased after the introduction of horses around 1730. While language barriers doubtless made difficult the transmission of factual details and extensive bodies of information, general information and impressions were widely transmitted among tribes. Not only did information about the Americans and some of their goods and technologies precede them, the diseases they dispersed also preceded them, as is evident from epidemics of smallpox that hit tribes in the region in the late eighteenth century. Somewhat later, but nonetheless an exemplification of this process, is the arrival in Montana, in 1816, of a group of twenty-four Iroquois who settled among the Flathead. Preceding missionaries, they brought elements of Christianity to the tribes. They had traveled a great distance and had been in contact with many tribes as well as European-Americans. Their influence on tribes in the area is believed to have greatly shaped the subsequent history of the cultures indigenous to the area.[3]

Following Lewis and Clark into the area were other explorers. David Thompson, an explorer of the North West Company, entered the area in 1811, followed by others in 1814. These were probably the first significant contacts. One outcome was the immediate flow of information to the European-American populace in the East, telling of the region's enormous potential for trapping, missionization, and agricultural settlement. Consequently, many trappers, missionaries, and settlers began to arrive in the area.

Henry Harmon Spaulding, a Presbyterian, arrived in 1836 to establish the first Protestant mission at Lapwai near present-day Lewiston, Idaho.[4] The first school was opened in 1837. Catholic missions appeared shortly thereafter. The mission influence grew slowly but steadily during a quarter-century period, gradually complemented by increasing numbers of settlers. The 1847 killing of the missionary Marcus Whitman and others attested to the growing uneasiness of Native Americans about the history that was unfolding all around them.[5]

With the establishment of the Washington Territory in 1853, a flood of settlers entered the area. The presence of Native Americans on land desired by settlers and the persistent threat they presented to the well-being and safety of the settlers were major issues for the new territorial government. The Indians were seen as deterrents to the advancement of civilization, as had been the case in many areas of the United States throughout the nineteenth century. Government policy at the time was to establish treaties with the natives, effecting their removal to established reservation lands.

In 1855, Isaac I. Stevens, then governor of the newly formed Washington Territory, made treaties with the Yakimas, Walla Wallas, Cayuses, and Nez Perces in which the principle of their general confinement to reservations was declared. But the principle was not easily or immediately instituted, and for several years war, resistance, outbreaks, and renegade actions were common. There was also an increase in the incidence of native millenarian movements, that is, movements that anticipated and prophesied cataclysmic events that would remove European-Americans and their influences and restore the Native American world as it had been, including commonly the return of the dead. The movement in which Smohalla played an important role, "the Dreamers," probably had its origin in the decade of the 1860s. The movement flourished among many tribes in the region during the decade of the 1870s, appealing primarily to Indians who refused to go onto reservations. It encouraged many to break out of reservation confinement to pursue a way of life in continuity with what had existed prior to the European-American presence.

Chief Joseph's heroic resistance to settlement and governmental pressures is well known. The capture of Joseph in 1877 marks the end of potentially successful military resistance efforts for all of the tribes in the area.

By the 1880s the "Indian problem" was largely solved in the region. There remained only a few resisters. For those Native Americans, it was a period of holding out and of "dreaming" and dancing to maintain their millennial expectations. Smohalla continued to avoid the pressures of the government and of settlement, yet his movement slowly lost its energy and was eventually transformed from a millenarian movement into a less expectant, more permanent and stable community. The movement had gained acceptance and lost some of its identity with protest and resistance. The incident at Wounded Knee in 1890, although occurring outside of this particular region, provides a suitable date to indicate the transformation of the resistance movements such as the Ghost Dance and the Dreamers into more institutionalized religious communities.

During this period many Native Americans followed the counsel of the government agents by occupying homesteads and attempting to farm. But even these efforts to comply with the American way were eventually denied them. Many Native American settlers were forced off their homesteads and back onto reservations in the early 1880s when their land was needed for the railroad being constructed across the area. The Northern Pacific Railroad opened in 1883.

Documentary Evidence of Belief in Mother Earth

Smohalla was not the only Native American in this area who is reported to have referred to the earth as a mother. The earliest examples appear among the proceedings of the 1855 treaty negotiations held at Walla Walla Valley. This council was called by Governor Isaac I. Stevens in order to get the Nez Perce, Walla Walla, Cayuse, Umatilla, Yakima, and other tribes to agree to live on designated reservations. The council began on May 28, 1855, and continued until the treaties were signed on June 9 and 11. Meetings were held nearly every day during this period. An official government record was kept of the proceedings and included the speeches that were made.[6] Furthermore, Lieutenant Lawrence Kip, who was a visitor at the meetings, wrote down some of the speeches.[7] Many Native Americans spoke during the council. Only three of these speeches make reference to the earth in terms that are somehow related to the notion of motherhood. Notable, however, is one statement found in Lieutenant Kip's report of the physical arrangements for the meeting. In his journal entry for Wednesday, May 30, 1855, one of the early days of the treaty council, Kip wrote, "The Indians sat on the ground (in their own words,) 'reposing on the bosom of their Great Mother'."[8]

We have in 1855 a report of a statement remarkably similar to the statement attributed to Tecumseh at an event forty-five years before and half a continent away. It is significant that Kip presents this statement as a quotation and that the English words "reposing" and "bosom" are central. I see no way to understand this statement as documenting a common belief between the Shawnee, along with other Eastern tribes, and these plateau tribes of the Washington Territory. It indicates to me rather that some of those present in Walla Walla were familiar with the Tecumseh statement so widely quoted by 1855. It could have been the interpreters (one of whom was a Delaware Indian), Kip, or the Indians themselves, for some were literate and familiar with American history and literature. This is evident for the Nez Perce man, Aleiya, called "Lawyer," who was a key figure in the treaty negotiations.

Kip described Lawyer, whom he observed on May 25, 1855. He was "surrounded by his family and reading a portion of the New Testament, while a German soldier of Governor Stevens' party was engaged in taking his portrait in crayon."[9]

Further, on June 7, in perhaps the most eloquent speech of the entire meeting, Lawyer carefully traced the history of contact all the way across the continent, from the voyages of Columbus to the explorations of Lewis and Clark into the Nez Perce region. Beyond demonstrating a knowledge of the shape of the world and the impact of American history on Native Americans across the continent, he showed in his speech a clear understanding of U.S. government processes and policies and a keen sense of the skills of negotiations.[10]

There is every reason to believe that by 1855 at least some of the Native Americans attending the treaty negotiations at Walla Walla and, most certainly, any number of the European-Americans present had heard or read, to the point of familiarity, the statement attributed to Tecumseh, during its florescence in the second quarter of the nineteenth century. It would be difficult to account for the extent of the similarity of the statements in any other way.

There are other references to the earth as mother by native speakers at these negotiations. On June 5 the Cayuse chief, Stachas, spoke. It appears that he was desperately attempting to communicate accurately to the government officials.

> My friends I wish to show you my mind, interpret right for me. How is it I have been troubled in mind? If your mothers were here in this country who gave you birth, and suckled you and while you were sucking some person came and took away your mother and left you alone and sold your mother, how would you feel then? This is our mother this country as if we drew our living from her.
>
> My friends all of this you have taken. Had I two rivers I would be content to leave the one and live on the other.
>
> I name three places for myself, the Grande Ronde, the Touchet towards the mountain and the Tucannon.
>
> That is all I have to say.[11]

Two days later, the Nez Perce spokesman, Lawyer, spoke to support the reservation policy being presented. His view was not generally shared by the others. For example, the Cayuse chief named "Young Chief" spoke of his confusion. The complexity of his speech seems to have defeated the translator, but some semblance of the intent perhaps survives.

> Us Indians are blind the reason we do not see the earth well, the Lawyer sees clear. The reason that I do not know anything about this ground is I do not see the offer you have made as yet. If I had the money in my hand then I would see: the country is very large is the reason this land is afraid. I wonder if this ground has anything to say: I wonder if the ground is listening to what is said. I wonder if the ground would come to life and what is on it; though I hear what this earth says, the earth says, God has placed me here. The Earth says, that God tells me to take care of the Indians on this earth: the Earth says to the Indians that stop on the Earth feed them right. God named the roots that he should feed the Indians on: the water speaks the same way: God says feed the Indians upon the earth; the grass says the

same thing: feed the horses and cattle. The Earth and water and grass says God has given our names and we are told those names; neither the Indians or the Whites have a right to change those names: the Earth says, God has placed me here to produce all that grows upon me, the trees, fruit, etc. The same way the Earth says, it was from her man was made. God on placing them on the Earth desired them to take good care of the earth and do each other no harm. God said. You Indians who take care of a certain portion of the country should not trade it off unless you get a fair price.[12]

This speech was among those recorded and published by Lieutenant Lawrence Kip. Kip sat at the table with the interpreters and recorders. His text is very similar to the official record. Kip refers to "ground" rather than "earth" and to "Great Spirit," not to "God."[13]

Young Chief's speech as recorded here is difficult to understand. One theme seems to be his concern about clearly seeing the terms of the agreement. But the speech perhaps also reflects a Cayuse theory of names in which the bestowing of a name on an object or place gives it existence, that is, personhood. While it cannot be clearly determined, the speech may reflect a Cayuse belief in the personification and personalization of aspects of material reality such as earth, grass, and water that seem to be bestowed with speech. These may be theological or religious conceptions, but the most overt theological presence in the speech has to do with the powerful figure known variously as "God" or "Great Spirit." The extent to which this nominalization is Cayuse or Christian is perhaps impossible to determine, for usually the specifically tribal names of Native American deities have been translated by either of these common English appellations. An examination of the relevant materials of this region suggests that the terms are ambiguous, that for both Native Americans and European-Americans they may refer loosely to either the Christian God or powerful tribal spiritual figures. In negotiations the differences were doubtless minimized by both parties.

On the same day that Young Chief spoke, Owhi, a Yakima chief, spoke of the relationship of his people to the earth they were being asked to give up.

God ["Great Spirit" in Kip] gave us day and night, the night to rest in, and the day to see, and that as long as the earth shall last, he gave us the morning with our breath; and so he takes care of us on this earth and here we have met under his care. Is the earth before the day or the day before the earth. God was before the earth, the heavens were clear and good and all things in the heavens were good. God looked one way then the other and named our lands for us to take care of. God made the other. We did not make the other, we did not make it, he had it to last forever. It is the earth that is our parent or it is God is our elder brother. This leads the Indian to ask where does his talk come from that you have been giving us. God made this earth and it listens to him to know what he would decide. The almighty made us and gave us breath; we are talking together and God hears all that we say today. God looks down upon his children today as if we were all in one body. He is going to make one body of us; we Indians present have listened to your talk as if it came from God.

God named this land to us that is the reason I am afraid to say anything about this land. I am afraid of the laws of the Almighty, that is the reason I am afraid to speak of the land. I am afraid of the Almighty that is the reason of my hearts being sad: this is the reason I cannot give you an answer. I am afraid of the Almighty. Shall I steal this land and sell it? or what shall I do? this is the reason that my heart is sad.

My friends, God made our bodies from the earth as if they were different from the whites. What shall I do? Shall I give the lands that are part of my body and leave myself poor and destitute? Shall I say that I will give you my lands? I cannot say. I am afraid of the Almighty.

I love my life is the reason why I do not give my lands away. I am afraid I would be sent to hell. I love my friends. I love my life, this is the reason why I do not give my lands away.[14]

Despite some rather likely failings in translation, Owhi's speech is relatively clear. He affirms his belief that God made the world and all that is within it, the day and night, the earth and the people in whose care he named the earth. Owhi sees his people's relationship to the land as based in the act of creation and amounting to a responsibility that is inviolable. He then seems to challenge the basis of authority on which the white officials are asking the Indians to relinquish their lands. While it appears that he feels that the Indians are expected to listen to the white officials as though they spoke on behalf of God, Owhi seems to be questioning this. It follows that, if they do not speak as God, then there is good reason for Owhi to fear giving up his land, for "the Almighty," who obviously has greater power and precedence, had intended that it be otherwise. Owhi appeals to a color similarity between Indians and the earth to demonstrate that the Indians are "different from the whites." Because of their immediate derivation from the earth and the God-given responsibility they bear to the land, they cannot simply sell or give up their lands, for fear of the "Almighty." Owhi speaks of the earth as "parent" in the sense of being the stuff from which one is made, and for whose care one is responsible.

Largely overlooking the concerns and careful reasoning of the various Indian spokespersons, and depending upon the support and influence of the Nez Perce leader named Lawyer (the Nez Perce people later indicated that Lawyer had no authority to speak on behalf of the tribe),[15] the government officials drew up treaties, which were signed by the Indians. It is clear that the tribal leaders were pressured into signing and that they did not have full knowledge of the implications of the treaties. In the fifteen years that followed, many Indians refused to take residence upon reservation lands. Further, the rights guaranteed the Indians, especially their right to control access to their lands, were simply ignored. An obvious violation of this right accompanied the discovery of gold on the Nez Perce reservation. By 1860 there were as many as 10,000 people in Nez Perce country looking for gold. A mining town sprang up on the reservation. To resolve this situation, which stood in violation of the treaty of 1855, a new council was called and a new treaty (1863) was established that effectively reduced reservation lands so that mining activity could continue.

Many Native Americans found such actions difficult to accept, and there continued to be uncooperative groups roaming the area attempting to maintain continuity with their old lifeways. In the attempt to resolve some of this strife, government commissions were occasionally sent to meet with uncooperative Indians. In 1871 a commission was sent to the Umatilla and other reservations to give native peoples a chance to speak about their situation. During one of these hearings, a Cayuse chief, described as Catholic and as dressed as an American farmer, spoke. He reportedly said,

> This reservation is marked out for us. We see it with our eyes and our hearts. We all hold it with our bodies and our souls. Right out here are my father and mother, and brothers and sisters and children, all buried. I am guarding their graves. My friend, this reservation, this small piece of land, we look upon it as our mother, as if she were raising us. You come to ask me for my land. It is like as if we who are Indians were to be sent away and get lost.[16]

This Cayuse chief is using the language of kinship with the earth as a means of expressing the responsibilities he feels for the graves of deceased members of his family, for the continuity of his lineage and heritage, and for his inherited rights to the land.

In 1876 and again in 1877, U.S. government officials met with leaders of a group of Nez Perce who had refused to acknowledge the treaties, in an attempt to settle what appeared to be growing unrest among them. Joseph, the son of the older Chief Joseph who had signed the treaty of 1855 establishing reservations, was a leader of this faction. A report to the Commissioner of Indian Affairs described a meeting at Lapwai, Idaho, in November 1876, between the Nez Perce leadership and a government commission. The principal issue concerned the Wallowa Valley. Joseph and his followers spent much of their time in the valley, but the government claimed title to the land and had proceeded to survey it for settlement. The commission, upon meeting with Joseph, explained the basis of the government's right to the land, citing treaties and executive orders. Joseph was unimpressed with their arguments, and the substance of his response, though not in his words, is summarized in the report.

> The reply to all such suggestions, seriously made and often repeated both by Joseph and his brother, was to the effect that the "Creative Power," when he made the earth, made no marks, no lines of division or separation upon it, and that it should be allowed to remain as then made. The earth was his mother. He was made of the earth and grew up on its bosom. The earth, as his mother and nurse, was sacred to his affections, too sacred to be valued by or sold for silver and gold. He could not consent to sever his affections from the land that bore him. He was content to live upon such fruits as the "Creative Power" placed within and upon it, and unwilling to barter these and his free habits away for the new modes of life proposed by us. Moreover, the earth carried chieftainship, (which the interpreter explained to mean law, authority, or control,) and therefore to part with the earth would be to part with himself or with his self-control. He asked nothing of the President. He was able to take care of himself. He did not desire Wallowa Valley as a reservation, for that would subject him and his band to the will of and dependence on another, and to laws not of their own making. He was disposed to live peaceably. He and his band had suffered wrong rather than do wrong. One of their number was wickedly slain by a white man during the last summer, but he would not avenge his death. But unavenged by him, the voice of that brother's blood, sanctifying the ground, would call the dust of their fathers back to life, to people the land in protest of this great wrong.

In summarizing for the Commissioner of Indian Affairs in Washington the cause of the trouble with this group of nontreaty Indians, the commission noted that Joseph and his group had "fallen under the influence of the 'dreamers,' (Smohallah,) a modern spiritualistic mysticism, known of late among the Indians of this region." For the commission, herein lay the cause of the trouble.

> The dreamers, among other pernicious doctrines, teach that the earth being created by God complete, should not be disturbed by man, and that any cultivation of the soil or other improvements to

interfere with its natural productions, any voluntary submission to the control of the government, any improvement in the way of schools, churches, etc., are crimes from which they shrink. This fanaticism is kept alive by the superstitions of these "dreamers," who industriously teach that if they continue steadfast in their present belief, a leader will be raised up in the East who will restore all the dead Indians to life, who will unite with them in expelling the whites from their country, when they will again enter upon and repossess the lands of their ancestors.[17]

Although these reflections on the Nez Perce and the perspectives of "the dreamers" are written by white government officials, one can perhaps see how the issues of contention were shaped during the period beginning with the 1855 treaty negotiations. The conflict came to center on conflicting conceptions of the land. From the government point of view, land is made meaningful and productive when it is divided, possessed as personal property, and transformed into farms and cities. The very term "settlement" implies that land gains value when it is divided, possessed, settled, cultivated, civilized. Certainly the occupation of the entire United States was based on this principle. The nontreaty Indian groups in this region, while first expressing an opposed conception in somewhat awkward terms in 1855, came, partly through the development of millenarian movements like that of "the dreamers," to articulate their position more clearly. That position rests upon the precedent of creation, that is, the land was created as it was before the Americans arrived. It was God, not humans, who not only created the land but established its proper relationship with the people. The Indian people were created by God from the earth, as the similarity in color indicates, and the earth therefore is like a mother to them. In the terms of this relationship the Indian people understood they had been given responsibility for the land. By the mid-1870s this conception of responsibility was spoken of in the terms of "chieftainship," formally emphasizing the elements of law, authority, and control.

It is important to recognize that these conceptions, while very likely continuous with the conceptions of ancient tribal traditions, were expressed in these council settings in a language conceived and refined to meet the exigencies of the threat at hand.

There is further evidence of these lines of argument from the meeting that occurred in April 1877, again between the Nez Perce nontreaty leadership and the officials of the government. General Oliver O. Howard of the commission reported the substance of the preliminary remarks made by the Nez Perce spokesman, Too-hul-hul-sote.

He had the usual long preliminary discussion about the earth being his mother, that she should not be disturbed by hoe or plough, that men should subsist on what grows of itself, etc. He railed against the violence that would separate Indians from lands that were theirs by inheritance. He repeated his ideas concerning "chieftainship," chieftainship of the earth. Chieftainship cannot be sold, cannot be given away.[18]

Howard's reply to Too-hul-hul-sote is notable. As he reports it, he said,

We do not wish to interfere with your religion, but you must talk about practicable things. Twenty times over you repeat that the earth is your mother, and about chieftainship of the earth. Let us hear it no more, but come to business at once.

What followed was an embittered discussion, and even Howard's own account shows him to have been curt and impatient with the insistence of Too-hul-hul-sote that the land cannot be measured and divided even by the authority of the president of the United States, the authority that Howard invoked. When Howard pressed Too-hul-hul-sote to agree to move onto the reservation, he was told, "So long as the earth keeps me, I want to be left alone. You are trifling with the law of the earth."[19]

Howard's demand that the Indians cease talking of their religion (which he assures them he wishes not to violate) and get on to practical matters demonstrates the irreconcilability of the two positions. Howard appealed to land rights resting in the authority of the U.S. government, in its laws and legal agreements such as treaties and executive orders. The Indians appealed to creation and the authority of God-given precedent, and, subsequently, to the chieftainship that was thereby implied. To one party the matter was political and legal, for the other it was basically religious but was recast as legal. This distinction is more clearly seen in the discussion of the statement attributed to Smohalla.

First, it is important to recall that this meeting of the Nez Perce group with General Howard in 1877 ended with the arrest of Too-hul-hul-sote, thus creating the tensions that led to the flight and eventual capture of Chief Joseph and the subjugation of his people. Joseph was never allowed to return to his homelands but was sent to Oklahoma, where he lived out the balance of his life. In Oklahoma, Joseph had occasion to record his recollections and views on his earlier meetings with government officials.

I have been in a great many councils, but I am no wiser. We are all sprung from a woman, although we are unlike in many things. We

cannot be made over again. You are as you were made, and as you
were made you remain. We are just as we were made by the Great
Spirit (Ah-cum-kin-i-ma-me-hut), and you cannot change us; then
why should children of one mother and one father quarrel—why
should one try to cheat the other? I do not believe that the Great
Spirit gave one kind of men the right to tell another kind of men what
they must do. . . . All men were made of the same Great Spirit Chief.
They are all brothers. The earth is the mother of all people, and all
people should have equal rights upon it.[20]

The most well-known statements made by Native Americans in
this area about the earth as mother are, of course, those attributed to
Smohalla dated around 1884 and 1885. These occurred at a time
when most tribes had finally been confined to reservations. There
were fresh grievances about the land in the early 1880s when the
railroad displaced some Indian homesteaders. Smohalla and his little
group of followers lived at Priest Rapids on the Columbia River,
trying to hold to the old ways of sustaining themselves. They had
never made a formal treaty with the U.S. government.

One report of the views voiced by Smohalla comes from E. L.
Huggins of the Second Cavalry. Around 1884, Huggins, traveling
through the area in which Smohalla lived, endeavored to meet the
famed leader of the Dreamers.[21] After much effort and several disap-
pointments, a brief meeting eventually took place. The two men ex-
changed views on the settlement of the lands in the area. Smohalla's
initial assumption was that Huggins had come to take his lands away
from him. Huggins assured him that this was not his purpose, but
Smohalla nonetheless recounted the history of "white" encroachment.

> White men come from these very countries, and say the Indian
> must not keep his land because he hunts over it instead of plowing it. I
> know a man on the lower Columbia, who for years has had a big piece
> of bottom land that is neither plowed up or grazed over, but no one
> disturbs him, because he is a white man. I will not plow my land, but
> if I did, it would not protect me. Joseph's people had good fields and
> gardens, but they were driven away. I have no pity for them. They had
> no business to plant fields like white men. Many Indians are trying to
> live like white men, but it will do them no good. They cut off their
> hair and wear white men's clothes, and some of them learn to sing out
> of a book.[22]

Huggins reminded Smohalla that the country was rapidly filling
with European-Americans and that the Native Americans must learn
these new ways. Smohalla responded, "My young men shall never

work. . . . Men who work cannot dream, and wisdom comes to us in dreams."

Huggins retorted, "But your young men have to work hard during the fishing season to get food for winter."

To which Smohalla said, "This work only lasts for a few weeks. Besides, it is natural work and does them no harm. But the work of the white man hardens soul and body: nor is it right to tear up and mutilate the earth as white men do."

Not to be bested, Huggins said, "But you also dig roots. Even now your people are digging cammas roots in the mountains."

> "We simply take the gifts that are freely offered," Smohalla replied. "We no more harm the earth than would an infant's fingers harm its mother's breast. But the white man tears up large tracts of land, runs deep ditches, cuts down forests, and changes the whole face of the earth. You know very well this is not right. Every honest man knows in his heart that this is all wrong. But the white men are so greedy they do not consider these things."[23]

Smohalla's concern is with the treatment of the land by the intruding culture and the pressure the "white men" exert to convert the native peoples to their ways. He clearly distinguishes the alternative relationships to the land and argues with clear reasoning the error of the "white man's" ways. In defense of the practice of root-digging as consistent with the relationship to the land he espouses, he presents the metaphor that it is like an infant feeding at its mother's breast.

Another report from Smohalla comes from about the same time, 1885. General N. A. Miles sent Major J. W. MacMurray to confer with the native peoples who continued to refuse settlement and treaty. MacMurray spent about a year on this mission, with a portion of it at Priest Rapids where he spoke with Smohalla and observed his religion.

Notable is an exchange reported by MacMurray which took place on an occasion when he used a checkerboard to illustrate the homestead plan and how the government wanted the land divided. He urged the Native Americans to apply for land and to settle it on the pattern of the European-Americans. Smohalla responded that he could not accept this and proceeded to tell his story of the creation of the world.

> Once the world was all water, and God lived alone; he was lonesome, he had no place to put his foot; so he scratched the sand up from the bottom, and made the land and he made rocks, and he made

trees, and he made man, and the man was winged and could go anywhere. The man was lonesome, and God made a woman. They ate
fish from the water, and God made the deer and other animals, and he
sent the man to hunt, and told the woman to cook the meat and to
dress the skins. Many more men and women grew up, and they lived
on the banks of the great river whose waters were full of salmon. The
mountains contained much game, and there were buffalo on the
plains. There were so many people that the stronger ones sometimes
oppressed the weak and drove them from the best fisheries, which
they claimed as their own. They fought, and nearly all were killed, and
their bones are to be seen in the sand hills yet. God was very angry and
he took away their wings and commanded that the lands and fisheries
should be common to all who lived upon them. That they were never
to be marked off or divided, but that the people should enjoy the
fruits that God planted in the land and the animals that lived upon it,
and the fishes in the water. God said he was the father, and the earth
was the mother of mankind; that nature was the law; that the animals
and fish and plants obeyed nature, and that man only was sinful. This
is the old law.

Smohalla also told MacMurray,

Those who cut up the lands or sign papers for lands will be de-
frauded of their rights, and will be punished by God's anger. . . .

It is not a good law that would take my people away from me to
make them sin against the laws of God. You ask me to plough the
ground? Shall I take a knife and tear my mother's bosom? Then when
I die she will not take me to her bosom to rest.

You ask me to dig for stone! Shall I dig under her skin for her
bones? Then when I die I can not enter her body to be born again.

You ask me to cut grass and make hay and sell it, and be rich like
white men, but how dare I cut off my mother's hair?

It is a bad law and my people shall not obey it. I want my people to
stay with me here. All the dead men will come to life again; their
spirits will come to their bodies again. We must wait here, in the
homes of our fathers, and be ready to meet them in the bosom of our
mother.[24]

Neither Huggins nor MacMurray knew the native languages and
had to depend upon translations through even more than one language. Neither was trained in observing and recording such encoun-
ters. Indeed, Huggins's account may well be based on recall of an
incident that happened years earlier. Beyond the shadow cast by these
factors there are other reservations about the adequacy of these documents and the others we have considered as the basis for establishing

the general Native American belief in Mother Earth or an earth goddess. It is clear, in light of other historical contexts, that even the
earliest statements referring to the earth as mother—those in the
speeches of the treaty negotiations of 1855—were made in response
to the threat of the loss of land on an enormous scale. By the time of
the statements of the Nez Perce nontreaty leaders in the late 1870s the
fate of the native peoples of the area was all but sealed. Nez Perce
religious traditions had already undergone major transformations.[25]
By the time of the statements of Smohalla in the mid-1880s, settlement was advanced, the railroad connecting the region with the East
had been opened, and only a handful of native peoples continued to
hold out and to expect the reversal of history. Since the 1860s,
Smohalla had led a protest movement, millenarian in style and considerably influenced by Christianity. Given this historical context for
these statements, they have little value in documenting traditional and
ancient Native American tribal religious beliefs. The strongest evidence in the speeches attests to the Native American belief in a creator
deity, known in English as "God" or the "Great Spirit." In themselves
these speeches do not even document a belief in this figure in the tribal
traditions, since the figure may very well have derived in some measure from the Native American utilization of Christian teachings in
order to express native views about land to Christian Americans. The
earth is certainly referred to as the mother of the Indians, sometimes as
the mother of all people, but it is referred to in much more metaphorical terms than is the creator figure in the speeches. The basic
point is simply that the speeches cited are not adequate documentation for the claims that have been made for them regarding the existence of a general Native American belief in a figure known as Mother
Earth, or even for belief in an earth goddess. Corroborative evidence
must be sought elsewhere.

The Prophet Dance Controversy

A great deal of attention has been directed toward discerning a continuity between the late-nineteenth-century millenarian movements
and the religious traditions of the pre- and early contact periods. The
issue has been the degree to which these later religious movements
are crisis cults that arose explicitly to compensate for the deprivations
suffered at the hands of Americans entering the area.

This was the issue that led James Mooney, in his study of the
Ghost Dance of 1890, to examine such earlier movements as "the

Dreamers" and the Ghost Dance of 1870. His contention was that
all of these movements arose in response to the crises created by
American expansion into the area.

Countering this view in the 1930s was the study conducted by
Leslie Spier.[26] His principal objective was to propose the existence,
prior to contact with the settlers, of a prophetic movement which he
called the Prophet Dance. In his reasoning, the existence of the
Prophet Dance would establish that the later movements in the nineteenth century were wholly native in development rather than responses to outside pressures.

Spier's view was not seriously challenged for many years and
seemed to be extended by several studies. Eventually, however, evidence for the impact of mediate, or precontact, influence began to
emerge more clearly. David Aberle [27] and later Deward Walker,[28] by
examining a wide range of materials, showed that, with the acquisition of the horse, cultures of the region underwent great transformations as early as the 1730s. They present considerable evidence that
deprivation was experienced prior to the time Lewis and Clark entered the area. One undeniable element of deprivation is the documented occurrence of epidemic disease in the 1770s. Walker, upon
examining a range of ethnographic and archaeological evidence, concludes that "it seems quite reasonable that indirect White influence
could have played a substantial part in the origin of the Prophet
Dance."[29] Especially important for our present concerns, Walker
also shows that there is evidence that even these precontact movements had borrowed and incorporated elements from Christianity.

Even if Spier had been successful in documenting a native crisis-
cult that was motivated by something other than contact, his conclusions about later movements would still not hold. The demonstration of the precontact existence of a millenarian movement does not
necessitate, as Spier argues, that postcontact millenarian movements
are not influenced by the contact culture or that they cannot be motivated by crises attributable to the contact culture.

The studies that have contributed to the Prophet Dance controversy show that it is even more difficult to utilize the statements that
are part of these cult movements as documentation for any aboriginal tribal religious beliefs. The convincing arguments of Deward
Walker lead us rather to expect that these movements, including that
of "the Dreamers," stand within a religious heritage that is specifically motivated by and directed toward resolving the crises and deprivations suffered by mediate, expected, or immediate contact with
majority American culture, and that these movements showed Chris-

tian influence even before immediate contact. Put simply, it is likely that European-American influences had an effect on cultures in the interior plateau areas, particularly in giving rise to millenarian movements with elements of Christian influence, as much as a century before the earliest of the evidences we have considered. Thus, particularly for the occasions of disputes and negotiations over land—the core of the crisis situation—a large measure of caution must be exercised in considering these statements of Native Americans as revealing aboriginal religious beliefs.

The Earth-Woman Doctrine

One likely area to investigate for corroboration of these beliefs is the ritual and oral traditions of the tribal cultures. Caution must be taken with these materials as well, but one might reason that tribal traditions would be less subject to radical change and the incorporation of external influence than would crisis-cult activities. In Spier's study of the Prophet Dance, he traced the record of the existence of the movement among tribes throughout the interior plateau area, although he noted the fragmentary nature of the data on which to establish the extent and character of the movement and its variations. He identified as the common doctrinal background what he called "the Earth-Woman doctrine." In his analysis the doctrine held that the earth is personified as a woman whose life is limited. When her life comes to its end the world will be destroyed. When the world is destroyed, the creator will return with the dead. Prior to the world destruction, prophets will, from time to time, visit the land of the dead and return with messages. There appears to be no necessary continuity between the personification of the earth as a woman and the millenarian expectations of the movement, and Spier acknowledges that "the Earth-Woman concept is more narrowly limited in its distribution than the belief involved with it that the world has a definite life span." He then notes that "in addition to Northern Okanagon, Thompson, and Shuswap, [the Earth-Woman concept] reappears repeatedly through the southern plateau in the statements of followers of the Smohallah cult at the time of the Nez Perce war (circa 1877)."[30]

As Spier's principal evidence for this Earth-Woman doctrine he cites a Nespelim tale called "Old-One." This is the Northern Okanagon example to which he referred. It is to be noted that the balance of his evidence for the concept or doctrine is none other than the several statements we have already examined. Spier's concern in pre-

senting the doctrine is to demonstrate the precontact ideology of the
Prophet Dance. The portion of the Nespelim tale he quotes is from
near the end of the story:

> He [Old-One, the Chief] said, "I will send messages to earth by
> the souls of people that reach me, but whose time to die has not yet
> come. They will carry messages to you from time to time; and when
> their souls return to their bodies, they will revive, and tell you their
> experiences. Coyote and myself will not be seen again until the Earth-
> Woman is very old. Then we shall return to earth, for it will require a
> new change by that time. Coyote will precede me by some little time;
> and when you see him, you will know that the time is at hand. When I
> return, all the spirits of the dead will accompany me, and after that
> there will be no spirit-land. All the people will live together. Then will
> the Earth-Woman return to her natural shape and live as among her
> children. Then will things be made right, and there will be happiness."
>
> The Earth-Woman is now very old, and even her bones (the rocks)
> are crumbling away. Therefore the time cannot be far away when the
> earth will be transformed again, and when the spirits of the dead will
> come back. The Chief has sent messages from time to time. The Indi-
> ans have learned from these that to be good, speak good, pray, and
> dance will hasten the return of Coyote, and therefore the Indians in
> many places often danced; and when dancing, they prayed much.[31]

What Spier fails to tell his readers is that this story is among the
Okanagon tales that James A. Teit collected between 1907 and
1917. Nor did Spier present or consider the full text of the story. It
is essential to do so. The story begins as a creation story.

> Old-One, or Chief, made the earth out of a woman, and said she
> would be the mother of all the people. Thus the earth was once a
> human being, and she is alive yet; but she has been transformed, and
> we cannot see her in the same way we can see a person. Nevertheless
> she has legs, arms, head, heart, flesh, bones and blood. The soil is her
> flesh; the trees and vegetation are her hair; the rocks, her bones; and
> the wind her breath. She lies out there, and we live on her. She
> shivers and contracts when cold, and expands and perspires when hot.
> When she moves, we have an earthquake.

The story goes on to describe how Old-One took mud or clay and
rolled it into balls from which he made the beings of the ancient
world.

> These beings had some of the characteristics that animals have
> now, and in some respects acted like animals. In form, some were like
> animals, while others more nearly resembled people. Some could fly
> like birds, and others could swim like fishes. All had greater powers,

and were more cunning, than either animals or people. They were not well balanced. Each had great powers in certain ways, but was weak and helpless in other ways. Thus each was exceedingly wise in some things, and exceedingly foolish in others. They all had the gift of speech. As a rule, they were selfish, and there was much trouble among them. Some were cannibals, and lived by eating one another. Some did this knowingly, while others did it through ignorance. They knew that they had to live by hunting, but did not know which beings were people, and which deer. They thought people were deer, and preyed on them. . . .

Old-One made each ball of mud a little different from the others, and rolled them over and over. He shaped them, and made them alive. The last balls of mud he made were almost all alike, and different from any of the preceding ones. They were formed like Indians, and he called them men. He blew on them, and they became alive. They were Indians, but were ignorant and knew no arts. They were the most helpless of all things created; and the cannibals and others preyed on them particularly. The people and animals were made male and female, so that they might breed. Thus everything living sprang from the earth; and when we look around, we see everywhere parts of our mother.

At this point in the narrative there seems to be the promise of documentation within a tribal tradition of the Mother Earth concept; however, the next passages of the story, as recorded by Teit, cast all of this in a new light. Unfortunately, at this point, Teit changes the style in which he has been presenting the story. He abandons the words of the storyteller and in parentheses presents the following description of what the storyteller related:

(Here my informant narrated the story of the Garden of Eden and the fall of man nearly in the same way as given in the Bible. Then he followed by saying the people were much oppressed and preyed on; and so much evil prevailed in the world, that the Chief sent his son Jesus to set things right. After travelling through the world as a transformer, Jesus was killed by the bad people, who crucified him, and he returned to the sky. After he returned, the Chief looked over the world, and saw that things had not changed much for the better. Jesus had only set right a very few things. He had done more talking than anything else. Here the narrator tried to explain that Jesus worked only for the people's spiritual benefit; that he had tried to induce them to be good, and taught them to pray to the Chief. He taught them no arts, nor wisdom about how to do things, nor did he help to make life easier for them. Neither did he transform or destroy the evil monsters which killed them, nor did he change or arrange the features of the earth in any way.)

Teit then lets the storyteller speak again.

> Now, the Chief said, "If matters are not improved on earth soon there will be no people." Then he sent Coyote to earth to destroy all the monsters and evil beings, to make life easier and better for the people, and to teach them the best way to do things.

In another parenthetical interlude, Teit summarizes his story-teller's discussion of the controversial nature of Coyote. Then the story continues:

> Coyote then traveled on the earth, and did many wonderful things. He destroyed the powers of all the monsters and evil beings that preyed on the people. He transformed the good ancients into Indians, and divided them into groups or pairs, and settled them in different places; for the Chief desired the earth to be inhabited everywhere, and not only in a few places. He gave each people a different name and a different language. These pairs were the ancestors of all the present Indian tribes; and that is why there are so many Indian tribes and languages now, and why Indians live all over the country. He taught the people how to eat, how to wear clothes, makes houses, hunt, fish, etc. Coyote did a great deal of good, but he did not finish everything properly. Sometimes he made mistakes; and although he was wise and powerful, he did many foolish things. He was too fond of playing tricks for his own amuse-ment. He was also often selfish, boastful, and vain. He sometimes overreached himself, and occasionally was duped by persons whom he intended to dupe. He was ugly, and women generally did not like him. He often used cunning to gain his ends. He was immortal, and did not die as we die.
>
> Coyote had done nearly everything he could think of, and was travelling from place to place to learn of other things that remained to be done. Chief looked over the earth, and said, "Coyote has now done almost everything that he is capable of doing. I will relieve him." Chief came down, and travelled in the shape of a poor old man. He met Coyote, who said to him, "I am Coyote. Who are you?" Chief answered, "I am Chief of the earth. It was I who sent you to set the world right." Coyote said, "No, you never sent me. I don't know you. If you are Chief, take that lake and place it yonder." Chief said, "No. If you are the wonderful Coyote, let me see you do it!" Coyote did it. Chief said, "Place it back again." Coyote tried, but could not do it. He thought this strange. Chief placed it back. Coyote said, "Now I know you are Chief." Chief said, "Your work is finished. You have travelled far and long, and done much good. Now, you shall go to where I have prepared a home for you." Coyote disappeared, and no one knows where he is.

This is followed by the passage quoted by Spier. Then the story-teller concludes:

Nowadays they pray differently, according as the priests have
taught them; and they build churches, and kneel, praying in them.
They do not now dance as they used to do. The priests say the dancing
is unnecessary, and prayers must be as the Chief's son Jesus taught the
whites. Most Indians agree with this, and think it is the same thing.
Some think that the whites may know better about this, because it
seems that they have been taught more by the Chief, and may be
superior to the Indians in this respect. The Chief must have sent many
wise messages to them.[32]

The purposes for which Spier quoted the passage from this story
are wholly negated when the date of the recitation of the story is
known and the full account is presented. The story assimilates many
Christian elements into a native tradition obviously shaped by millenarian concerns. This is most clearly seen in the conjunction of Jesus
and Coyote as messengers from Old-One sent to earth to set things
right. The Earth-Woman element of the story is striking since clearly
the earth is presented as a female figure, with physical correspondences between body parts and earth features. This element seems to
confirm the existence of a Native American belief in the figure of
Mother Earth, so commonly attributed to Native Americans. There
is little doubt that the inclusion of this figure in the story reflects
such a belief that existed at the time of collection, but there is much
in the story that indicates the belief to be very recently acquired in
the context of a highly creative and dynamic historical situation. We
must be especially cognizant that the inclusion of a personified earth-
woman in this story that was collected after 1907 has no precedent
in any other known Native American story from this region. It does
have precedent in two anthropological works, one by Albert S.
Gatschet, the other by James Mooney.

In 1890, Albert S. Gatschet published an ethnography of the
Klamath people of southwestern Oregon. In this work, Gatschet
states:

> Among all nations of the world we find the idea, which is real as
> well as poetical, that the Earth is our common mother. "She is deal-
> ing out her bountiful gifts to her children, the human beings, without
> envy or restraint, in the shape of corn, fruits, and esculent roots. Her
> eyes are the lakes and ponds disseminated over the green surface of the
> plains, her breasts are the hills and hillocks; and the rivulets and
> brooks irrigating the valleys are the milk flowing from her breasts."
> [Gatschet does not indicate the source of his quotation.]

Gatschet cites several Klamath songs as referring to the earth (*käila*
in Klamath language). The song phrases he refers to are: "I am sing-

ing my earth song," "I, the earth, am resounding like the roll of thunder," "In the morning the Earth resounded,/ Incensed at us was the Earth/ For to kill us wanted the Earth," and "I take the Earth up in my arms and with it whirl around in a dance." He provides no other Klamath evidence on which to base his interpretive statement, but he gives corroborative evidence from a neighboring tribe:

> The Indian prophet Smúxale [Smohalla] at Priest Rapids, on Middle Columbia River, and his numerous followers, called the "Dreamers," from the implicit faith these Sahaptin sectarians place in dreams, dissuade their adherents from tilling the ground, as the white man does; "for it is a sin to wound or cut, tear up or scratch our common mother by agricultural pursuits; she will revenge herself on the whites and on the Indians following their example by opening her bosom and engulfing such malefactors by their misdeeds." [Gatschet does not indicate the source of this quotation either.][33]

And to demonstrate the universality of the first observations cited above, Gatschet provides evidence among tribes distant from the Oregon area.

> This is the poetical imagery in use among the Eastern Indians when the Earth is mentioned to them. [And in a footnote to this sentence he provides the following example.] After Tecumseh had delivered a speech to Governor Harrison at Vincennes, in 1811, he was offered a chair by the interpreter, who said to him: "Your father requests you to take a chair." To this Tecumseh made, with great dignity of expression, an answer which has since become classical: "*The sun is my father, and the earth is my mother; and on her bosom will I repose.*" and immediately seated himself, in the Indian manner, upon the ground. [Gatschet's italics.][34]

These examples constitute the total evidence for Gatschet's conclusions, for he explains:

> The Earth is regarded by these Indians as a mysterious, shadowy power of incalculable energies and influences, rather mischievous and wicked than beneficial to mankind. The Indians ascribe anger and other passions to it, but never personify it in clearer outlines than the ancients did their 'Επα or *Tellus;* and it never appears as an active deity in the numerous mythic tales gathered by Mr. [Edward S.] Curtis for the collection of the Bureau of Ethnology. I know of it only through the song-lines gathered by myself from individuals of both tribes.[35]

In James Mooney's 1896 publication on the Ghost Dance he makes a similar leap from the statements of Smohalla to a theological universal of an earth-mother goddess. Mooney presents the statement of Smohalla as evidence that the idea that the earth is the mother of all created things lies at the base, not only of the Smohalla religion, but of the theology of the Indian tribes generally and of primitive races all over the world. This explains Tecumtha's reply to Harrison: "The sun is my father and the earth is my mother. On her bosom I will rest." In the Indian mind the corn, fruits, and edible roots are the gifts which the earth-mother gives freely to her children. Lakes and ponds are her eyes, hills are her breasts, and streams are the milk flowing from her breasts. Earthquakes and underground noises are signs of her displeasure at the wrongdoings of her children. Especially are the malarial fevers, which often followed extensive disturbance of the surface by excavation or otherwise, held to be direct punishment for the crime of lacerating her bosom.[36]

Of these statements and their notable connection with the Tecumseh statement, more will be said shortly. The central point here is that these studies were published and extant in the region long before the collection of the Okanagon tale by Teit. Since that tale shows extensive Christian influence and a history of encounter with European-Americans, there is every reason to believe that its identification of elements of the physical earth with parts of a female earth-mother may well have been derived from these scholarly sources.

The evidence cited by Spier for the Earth-Woman doctrine of the early Prophet Dance all comes either from the situations of the negotiations over land influenced by crisis-cult developments or from the highly unusual incorporation of this Earth-Woman concept into tribal oral traditions as in the case of the Okanagon story.

To demonstrate that there is no evidence in the interior plateau area for the existence of a mother-earth concept outside of the situation of crisis, is not in any sense to denigrate the figure or the native persons who developed and used the statements cited. However, once it is seen that these statements and stories do not attest to the general belief in a major earth-mother goddess, there is freedom to interpret and appreciate them much more fully. This is the task to which we now turn.

The Longed-for Triumph over Civilization

There are notable peculiarities in the documents that reflect the Native Americans' attitudes toward land and toward the Americans and their policies that would deprive them of their land, but there are some key elements that can be identified and discussed.

Here, as throughout the history of contact, the issue is land, the earth. This issue continues the imagery of savagism versus civilization. American policy centers upon the transformation of native hunters (gatherers and fishers) into cultivators (miners and builders). It is an issue of property and ownership. In the native lifeways the land is not divided and owned as personal property, while this division, settlement, and personal ownership is essential to European-American ways of life. The issues, the contrasting imagery, changed little as the United States spread across the continent.

Yet something new developed in the course of this northwestern encounter. The Native Americans of this region developed during the last half of the nineteenth century a reasoned, sophisticated, and well-articulated argument to support their point of view and with which to criticize the actions of the Americans.

Ultimately the position is founded in and based upon a religious perspective. This is reflected in the constant appeal to the actions of a creator figure who established the proper order in the act of creation. This creator existed before the earth. This creator made the earth. This creator, sometimes using elements of the earth, made the people and all things living on the earth and named them, thus giving them identity and responsibility.

From this base in creation a number of issues and principles are derived. Since people were made from the earth, that is from balls of mud, there is a special earth kinship of the Indian peoples, whose skin is darker than that of European-Americans. Further, since the creation established the native peoples as hunter-gatherer-fishers and did not cause the land to be divided for purposes of cultivation, there is a rightness to the Indian way and a wrongness to the proposed settlement ways.

In some native statements and stories, a history of oppression is described (especially in the stories of Smohalla and the Okanagon) or easily inferred. In this history some people get stronger than others and, as a result, they oppress the weaker and deprive them. The creator, therefore, takes action, killing or reorienting these oppressors. This is a thinly veiled way of criticizing the ways of Americans. In the Okanagon story, Christianity itself is addressed and absorbed into the native traditions. Jesus is first sent by the creator to set the world right, but, while doing some good, he does not do enough. Coyote is the successor to Jesus and does the job well, but he lets the trickster aspect of his character dominate at times. Thus the world is still not fully oriented as desired by the creator. This gives the basis for the expectation of future intervention, even of a cataclysmic event, mediated by and foretold to human prophets. It also establishes a way of comprehending why the millennium has not yet arrived, for the European-Americans have had more prophets and they have established a closer relationship with the creator. This religious base was translated into the ritual practice of millennial movements by prophets who communicated with the creator.

It was also carefully translated into legal terms and practical policy, which are particularly clear in the statements made by Nez Perce nontreaty leaders in the late 1870s. Upon this religious base, they developed the notion of the chieftainship of the land. This is a political and legal extension of the creation doctrine. That is, given the events and outcome of creation, native peoples have the creator-given charge to maintain certain responsibilities toward land, heritage, and lifeways. Furthermore, this is the basis for the inherited rights to the lands. All this amounts to law whose authority is none other than the creator of the world. No other authority can supersede this, not even that of the president of the United States. Therefore, treaties and executive orders are of no use or effect, so there is no need to reverse or nullify them. As put so clearly in the Nez Perce negotiations, the Indians asked nothing of the president of the United States. Smohalla articulated the Indian view when he spoke of the "old law." Even in 1855, Owhi, the Yakima chief, asked, "Where does his talk [the governmental official's] come from that you have been giving us?" In other words, how can you tell us to sell and give away the land unless you speak as the creator (and we already know how the world was created)?

The Native American perspective was fairly consistent and articulated with increasing clarity throughout the last half of the nineteenth century. The perspective is distinct in presenting an indisputable basis for the perpetuation of the Native American relationship with the land; for articulating the meaning, value, and imperative of this way; and for recognizing it as superior to the land relationship being proposed and implemented by European-Americans. Further, the perspective established a base for a movement nativistic, primitivistic, millenarian in character and for the performance of millennial rituals.

The role of the earth goddess in this development must also be considered. Prior to 1877, the earth is referred to in rather nonexplicit terms: "this is our mother this country" (Stachas, 1855); "the Earth says, that God tells me to take care of the Indians" (Young Chief, 1855); "God made our bodies from earth" (Owhi, 1855); and "this reservation, this small piece of land, we look upon it as our mother" (a Cayuse chief, 1855).

These references to the earth are metaphorical, not theological. The Native Americans seek in the metaphor of motherhood some commonality with their oppressors by which to communicate effectively their reluctance to be severed from their lands. They say simply that their traditions, cultures, heritages, and very existence depend upon their land as a child depends upon its mother.

The first indication of the earth as a major religious conception, after that recorded by Kip in 1855, is found in General Howard's response to the Nez Perce in 1877. Clear and explicit evidence for the personification of the earth as female begins to appear in 1885 with MacMurray's record of Smohalla's statement. This is developed into a theological position of some proportions by A. S. Gatschet in 1890[37] and expanded by James Mooney in 1896. It appears again in the Okanagon story told between 1907 and 1917, where not only is the earth a female goddess personified but the goddess's life cycle coincides with the evolution and destruction of the earth.

When this history of documents is carefully examined, it strongly suggests that the emergence of the notion of the earth as a female goddess is inseparable from and derived from the major theological statements made by Mooney and Gatschet. In turn, these theological interpretations are derived more directly from the expectations of the imagery developed in the eastern United States than from clear and demonstrative ethnographic evidence from the tribes in question. The Tecumseh-derived statement recorded by Kip in 1855 and the statements of Gatschet and Mooney, both citing the Tecumseh statement as a primary source, are accessible and likely sources for the development of the earth-goddess concept in Native American cultures in the interior plateau region. The record of the Okanagon story documents a notable creative moment in tribal religious history where ambient imagery of non-native origin is appropriated and put to meaningful use by tribal traditions, even incorporated into oral traditions.

Statements about the earth that were metaphorical and political, though contained within a basically religious perspective, were consistently misinterpreted as theological. In time (not such a very long time, really), these misinterpretations were appropriated by Native Americans who transformed metaphor into divinity.

Reflections on Story and History

Comparison of these two story traditions that center on Tecumseh and Smohalla reveals something of the interdependence of story and history. One story was created by European-Americans about the encounter between themselves and Native Americans, the story of the encounter of Tecumseh and Harrison. The other, created by Native Americans, emerges during the history of encounter between themselves and European-Americans, the story of creation as told variously by Smohalla and by the Okanagon raconteur. Both reinterpret history so as to give it meaning. Both serve not only to create history in the reinterpretation of the past, but in the sense of providing a base, an authority, a course for the actions that open to the future. Both stories seek an unquestionable base for their validity and authority. For the European-American story this base is history itself. The story attributes Tecumseh's statement to a specific historical situation. This concept of authority is evident in the northwest, where European-Americans frequently argued that signed treaties and executive orders were authoritative. Authority in the Native American story is based in the primordium and in the acts of the creator, what might be called the authority of religion. The difference in the basis for authority is fundamental and in it much may be learned about the differences between Americans with European ancestry and Native Americans.

The comparative consideration of these two examples shows that European-American and Native Americans do not differ as radically and clearly as is usually indicated by the distinction between history and story, a difference parallel to that between literate and nonliterate, civilized and savage. History is taken seriously, seen as connected with reality and with the true past. In contrast, story is usually seen as fictive, imaginative, nonhistorical, and, therefore, not to be taken seriously, especially if it is the story of the folk. Consideration of the Tecumseh and Smohalla stories shows that the careful distinction between story and history is fundamental and essential, but that it does not distinguish between Native Americans and European-Americans. Neither the story of Tecumseh nor the creation story told by Smohalla and the Okanagon is historical, but history is behind and within both. The careful analysis of these examples warns against continuing to make radical distinctions and a host of assumptions on the basis of a genre distinction alone. There is an important interdependence between story and history. Story is a manifestation of the power of the word to render history and, consequently, human life meaningful. As I have come to think of it, when the facts of history come together for someone in a way that reveals their meaning or in a way that enables their fuller meaning to be sought, a story is born. History lacks meaning without story. Story lacks substance and relevance without history. What distinguishes these traditions and those who bear the traditions is not that one presents history and the other tells stories, for they both tell stories; the distinction is the authority underlying the stories told. For the European-American story tradition the authority is history, even though the story is not strictly historical; for the Native American story tradition the authority is religious and outside of history, even though the story reflects history.

Elsewhere in native North America, Mother Earth is commonly recognized as part of story traditions. It is to a pair of these examples that we now turn.

▲ 4 ▲

Metamother Earth: The Zuni and the Pueblo Idea of Fertilization

From the lying together of these twain [the Fourfold-Containing Mother Earth and the All-Covering Father Sky] upon the great world-waters, so vitalizing, terrestrial life was conceived; whence began all beings of earth, men and the creatures, in the Fourfold Womb of the World.

This Zuni account of creation, presented by nineteenth-century ethnologist Frank Hamilton Cushing, is commonly quoted as evidence that the Zuni people, of what is now New Mexico, exemplify a classic world-parent cosmogony, that is, the belief that Father Sky and Mother Earth are progenitors of the world. Among all tribes in North America, the Zuni have stood as the prime example of this cosmogony, yet the belief has been attested as existing much more widely. H. K. Haeberlin, in his classic monograph, "The Idea of Fertilization in the Culture of the Pueblo Indians,"[1] holds that the belief in Mother Earth and Father Sky exists among all the Pueblos and among Native Americans generally, throughout the United States excepting only the Northwest Coast. Haeberlin saw the belief in Father Sky and Mother Earth as corresponding closely with the practice of agriculture and, to a lesser degree, pottery-making.

Haeberlin's study has been widely influential, affecting not only the way Pueblo cultures are understood but supporting the widely held view that the American Southwest is the stronghold of Mother

Earth. It is essential to consider Haeberlin's study carefully and critically and then move beyond it to the materials related to Mother
Earth and other goddesses in the ethnographic record of the Zuni
and other Pueblo tribes.

Haeberlin's Idea of Fertilization

The tribes in the American Southwest referred to as "Pueblo" have
similar lifeways, but they are far from being homogeneous. Among
these tribes four language-families are represented and each tribe
speaks a language that is unintelligible to all the others, except for
several tribes whose languages are dialectically related. The histories
of the Pueblo tribes have been intertwined for centuries due to physical proximity, but individual tribal traditions are distinct.

The simple fact of the diversity is essential background to any
critical appraisal of Haeberlin's article because, as the title implies, he
holds that there is a monolithic Pueblo culture, not several distinct,
although related, Pueblo cultures. This assumption permits him to
draw freely, even randomly, from any of the Pueblo tribes without
placing his evidence in the context of particular tribal or regional
traditions. Haeberlin believes that there is a near universality of the
idea of Father Sky and Mother Earth in North America, with its
historical roots in Mesoamerica. Yet because of this understanding,
Haeberlin cannot simply present the Pueblo belief in the Father Sky
and Mother Earth deities as distinguishing Pueblo thought, or "psychology" as he consistently terms it. While he holds that this fructifying pair is central to Pueblo psychology, he must give it specificity by
showing how it is uniquely interpreted by the Pueblos. Thus, for
Haeberlin, the key is the association of Father Sky and Mother
Earth with a distinctively Pueblo idea of fertilization. In Haeberlin's
words,

> the idea of the complementary sky and earth beings itself does not
> constitute a unique characteristic of the Pueblo. I shall, however, at-
> tempt to show that on account of the typical associations which this
> idea has met with in the culture of these peoples, it has found a specif-
> ic expression characteristic of the center of the Southwestern culture
> area.[2]

To evaluate his argument it is necessary to review critically the
evidence Haeberlin presents to support his contention of the Pueblo
belief in the sky-earth creators. His most extensive discussion is of
the Zuni, and it is based almost exclusively upon Cushing's account,

which will be considered in more detail below. For evidence of this belief among the Hopi, he cites a remark made by J. Walter Fewkes to the effect that, in Hopi belief, the earth has always existed and is analogous with growing vegetation, and further that the earth is the mother of lesser gods and animals and the original ancestor or first member of the human race.[3] In evidence for this belief among the eastern Pueblo tribes, Haeberlin notes that "the Tewa and the Keres regard sun-father and moon-mother as their principal deities."[4] Haeberlin holds that there are common associations that may fuse Earth Mother and Moon Mother. While he holds that it is inaccurate to conclude that the native people conceive of the moon and earth goddesses as identical, Haeberlin allows himself to effectively identify them by arguing that

> the decisive point seems to be that the beings that figure in primitive religion and mythology, never having undergone a logical specification and systematization, are not clearly definable, and not "finished" products of the human mind, but are rather subject to kaleidoscopic changes due to the shifting angle of apperception of the folk as a whole as well as of its constituent individuals.[5]

This principle permits Haeberlin to find Mother Earth anywhere a female figure with certain traits is mentioned, whatever her name or domain. We must see that the disparity of names and identities for Mother Earth that Haeberlin attempted to reconcile was not introduced by the Pueblos but by Haeberlin's insistence that these figures were all appearances of one figure, Mother Earth.

Cushing's account of Zuni creation is the only explicit evidence Haeberlin has to document the Pueblo belief in sky-earth world-parent creators. He adds to this several nonexplicit references to the earth he finds in other Pueblo tribes. From his belief in the primitive mentality of the Pueblo peoples, Haeberlin can identify figures such as Moon Mother with Earth Mother to further his documentation. In this manner, he establishes, all too thinly, what he sees as the central expression of the Pueblo idea of fertilization. Belief in this fructifying pair of world parents is not in Haeberlin's understanding unique to the Pueblos, so he proposes that Pueblo psychology is distinguished by the way in which this creator pair can be related to other cultural forms by means of the idea of fertilization. Thus, the Mother Earth–Father Sky creator pair become the central link on which are hung several chains of association all interlinked by the idea of fertilization.

The first chain of associations begins with the notion that the sexual union of the sky and the earth fertilizes the earth. Parturition from the womb within the earth takes place through a birth channel that Haeberlin recognizes as the hole of emergence common to various Pueblo story traditions. Haeberlin looks to Hopi culture as exemplary, considering associations with the *sipapu*. He notes that in Hopi culture the *sipapu* is the earth opening through which the figure Müwiñwû sends the germs of all living things. Assuming, therefore, that the *sipapu* is predominantly associated with the idea of germination and fertility, Haeberlin moves to the next link in this chain:

> When one bears in mind that water and fertility are practically synonyms in the mind of the Pueblo, it is readily understood why the Great Waterserpent, the Palülükoñ of the Horn, should be conceived in a way that is very similar to Müwiñwû.[6]

Through this association, Haeberlin enters finally into a discussion of the Great Waterserpent.

The final association in this chain is that the return of the dead to the underworld is homologous with agricultural cycles.

This chain of associations begins with the sky-earth pair. Their creative act suggests birth from the earth womb, which reminds Haeberlin of the Hopi *sipapu* and then of Müwiñwû, the germinator, who in turn reminds him of Palülükoñ, the Great Waterserpent. The emergence, on the other hand, suggests to Haeberlin the return of the dead to the underworld and the associated idea of fertilization.

Beginning once again with the assumed world-parent act of creation, Haeberlin enters another chain of associations. This time he discusses the twin war gods, because they were born of a maiden (whom Haeberlin can quickly recognize as the Earth Mother) who is impregnated by the sun. The topic of the twins leads Haeberlin to consider lightning (with which the twins are armed), hoops, rings, and the dart and hoop game (for the twins played with hoops and rings).

Throughout this associative chaining process, Haeberlin selects evidence from any of the Pueblo tribes as needed and never indicates anything of the historical or cultural contexts relative to the specific tribes. He firmly holds to the homogeneity of Pueblo culture and the Pueblo mind.

Haeberlin's own summation reviews his reasoning and deserves being quoted at length.

> The idea of Sky-father and of his complement, Earth Mother, which, when considered independently, is by no means restricted to the

Pueblo, gains its characteristic connotations through the associations into which it enters in this culture. Important associations of this kind appear in the myths of the Snake society of the Hopi. The same idea is also associated with that of parturition and of the emergence of the people through the *sipapu*. A further link in the chain of associations is the idea of the *sipapu* as a *lagune* and of springs as the natural passages of communication with the gods of the underworld and of fertility. The water serpent is the deity of the fertilizing water of these springs, as well as God of the Underworld, the place of germination. The deceased return to the underworld whence they work for rain and fertility in the behalf of the living. This belief is an important psychological factor in the Katcina cult, without explaining its origin historically. The Twin War Gods offer a similar example of secondary psychological associations. These gods and their societies are associated with war, on the one hand, and with the idea of fertilization, on the other. Their weapons are simultaneously weapons of war and symbols of fertilization. The unequivocal meaning of the hoop or annulet, whether it be associated with the Twin War Gods or not, is always that of fertilization of the fields. Finally, the dart and wheel game, which is the game par excellence of the war-gods, is employed in the women's dances of the Hopi as magic of fertilization. . . .

This summary indicates the common trend or setting of the Pueblo culture. That this setting is not comprehensible as a summation of diffused elements is proven by the reinterpretation of heterogeneous traits according to a uniform scheme of interrelated ideas.[7]

Haeberlin begins with the assumption of the near universal existence of the Father Sky and Mother Earth pair and the contention that the fertility associations that the Pueblo form with this pair serve to distinguish Pueblo psychology. The construction of a series of associations selected seemingly upon a connection with fertility is intended to demonstrate that the idea of fertilization is a characteristic of each of the associations. This leads Haeberlin to claim proof for both the existence of Father Sky and Mother Earth as well as for the conjoined idea of fertilization as the distinguishing feature of Pueblo psychology.

This type of argument is faulty in several respects. Haeberlin's principles of selecting and interpreting data to establish the idea of fertilization are too heavy-handed. On his terms, there is no question that he will find ample support for his concern. Furthermore, there is no negative evidence to demonstrate that other tribes, who in Haeberlin's view believe in the sky-earth pair, do not also hold to the idea of fertilization. Haeberlin's belief that the sky-earth pair is nearly conterminous with the area of agriculture suggests that the idea of fertilization might likewise correspond with the area. In any case, the idea of fertilization is so general that it loses any sense of precision or distinctiveness. Such a broad idea might be and commonly has been found among cultures the world over. Finally, and most importantly, while Haeberlin's fundamental contention, the link on which all others seem to hang, is the fructifying act of Father Sky and Mother Earth, all of the associations he identifies are based upon the general idea of fertilization. Thus these claims of association are actually independent of the creator pair and therefore do not constitute acceptable evidence for the general Pueblo belief in Father Sky and Mother Earth beyond his single specific example, Cushing's account of Zuni creation.

Metamother Earth, Cushing's Myth of the Zuni

Frank Hamilton Cushing is one of the most colorful, yet controversial, figures in the history of American ethnography.[8] One element of controversy centers on his accounts of the Zuni story of their origin. His accounts appear in his "Zuñi Breadstuff" (1884) and his "Outlines of Zuñi Creation Myths" (1896). Both of these accounts begin with the progenitive act of a Sky Father and an Earth Mother. The earlier version includes the following passage:

> First, there was sublime darkness, which vanished not until came the "Ancient Father of the Sun," revealing universal waters. These were, save him, all that were.
> The Sun-father thought to change the face of the waters and cause life to replace their desolation.
> He rubbed the surface of his flesh, thus drawing forth *yep'-na*.
> The *yep'-na* he rolled into two balls. From his high and "ancient among the spaces," (*Te'-thlä-shi-na-kwin*) he cast forth one of these balls and it fell upon the surface of the waters. There, as a drop of deer suet on hot broth, so this ball melted and spread far and wide like scum over the greater waters, ever growing, until it sank into them.
> Then the Sun-father cast forth the other ball, and it fell, spreading out and growing even larger than had the first, and dispelling so much of the waters that it rested upon the first. In time, the first became a great being—our Mother, the Earth; and the second became another great being—our Father, the Sky. Thus was divided the universal fluid into the "embracing waters of the World" below, and the "embracing waters of the Sky" above. Behold! this is why the Sky-father is blue as the ocean which is the home of the Earth-mother, blue even his flesh, as seem the far-away mountains—though they be the flesh of the Earth-mother.

Now while the Sky-father and the Earth-mother were together, the Earth-mother conceived in her ample wombs—which were the four great underworlds or caves—the first of men and creatures. Then the two entered into council that they might provide for the birth of their children.[9]

The later version begins as follows:

Before the beginning of the new-making, Áwonawílona (the Maker and Container of All, the All-father Father), solely had being. There was nothing else whatsoever throughout the great space of the ages save everywhere black darkness in it, and everywhere void desolation.

In the beginning of the new-made, Áwonawílona conceived within himself and thought outward in space, whereby mists of increase, steams potent of growth, were evolved and uplifted. Thus, by means of his innate knowledge, the All-container made himself in person and form of the Sun whom we hold to be our father and who thus came to exist and appear. With his appearance came the brightening of the spaces with light, and with the brightening of the spaces the great mist-clouds were thickened together and fell, whereby was evolved water in water; yea, and the world-holding sea.

With his substance of flesh (*yépnane*) outdrawn from the surface of his person, the Sun-father formed the seed-stuff of twain worlds, impregnating therewith the great waters, and lo! in the heat of his light these waters of the sea grew green and scums (*k'yanashótsiyallawe*) rose upon them, waxing wide and weighty until, behold! they became Áwitelin Tsíta, the "Four-fold Containing Mother-earth," and Aponyan Tä'chu, the "All-covering Father-sky."

From the lying together of these twain upon the great world waters, so vitalizing, terrestrial life was conceived; whence began all beings of earth, men and the creatures, in the Four-fold womb of the World (*Áwiten Téhu'hlnakwi*).[10]

These two accounts of creation differ in some detail, but they are roughly parallel. The primal condition is one of darkness in which dwells "Ancient Father of the Sun" (1884) or "Áwonawílona, the Maker and Container of All" (1896). This primal being initiates a process of creation that leads to the appearance of a pair whose union creates a second pair, the earth and sky, whose union in turn is the act of conceiving the humans and creatures that will inhabit the world. The first conception is made via flesh, that is in one case the substance of earth and sky (1884) and, in the other, the seed stuff that fertilizes the waters from which grow the substantial sky and earth (1896). In both versions, the sky is conceived as father, the earth as mother, and it is through their union that humans and creatures, inhabitants of the earth, are conceived in the wombs of the earth.

In both texts Cushing grounds the English language with some Zuni terms, and, in the 1884 account, he places an occasional phrase in quotation marks, suggesting a strict Zuni equivalent, as in a literal translation.

While we do not have the Zuni language texts, nor are we told the name of the storyteller or the situation under which the story was told, and while there are certain differences between the two accounts that call for clarification, the texts appear to accurately document Zuni story tradition. The problems arise when we seek accounts of these stories from other students of Zuni oral tradition and thereby learn of their frustrating attempts to corroborate Cushing's versions. For example, in a summary version of the Zuni story of creation published by Matilda C. Stevenson in 1904 is the following:

> In the beginning A'wonawil'ona with the Sun Father and Moon Mother existed above, and Shi'wanni and Shi'wano'kia, his wife, below. Shi'wanni and Shi'wano'kia were superhuman beings who labored not with hands but with hearts and minds....
>
> All was shi'pololo (fog), rising like steam. With the breath from his heart A'wonawil'ona created clouds and the great waters of the world. He-She is the blue vault of the firmament. The breath clouds of the gods are tinted with the yellow of the north, the blue-green of the west, the red of the south, and the silver of the east of A'wonawil'ona. The smoke clouds of white and black become a part of A'wonawil'ona; they are himself, as he is the air itself; and when the air takes on the form of a bird it is but a part of himself—is himself. Through the light, clouds, and air he becomes the essence and creator of vegetation. The Zuni conception of A'wonawil'ona is similar to that of the Greek of Athena....
>
> After A'wonawil'ona created the clouds and the great waters of the world, Shi'wanni said to Shi'wano'kia: "I, too, will make something beautiful, which will give light at night when the Moon Mother sleeps." Spitting in the palm of his left hand, he patted the spittle with the fingers of his right hand, and the spittle foamed like yucca suds and then formed into bubbles of many colors, which he blew upward; and thus he created the fixed stars and constellations. And Shi-wanni was well pleased with his creation. Then Shi'wano'kia said "See what I can do," and she expectorated into the palm of her left hand and slapped the saliva with the fingers of her right, and the spittle foamed like yucca suds, running over her hand and flowing everywhere; and thus she created A'witelin 'Si'ta (Earth Mother).[11]

In Stevenson's version Shi'wanni and Shi'wano'kia were the parents of the Zuni people. They were created within the earth. The Sun created two sons, war gods, who entered the earth to release the peoples and lead them to the earth's surface.

We may note some of the crucial differences in these three accounts. The figure of A'wonawil'ona (*?a'wona'wil?ona*) varies among the accounts. In Cushing's first account there is no mention of such a figure, although the part is played by a figure Cushing calls "Ancient Father of the Sun." Cushing's second account designated the figure as the original being, "the Maker and Container of All, the All-father Father." In Stevenson's account A'wonawil'ona is one of the original beings joined by Sun Father and Moon Mother and by Shi'wanni and Shi'wano'kia. A'wonawil'ona is addressed sometimes as a male (although there are suggestions of androgyny) and as such is identified as "the vault of the firmament," as well as "the essence and creator of vegetation." The role of the Sky Father and Earth Mother shifts markedly also. In Stevenson's account they do not appear as Cushing placed them, as a second pair of creator figures, those most responsible for creating humans and earth's creatures. The Sky Father even fails to appear and the Earth Mother is one of the results of the creative process.

While these differences are important, even more important ones appear with Ruth Bunzel's works on the Zuni. A statement from Bunzel's "Introduction to Zuñi Ceremonialism" (1932) helps to define the issues that must be resolved in relation to the Zuni belief in a Sky Father and Earth Mother:

> Zuni myth and ritual contain innumerable expressions of what Haeberlin calls the "idea of fertilization," but to the Zuni these are unrelated episodes—they do not view them as parts of a great cosmological concept. There are many tales of a maiden being impregnated by the sun or the rain; the sun is called "father," the earth "mother"; and the people are believed to have originated within the earth in the "womb." [Here Bunzel notes that *tehulikwin* is a word used for womb, but also for any dark enclosed place and literally means "inside space."] Yet the general concept of the sexuality of the universe as the source of life, . . . is not known at Zuni. Cushing records the myth of the sky cohabitating with the earth to produce life, indicating that the notion was current in that day. It has completely vanished at the present time. I have recorded Zuni creation myths from priests and laymen, in secular and ritualistic form, and all commence the same way. . . .[12]

Alas! the vivid image of creation as the sexual act of the Father Sky and Mother Earth has, by Bunzel's time, disappeared from Zuni altogether. Bunzel further calls attention to the confusion of both Cushing's and Stevenson's accounts by showing that A'wonawil'ona is not a bisexual deity but rather a term that refers to a great class of supernaturals.[13]

As the various students of Zuni culture and oral traditions are reviewed, it becomes clear that Cushing is the only source for evidence of the Zuni belief in Father Sky and Mother Earth as creators, yet there is scattered evidence among the sources attesting to Zuni belief in various figures who are personalized, and some anthropomorphized, such as Earth Mother, Moon Mother, Sun Father, and Corn Father. Bunzel left open the possibility that the belief Cushing described had existed in his day but had since disappeared. That is one issue that must be addressed. The other is the need to document carefully the Zuni belief in a figure they refer to as Mother Earth or Earth Mother, in Zuni language ?*awitelin citta*.

The first concern is illuminated by reviewing Cushing and his adventures at Zuni. Cushing was ethnologist on a Smithsonian expedition to Zuni in 1879. The expedition was to last approximately three months. The members of the expedition camped at a distance from Zuni and began their investigations. Cushing was eager to make personal contact with the Zuni people and after failing in several attempts to establish the kind of rapport he desired, he believed that his physical separation from them was his problem. His solution was to move, uninvited, into the house of the governor of Zuni. Discovering that Cushing had taken residence in his house, the governor inquired how long he was to be his host, and Cushing responded, "Two months." What, no doubt, had looked to be a long two months for his Zuni hosts turned out to be four and a half years. The challenge to understand made Cushing determined to devote himself to "becoming Zuni." The other members of the Smithsonian expedition, upset by Cushing's approach, left him at Zuni, apparently without provisions or encouragement. The Zuni eventually accepted Cushing and resolved to make him as Zuni as they could. He became fluent in Zuni language. He was initiated into a Zuni ceremonial order and came to hold the prestigious office of "First War Chief." In fact, his departure from Zuni was not of his choosing but the result of his acting as Zuni war chief. He attempted to protect Zuni lands from the insatiable land desires of Americans. Because he tangled with interests of relatives of a United States congressman, the continuance of government funding for the Bureau of Ethnology came to depend upon his departure from Zuni. Cushing's character as well as his style of ethnology is captured in the epithet he attached to his signature: "1st War Chief of Zuni, U.S. Asst. Ethnologist."

Cushing has been praised and harshly criticized for his participant-observation style of ethnology. He was among the first professional ethnologists to use this method. There seems always to be some measure of exasperation in those who have written criticisms of Cushing's work. His devotion to Zuni, his knowledge of Zuni language, his insight and tenacity are generally recognized, yet his manner of reporting his findings has often left his readers unable to disentangle his observations from his imaginings. Cushing presents one of the first examples in the continuing debate in anthropological method between the polar positions of objective observation and complete absorption of the observer within the culture observed.[14]

This issue need not be resolved (it is perhaps more a matter of style than validity anyway) in order to evaluate Cushing's account of the Zuni origin story, but knowing Cushing's style and method helps us to understand the character and intent of his account of Zuni origin stories. There is a suggestive clue to be found even in the title of Cushing's more formal presentation of the story in his Bureau of Ethnology report. The title is "Outlines of Zuñi Creation Myths." In a fifty-page introduction to the Zuni creation stories, Cushing is relatively clear about the approach and intent of his task. At the time of writing, he had envisioned doing several related projects. The first, "Outlines of Zuñi Creation Myths," was to provide an overall scheme of Zuni mythology, presented so that the reader could grasp what Cushing believed was the general structure of the mythology, which was marked by a synthesis and wholeness that Cushing believed was known by only a few Zunis, those who took the responsibility of Kyä'klo, who tells the whole story of creation. The second, to follow his general "outline" work, would present detailed explanations of the Zuni stories, including his authority for framing and translating the stories. Unfortunately the second project was never completed. He described his intent in the following passage:

> I have entitled the originative division of this paper "Outlines of Zuñi Creation Myths," because, in the first place, this is but a preliminary rendering of these, and, properly speaking, they are a series of explanation-myths. Now, while such myths are generally disconnected, often, indeed, somewhat contradictory episode-legends with primitive peoples, they are, with the Zuñis, already become serial, and it is in their serial or epic form (but merely in outline) that I here give

them. Although each is called a talk, and is held specifically by a particular organization or social division, yet all are called "the speech."
This comes about in Zuñi by the presence in the tribal organization,
as already explained, of a class of men and priests there called the
"Midmost," or the "All," because hereditary in a single clan (the Ma-
caw), yet representative sacerdotally of all the clans and all the
priesthoods, which they out-rank as "Masters of the House of
Houses."

With them all these various myths are held in brief and repeated in
set form and one sequence as are placed the beads of a rosary or on a
string, each entire, yet all making a connected strand. Here, then, we
see the rudiment or embryo of a sacred epic such as that of the Kyä'klu
or "Speaker of all times whensoever."

As finally published, this paper will contain the most ample explanation of all these points and many others, and will not ask, as it does
today, catholic judgment and charitable interpretation.[15]

Cushing, perhaps because of his appreciation of the poetic style of
Zuni oral tradition and doubtless because he believed himself to have
become Zuni in thought, did not present his outlines as mere outlines. Rather he rendered them in literary form as stories with suggestions of a certain biblical style. Consider the style of such outline
passages as: "From the lying together of these twain . . . " and "the
Sun-father formed the seed-stuff of twain worlds, impregnating
therewith the great waters, and lo! in the heat of his light these waters of the sea grew green. . . . "

In a recent reflection on the scope of Cushing's work and the
contributions it makes, Jesse Green concluded that

> in truth, when all is said about Cushing's significance in the history of
> anthropology, it may be that one should admit, if pressed, that it is
> primarily as literature that his writings continue to merit attention—
> though they have received even less of it in the literary world than in
> the anthropological.[16]

It is clear that Cushing, as an ethnologist, knew the importance of
the tedious job of preparing explanation and documentation for his
presentation of the Zuni creation stories, but it is also clear that he
was wholly satisfied by his literary, interpretive presentation of them.

Even if Cushing had published the second part of his report on
Zuni oral traditions, the "outlines" would no doubt still have been
widely used as Zuni texts. It would have been a simpler task to evaluate the ethnographic contribution of these outlines. What must be
seen and taken into account is that the outlines are exactly what
Cushing says they are, "a preliminary rendering." We must recog-

nize the process of which the outlines are the product. Living among the Zuni, speaking their language, attempting to think like them, Cushing wrote an interpretive English rendering of the stories presented in a serial form similar to the epic told by Kyä'klu, the speaker of all times whensoever. Cushing, in effect, wrote a story incorporating Zuni story elements. He created a myth upon Zuni mythology. He presented a metamyth. His stories are an interpretation of Zuni mythology in literary form. There is not necessarily fault in this approach, nor did Cushing intend to deceive. He stated his intention to explain his interpretive presentation. Still, his approach, while decades ahead of its time,[17] has invited the wide misconception that what he is presenting is an exact record of Zuni creation stories. They have certainly been used as such. While *?awitelin citta* (Earth Mother) does not appear to be a principal creator at Zuni, there is no doubt that she is a figure well known to the Zuni. Thus we must now turn our attention to her, to learn of her character and her place in Zuni thought and religious belief.

Mother Earth at Zuni

Observers of Zuni, and certainly Cushing is to be included, have been impressed with the extent to which the Zuni personalize and often anthropomorphize the elements in their world. Ruth Bunzel wrote:

> To the Zuni the whole world appears animate. Not only are night and day, wind, clouds, and trees possessed of personality, but even articles of human manufacture, such as houses, pots, and clothing, are alive and sentient. All matter has its inseparable spiritual essence. For the most part this spiritual aspect of things is vague and impersonal.[18]

In terms of Zuni taxonomy there is a very wide class of beings, *?a·ho??i,* that may be roughly considered to be people. This category is divided into two subdivisions, or two kinds of persons: *k?apin ?a·ho??i,* or "raw people," and *?akna ?a·ho??i* or *tek?ohannan ?a·ho??i,* "cooked people" or "daylight people."[19] The raw people eat uncooked food, that is, food offered to them by daylight people, and they can change their form. Cooked or daylight people are human beings, or, more narrowly, human beings who live according to the Zuni way of life. Most importantly, the raw and the cooked peoples should behave as kinsmen toward one another. In the Zuni perspective they are dependent upon one another. The cooked people must feed the raw people by making offerings and prayers to them. The raw people in turn provide life for the cooked people in the ways ordinarily attributed to nature, controlling such elements as the rains, the plants, and the animals or being made manifest through them. The figures known as *ʔaˑwonaˑwillapʔona* (plural of *ʔaˑwonaˑwilʔona*) or, literally, "the ones who hold the roads," are raw people.

The kinship relationship to these many raw people is manifest through the use of kinship terms. Stevenson wrote that "many things which tend to nourish life are symbolized by the Zunis as mother."[20] Certainly the same is true for other kinship terms, especially "father," "grandmother," and "grandfather."

These observations are important in the effort to understand the place of *ʔawitelin citta* in Zuni thought and religion. Clearly the earth, as well as the sun, winds, moon, and corn, is recognized as an important "raw person" and is addressed, as are the others, in appropriate kinship terms. The earth is a female raw person who may be addressed formally as *ʔawitelin citta* or Earth Mother. As a "raw person" she might be given offerings and addressed in prayer. She can be recognized as the source of vegetable matter and game animals, vital elements of nourishment for the Zuni peoples. Their relationship with her is essential to Zuni life.

During their work among the Zuni in 1972, Dennis and Barbara Tedlock found that the Zuni people personalized the earth in feminine form, with trees and bushes representing her arms and hands.[21] And in a prayer collected by Bunzel, which will be considered in more detail below, *ʔawitelin citta* is robed in moss, flowers, and pollen and the earth's surface is spoken of as the "flesh of the earth mother."[22]

Thus, there is ample ethnographic evidence that the Zuni at times refer to the earth as mother. This is simply evident in the Zuni term *ʔawitelin citta* or Earth Mother. It is clear that this practice is consistent with a much broader aspect of Zuni worldview in which many aspects of the physical world are identified in comparable terms.

The roles that *ʔawitelin citta* plays in Zuni religious culture and worldview and what constitutes her character must now be considered.

While Cushing's account of the Zuni creation story has drawn a great deal of attention, it appears that the Zuni are not greatly interested in cosmogony, in cosmic origins. In the collections of oral tradition, including Cushing's "outlines," almost all of the material is devoted to the emergence and the migrations of the first Zuni peoples and to their search for the place where they might find life, that is, their search for "the middle place."

Zuni cosmology is fairly consistently described as a system of the cardinal directions, the zenith, the nadir, and the center place. The zenith includes the sky, physically conceived as a stone bowl inverted over the earth. Above the sky are four upper worlds, each identified with a particular bird. Below the earth's surface the Zuni describe four worlds. Sometimes these are referred to in translation as "wombs," but as already noted, the Zuni word thus rendered refers to any dark enclosed place. These lower worlds are given distinction by the rooms they contain or with which they are identified. Moving from the lowest upward, the worlds are called Sulphur Room, Soot or Moss Room, Gray or Mud Room, and Wing (sunray) Room. The world of the earth's surface is depicted as circular, surrounded by oceans on the four sides in each of which is a mountain bearing the color associated with that direction. The oceans are interconnected by underground passages or streams that in places rise to the surface as lakes, streams, and ponds. While *ʔawitelin citta* may be depicted as the personification of the earth, it appears that when the Zuni describe the earth as part of the cosmos, they do not personify the earth's surface as a reclining female figure.[23]

Students of Zuni since Cushing have consistently included *ʔawitelin citta* among the Zuni deities, yet all have recognized that the most central of figures in Zuni religion are Sun Father (*yatokka tačču*) and Moon Mother (*yaʔonakka citta*) or Moonlight-Giving Mother. They are nearly synonymous with "The Ones Who Hold the Roads" (*ʔa·wonaʔwilʔona*). They are considered the ultimate givers of life, a notion consistent with one of the ways the Zuni designate human beings, as daylight people. According to Dennis Tedlock, Sun Father is considered to be the husband of Moon Mother. His mother, or maternal grandmother, is White Shell Woman (*kʔohak ʔoka*) and his sister is Old Lady Salt (*maʔlokaccikʔi*). These central figures do not include *ʔawitelin citta,* and she does not appear as a character in story traditions. Further, Sun Father and Moon Mother appear in ceremony as masked figures. This is not the case with *ʔawitelin citta.*

Without a major role in oral tradition or public ceremony, *ʔawitelin citta* is most commonly found in the context of sustenance activities. She may be named and described in prayer, although it is not clear whether or not she is actually addressed in prayer. She may be influenced by the offering of prayers and the presentation of prayerstick offerings, although this may be the result of her being influenced by other deities.

The best evidence for the role and character of *ʔawitelin citta* is found in the Zuni prayers collected by Ruth Bunzel. She introduces them as examples of the many prayers which describe natural phenomena in anthropomorphic guise. Unfortunately, Bunzel did not give either the context for these prayers or delineate the beginnings and endings of the prayers. The prayers presented here show both the manner in which *ʔawitelin citta* is described and that other elements in the physical world are described in similar terms.

> That our earth mother may wrap herself
> In a fourfold robe of white meal;
> That she may be covered with frost flowers;
> That yonder on all the mossy mountains,
> The forests may huddle together with the cold;
> That their arms may be broken by the snow,
> In order that the land may be thus,
> I have made my prayer sticks into living beings.[24]

This appears to be a prayer accompanying the offering of prayersticks (short sticks manifesting spirit beings), to the end that the earth be covered with snow. By its identity with white meal and flowers, the snow is the benevolent and life-giving substance of the winters.

> Following wherever the roads of the rain makers come out,
> May the ice blanket spread out,
> May the ice blanket cover the country;
> All over the land
> May the flesh of our earth mother
> Crack open from the cold;
> That your thoughts may bend to this,
> That your words may be to this end;
> For this with prayers I send you forth.[25]

This prayer passage appears to be associated with much the same context and values as those of the previous one. Added here are phrases that indicate the Zuni view of the power of thought and speech, as well as the power of prayer acts.

> When our earth mother is replete with living waters,
> When spring comes,
> The source of our flesh,
> All the different kinds of corn,

We shall lay to rest in the ground.
With their earth mother's living waters,
They will be made into new beings.
Coming out standing into the daylight
Of their sun father,
Calling for rain,
To all sides they will stretch out their hands.
Then from wherever the rain makers stay quietly
They will send forth their misty breath;
Their massed clouds filled with water will come out to sit down with
    us;
Far from their homes,
With outstretched hands of water they will embrace the corn,
Stepping down to caress them with their fresh waters,
With their fine rain caressing the earth,
With their heavy rain caressing the earth,
And yonder, wherever the roads of the rain makers come forth,
Torrents will rush forth,
Silt will rush forth,
Mountains will be washed out,
Logs will be washed down,
Yonder all the mossy mountains
Will drip with water.
The clay-lined hollows of our earth mother
Will overflow with water,
From all the lakes
Will rise the cries of the children of the rain makers,
In all the lakes
There will be joyous dancing—
Desiring that it should be thus,
I send forth my prayers.[26]

Rain makers are personified beings. This prayer is for rain, including recognition not only of its fructifying powers but also of its enormous physical powers.

That our earth mother
May wear a fourfold green robe,
Full of moss,
Full of flowers,
Full of pollen,
That the land may be thus
I have made you into living beings.[27]

This appears to be a prayerstick offering prayer like the one above, but one uttered in the spring rather than the winter.

With eagle's wing,
And with the striped cloud wings of all the birds of summer,
With these four times wrapping our plume wands
(We make them into living beings)
With our mother, cotton woman,
Even a roughly spun cotton thread,
A soiled cotton thread,
With this four times encircling them
And tying it about their bodies
And with a water bringing hair feather,
We made our plume wands into living beings.
With the flesh of our mother,
Clay woman,
Four times clothing our plume wands with flesh,
We made them into living beings.
Holding them fast,
We made them our representatives in prayer.[28]

This prayer appears to accompany the construction of feathered-wand prayer beings. Notably, as the earth is identified as mother, in this prayer we see that cotton and clay are so identified. They are essential elements of the plume wands.

In Zuni oral traditions ʔawitelin citta is not a major deity or figure. There are no stories in which she is a character. She appears most commonly in that broad pattern of Zuni thought and behavior in which things both animate and inanimate are personified, sometimes loosely anthropomorphized, and addressed in kinship terms. Among such things as trees, winds, rains, mountains, clay, and cotton, the earth is given personhood and referred to in kinship terms as mother, as ʔawitelin citta.

Conclusion

The contention which has motivated this investigation, that the Zuni and the Pueblos are a stronghold of Mother Earth and of world-parent cosmogony, has not only been challenged but an alternative understanding of at least one figure at Zuni has been advanced. A review of Haeberlin's discussion of the Pueblo "idea of fertilization" has not distracted from what undoubtedly is a major theme or idea among the Pueblo peoples, the idea of fertilization, although it is not unique to them. However, the linkage Haeberlin makes between the idea of fertilization and the existence of a world-parent origin theme has been found to be neither necessary nor defensible among the Pueblos. Most importantly, in Haeberlin's presentation at least, this linkage does not constitute adequate support for the existence among the Pueblos of a belief in Father Sky and Mother Earth as principal progenitors of the earth.

Further, Cushing's often quoted story of Zuni creation, which was Haeberlin's only explicit evidence for Father Sky–Earth Mother creators among the Pueblos, was found to be a metamyth, a story about a creation story. Thus the Mother Earth creator in his story is a figure we might more properly call Metamother Earth, a creation of Cushing's rather than an actual Zuni figure. In contrast, it has been possible to ascertain with some clarity the role and character, from the Zuni point of view, of *ʔawitelin citta,* their earth mother.

▲ 5 ▲

The Incestuous Rape of the Earth
The Luiseño Creation

With sighs he made her sleep, and after this she knew that she was to be a mother. He was ashamed of his deed, and went up in the sky. He was Tukmit, the Sky. When she found she was to bring forth, she was making ready. She made the same sort of sighing groans and thereby created a small piece of land. There was no land until then.

The Luiseño of southern California stand second only to the Pueblos among Native American peoples in being seen as exemplary for their world-parent type of cosmogony. Alfred L. Kroeber, for example, wrote that "the concept of prime origins by birth, instead of a process of making, is more thoroughly worked out [by the Luiseño] than by perhaps any other American tribe except possibly some of the Pueblos."[1] As was the case with the Zuni, this culture and its creation stories clearly deserve attention for the study of the history and origins of Mother Earth.

The Luiseño are one of a number of tribes in southwestern California collectively designated in this century as Mission Indians because of their association with Spanish missions that devoted themselves to their Christianization. Their tribal names are derived from the missions with which they were most closely associated. The term "Luiseño" thus comes from association with the mission San Luis Rey. Before being displaced from their lands, the Luiseño subsisted on the wide variety of foods available from the rich environment of southern California. Acorns were their most important food, yet they hunted a variety of animals and birds and procured foods from the sea. They gathered seeds, nuts, fruits, roots, bulbs, and berries from the area.[2]

The extensive history of the Luiseño, especially their contact with Europeans, is reflected by the division of that history into nine periods suggested by Raymond C. White:

1. Precontact
2. Early contact: from Cabrillo's voyage of 1542 to 1769
3. Initial mission: between 1769 and 1776
4. Early mission: from 1776 to 1798
5. Intermediate mission: from 1798 to 1825
6. Late mission: from 1825 to 1834
7. Postsecularization of the missions: 1834 to 1846
8. Early Anglo-American: 1846 to 1876
9. Reservation: 1876 to the present[3]

From 1776 until the time the missions were secularized, missionaries made a concerted effort to destroy or to greatly alter Luiseño culture. The old hunting-gathering economy was gradually replaced with herding and agriculture. The tribal political order declined as native "alcaldes" and "generals" were appointed to oversee the people's activities in relationship to the mission. The early period of American (non-Spanish) presence was one of massive encroachment upon the lands traditionally held by the Luiseño. This enormously increased the difficulties the people faced in supporting themselves. By 1891 their situation was so desperate that the United States Congress was asked to enact special legislation to secure their reservation lands. Through their acceptance of wage labor and by making a continuing effort at agriculture and livestock, the Luiseño have continued to the present to fend off the extinction of their culture.

The Luiseño Story of Creation

It is in light of Luiseño history that the existing accounts of their creation story must be considered, the story which has to Kroeber and others provided evidence that they believe in father-sky, and mother-earth deities who, through their procreative activities, gave birth to living things on the earth.

There are seven published accounts of the Luiseño creation story. The earliest is an account written by Father Geronimo Boscana, apparently in 1822.[4]

Even though Boscana's account is the earliest, it was recorded during the period of Luiseño history White characterized as "late mission." Thus in Boscana's time, few if any Luiseño people could have known a time when there had not been a dominating mission presence and intense pressure to accept Christianity and the demands of the missionaries. The accuracy and reliability of Boscana's entire account are subject to certain questions, and there is no way to obtain verification. Certainly he was rare among missionaries at the time for his belief that knowledge of the ways of native peoples would help to Christianize them, yet he was strongly predisposed to certain notions about Luiseño religious culture. This is evident in the introduction to his account of their creation story:

> . . . I am of the persuasion that if we are ignorant of the belief held by the Indians, of their usages and customs, it is very difficult to take them out of the error in which they live and to give them to understand the true religion, and to teach them the true way to their salvation.[5]

And in his comments introducing the Luiseño account of creation he wrote that,

> although one encounters in the narration many contradictions, we should not be surprised that certain crude Indians, without knowledge of the true God, without faith, without law or king, governed so long by the Father of Lies, without writings or characters, but having everything by mere tradition—we should not be surprised, I repeat, at their extravagancies and the little discernment in their acts, for since they were so ignorant, without being able to distinguish the true from the false, they did not know the path of light, and continually walked in darkness.[6]

Then in a brief summary Father Boscana presents, as he understood it, how the Luiseño believed the creation of the world took place.

Another account, collected in 1884, has only recently been published. It was recorded by Henry W. Henshaw while he was studying southern California languages.[7] Henshaw's account is an incidental one. The peculiar thing about it is its apparent linguistic deficiencies. In his preparation for its publication in 1972, Robert F. Heizer noted that Henshaw's recording of the names of deities varied considerably from other accounts. He attempted to reconcile these differences on the basis of phonetic similarities. Nothing is known of the Luiseño who gave the account to Henshaw.

Between 1904 and 1908 Constance Goddard DuBois published four accounts of the Luiseño creation. DuBois was a philanthropist and novelist with strong ethnographic interests. She surveyed and served the needs of the native peoples of southern California as she understood them. She was a highly sympathetic observer of Luiseño culture, and apparently had extensive experience with southern California cultures. She did not know Luiseño language, and there is no way to evaluate the competence of her interpreters or the reliability of her sources, except for the few general comments she made about them. Were it not for the fact that she collected a number of accounts of the original story from several different people, her contribution would be of doubtful value. Even she felt one of her accounts was questionable because it was told by a Luiseño man in Spanish and translated into English for her by a Spanish-speaking Anglo. The others were apparently told in Luiseño language (a Shoshonean language in the Uto-Aztecan family) and interpreted to her by a bilingual Luiseño. She described the process by which she attempted to find an adequate interpreter.[8]

The other known account was recorded by A. L. Kroeber in 1904 and published in 1906. It appears to be a highly abbreviated account.[9]

Significantly, all of the accounts except Boscana's were recorded and published during the last of White's nine periods. They derive from the culture after it had long been suffering the enormous pressures of Spanish missionization and land encroachment, pressures that resulted in almost a complete loss of land and culture. From this point of view it is remarkable that the stories survived at all and were recorded even in the small number that exist. From another point of view, it is without question that the stories must reflect this history and experience of the people. There are severe limitations on the degree to which the character and extent of that influence can be appreciated, because of the way in which the accounts were recorded and the brief span of history they represent. Not one exists in Luiseño language. Not one was recorded with much care. Only one dates from before the reservation period, and its validity is questionable. There are, then, serious reservations about the degree to which the available story accounts accurately reflect Luiseño views at any time and more particularly Luiseño views that were not strongly influenced by European-American contact.

With these reservations stated, the stories must still be considered, especially to the degree they may show evidence of the Luiseño conception of world parents and of Mother Earth. It is not impractical simply to recount the creation portions of all of the stories.

Boscana reported:

They relate that formerly there was nothing, only one above and another below; these two were brother and sister, man and woman, the one above, a man, which is properly the Heaven, and the one below, a woman, which is the Earth, but it was not the Heaven and the Earth as they are seen now, but of another nature which they do not know how to explain, but it was continually very dark night, without sun, moon, or stars. The brother came to the sister, and brought the light, which is the sun, telling her that he wanted to do many things with her; it meant that he wanted to cohabit with her. But the sister resisted declaring to him that they were brother and sister, and that therefore it was impossible to consent to what he desired, and for that reason he should go back and leave her in peace.

But at last in spite of all the resistance that she made, the sister became pregnant, and what she brought forth was earth and sand, but in a small quantity, after the shape and manner of a little plot of ground; this was the first childbirth.[10]

According to Henshaw's account,

Ke-wish-a-ta-wish [Kivish Atakvish] created the heavens and the earth. The heavens, Too-pash, and the earth, Tai-mai-ya-wurt, became the parents of the universe. The heavens hearing the voice of the earth inquired, "Who are you?" He could not see, for then all was darkness. Tai-mai-ya-wurt replied, "I am the earth. Who are you?" Too-pash answered, "I am the heavens," and he clasped her hand saying: "You are my sister." He afterwards placed his hand upon her head, and from this touch the virgin earth trembled and became the mother of all celestial and terrestrial creation.

When Tai-mai-ya-wurt told Too-pash she was with child, he declared he would destroy her, both were innocent, however, of the actual condition. She inquired, "with what weapon will you kill me?" He replied, "with my pipe." They both had long tubular stone pipes. The name of the heaven's pipe was, Ha-hol, and that of earth's Tamedol. Again the heavens spoke and said, "No, I will not slay you with my pipe. I will do it with darkness." The earth replied, "You cannot kill me with darkness, for I will defend myself with light." [Then the earth prepared herself in the fashion customary with Luiseño women and began to give birth to various things.][11]

DuBois' first published account of the origin was the Spanish-language version, given to her by an old man living on the La Jolla Reservation:

In the beginning Tu-co-mish (night) and Ta-no-wish (earth) sat crouching, brooding, silent. Then Tu-co-mish said, "I am older than you." Ta-no-wish said, "No, I am stronger than you." So they disputed. Then Tu-co-mish caused Ta-no-wish to go to sleep. When she woke she knew that something had happened, and that she was to be the Mother. She said, "What have you done?" "Nothing. You have slept." "No," she said. "I told you that I am stronger (morally) than you."

Soon within her grew all things and she sat erect and round.[12]

DuBois does not indicate her source for the next account. She appears to quote a storyteller in the first few sentences, but then she changes to a mode in which she simply describes the events of the story. The account describes that "in the beginning all was empty space," with Ke-vish-a-tak-vish as the only being. Then it presents a series of periods which preceded the creation of humans and their world. It reports a dialogue in which the male and female become aware of one another's presence and the nature of their relationship as brother and sister. DuBois indicates simply that "by her brother the Sky the Earth conceived and became the mother of all things."[13]

The final two versions of the story reported by DuBois are the most extensive. One version was contributed by Salvador Cuevas of the La Jolla Reservation. The beginning of this version follows. Apparently the parenthetical notes are DuBois' explanatory comments.

> Everything in the beginning was empty and quiet. Kivish Atakvish was the only being.
>
> Next came Whaikut Piwkut (whitish gray, unexplained).
>
> Whaikut Piwkut created two objects like great round balls called Maikumkush (meaning, something round, not having an end).
>
> They lay there three days and then were made alive, brought into being, after which they recognized each other. They were called Soimal-um (-um being the plural ending). They were male and female. Whaikut Piwkut, being the father of these two, left them and was no more seen.
>
> The two children (created beings) remained there. When they were by themselves, they quarreled: "I am older than you." "No, I am older than you." Each could read the thoughts of the other and this contention continued. The female being said that she was the older. She was Kivish Atakvish. The male began describing the color of the sky, by this to prove his earlier existence. "See, I am older than you." She got a stone smoking pipe, chahal, and showed it to prove herself the first. He got three kinds of pipes, kalulmul, nyatlumul, and chetmul, and held them up, and thus he silenced her and won (in this contention). Then with sighs (guttural breathings used in solemnities), he made her sleep, and after this she knew that she was to be a mother. He was ashamed of his deed, and went up in the sky (i.e., became the sky). He was Tukmit, the Sky.
>
> When she found she was to bring forth, she was making ready.

She made the same sort of sighing groans and thereby created a small piece of land. There was no land until then.[14]

DuBois' final version was given her by an old blind Luiseño man named Lucario Cuevish.

The first that came or appeared was Kivish, the man, Atakvish, the woman.

Then Omai, the man, Yamai, the woman.

When the two beings found themselves there, realized the existence of each other, the brother and sister each said to the other, "Who are you?"

The man called her sister. But when the thought of marrying her came to him, he changed the form of address and spoke to her in a different way. The woman asked, "Who are you?"

He answered, "Kivish no, Kivish no, Kivish no, Han-n-n-n-n. (I am Kivish, I am Kivish, I am Kivish, groan used in sacred narrative and ceremonies)."

The man asked, "What have you to say?"

She answered, "Atakvish no, Atakvish no, Atkavish no, Han-n-n-n."

[Then a similar exchange took place.]

Whaikut Piwkut was the man, the sky or Milky Way, whitish-gray. Harurai Chatutai was the woman, the earth.

Another transition and they became Tukmit, the sky, Tomaiyowit, the earth. These came after and from the previous states of existence, but were not born of them as their children.

The woman lay extended, her feet to the north, her head to the south. Her brother sat on the right hand by her side. "Sister, you must say who you are," he said. She answered, "I am Tomaiyowit." She asked, "Who are you?" He answered, "I am Tukmit." Tomaiyowit now, in a marvelous recitative, enumerates her attributes which it is distinctly explained do not belong to her but are prophetic of the completed state of being which is to come later.

"Non Obkit, non Opaykit, I am that which stretches out flat or is extended (from horizon to horizon).

"Non Yaramul, non Kworamul, I am that which shakes, and sounds with a loud noise, like thunder.

"Non Yinkit, non Yenankit, I am the earthquake.

"Non Punkit, non Choykit, I am that which rolls around and is round in shape.

"Non Manakit, I am that which goes out of sight and appears again." *After things were in shape it would be this way.*

Then Tukmit spoke:

"Non Tukmit, non Pamkit, I am that which arches over like a round lid or cover."

[He describes himself further as "something that goes up high and will rise high," as "death, that which will devour as if by taking all in, in one bit," as "he that from the east catches the spirits of man and sends them away off," and as "death."]

They said all this while she lay there and he sat by her side. It was in darkness, but he felt her and took her right hand. "What part of your body is this?" "That is my right hand." "And this?" "My left hand." In the same way he felt and she named her head, hair, the parting of the hair, the skull, the temple, brows, eyelids, cheek bones, teeth, etc. This is an extremely long enumeration, ending in that part of the story which the narrator omits from motives of delicacy...[here DuBois appeals to Father Boscana's delicate way of reporting the incestuous rape].

DuBois concludes this account with a noteworthy turn of events:

> She was with child and so large that she must lie down, falling backwards. She looked for something to help her, and Tukmit to deliver her took Sivut-paviut, the sacred stick with flint knife inserted on the end of it, and with this he cut her open from between the breasts downward. (Groaning recitative.) Then came forth her children in the order of their birth.[15]

Kroeber's very brief account adds nothing to these accounts.

While it will be important to consider these creation accounts in the wider context of Luiseño oral traditions and religious practices, to be done shortly, it is worth noting here something of the characteristics of the goddess in this story. Despite the questionable nature of these accounts, there is considerable agreement on some of her characteristics, on her relationship to the male figure, and on the creative process. Generally the stories seem not to make any identification of the female figure with the physical earth, although she has some association with the general orientation of being below the male figure; she is sometimes presented as being in a horizontal or reclining position, and in some versions there are other characteristics which identify her with the physical earth. Still the presentation of her features in all accounts if framed in a rather high degree of abstraction. She is often presented as one stage in a sequence of mysterious precreation transformations. Clearly, she does not appear to be a simple inspiration from the fructifying character of the earth as observed in nature. There is unanimity that these creator figures are brother and sister and that the creative act was an incestuous, as well as a rapacious, one in which the brother forced himself upon the sister against her will. In most versions the brother and sister argue with one another about who is the stronger; they show evidence of

their superiority as in a contest, but the brother eventually establishes his dominance. The created world, or aspects of it, is the result
of this power struggle. The brother is not portrayed as engaged in a
willful and conscious act of cosmic creation. He appears more driven
by sexual desire than by any other motive; it is suggested that, because he knows it is his sister he desires, this makes her all the more
intriguing to him. Yet he is disturbed by his cohabitation with her,
or more particularly by the pregnancy that results, to the point of
threatening to murder her. The most extreme form of this relationship and these characteristics of this creator pair is found in the
last of DuBois' versions, in which an act in something of the form of
a ritual sacrifice is performed by the brother so that the sister will
give birth to the world, yet his motives are not presented.

With this initial consideration of the narratives, the events of creation can be more fully understood in the context of other aspects of
Luiseño religious culture.

Luiseño Creation in Light of Luiseño Religion

In the recorded oral traditions of the Luiseño, these accounts of creation seem to be preliminary to the more developed story of Wiyot, a
male figure who is something of a culture hero.[16]

All things born at the time of origin were in the form of people.
Among these people was Wiyot. In some versions of the story, it
seems that the birth of Wiyot was the principal cosmogonic objective, yet in others his origin is not even told. As described in the
story, Wiyot was "very wise and knew more than anyone living. He
taught the people, watched over them, and made provision for their
needs, so that he called them all his children. They were not born to
him as children, but he stood to them in the relation of a father."[17]
Yet it seems that Wiyot was born to die, for the principal event of his
story is his death.

In Wiyot's time, it was the custom for people to bathe every
morning. When Wiyot went to bathe he noticed a beautiful woman
and he grew to admire her greatly. She had a beautiful face and long
hair that completely covered her back. One day when watching her
bathe, Wiyot noticed that her back was hollow and flat like that of a
frog and his admiration for her turned to disgust. She was, in fact, a
frog and was empowered by witchcraft. She knew Wiyot's thoughts
and set out to kill him. When he became ill, all of the doctors were
called, but none could save him. Importantly, it was not until Wiyot
knew that he was to die that he began to reveal to the people the

elements that were to characterize Luiseño culture. He told them the names of the months; he dispersed the peoples and set apart their languages; he revealed that he was to become the moon and that if they would run races and shout at the time when he returned to life as the new moon, they would live longer. As Wiyot knew he was about to die, he set forth the manner in which his body was to be treated. Wiyot was the first to die and his introduction of death not only set a pattern for Luiseño funerary customs it set the precedent for the many Luiseño religious themes that focus on death.[18]

Puberty rites for girls, one of the major Luiseño ceremonial occasions, dealt extensively with images and themes of death. The initiates were buried up to their necks in heated sand for several days. This practice combines the death and rebirth imagery of entering and emerging from the grave with that of cooking the initiate, both common initiatory motifs.[19]

Luiseño boys entered their formal religious lives in an initiation rite that involved their drinking a datura mixture. *Toloache,* the Spanish word for datura, is the term commonly used for this initiation ceremony. Intoxicated by the datura, the youths were assembled around a fire and given a display of the magical powers of the adepts. These were performances in a shamanic style in which all manner of mortal wounds were seemingly suffered, often self-inflicted ones, with the wounds then being miraculously healed. While the effects of datura were felt only during one night, the initiates continued to fast for a period of days. Three days after drinking the datura brew, the youths were taken to a pit in which a net representing the Milky Way had been placed, along with three stones forming a crude human shape. The Milky Way is the spirit to whom human spirits go when human beings die. The initiates had to enter the pit and leap from stone to stone. A misstep or fall presaged an early death. The danger of this crossing was heightened because the initiates had been fasting. Crossing the Milky Way expressed the Luiseño wish that, upon death, their spirits would be free from the earth and go to be caught in the net which is the Milky Way. The leaping from stone to stone enacted the escape of the spirit from the grave and enacted the pattern established by Wiyot at his death.[20]

Apart from initiation ceremonies, the Luiseño ritual practice centers upon funerary rites and mourning ceremonies in which the dead are remembered.

The Luiseño emphasis upon rituals of death and the extensive use of death imagery in religion are relatively common among California tribes, as Alfred L. Kroeber has shown.[21]

A suggestion of how Wiyot and the Luiseño emphasis upon death relate to the incestuous rape by which the elements of the world were created can be found in the oral traditions. After Wiyot's death the people met to consider its meaning for them. Some thought that should they die, they, like Wiyot, would return to life. Eagle, who was very wise, had attempted to find a place where death did not exist but returned to tell the others that death was everywhere. All had to die. The subject then turned to how, in death, some of them might be useful to the others. Some thought that Deer would be good to eat. They considered killing him and having a gathering in which the meat would be eaten. Deer did not care for the idea and an argument ensued. It is of such importance that one example of the argument must be presented, although this theme is well developed in most versions.

> They told him [Deer] they would kill him with the sacred stones. He said, No, he had the same. Then they got a stone arrow-straightener and said they would kill him with that. He said, No, he had that too. They said they had the feathers for the head-dresses and would kill him with them. He said, No, he had some of them too. They showed him arrowheads and said they would kill him with them. He said, No, he had those also. They showed him a bow and said they would kill him with that. Deer said he also had that. They told him they had sinew and would kill him with that. He said, No, he had that too. They told him they would kill him with blood. Deer said, No, he had that. They told him they would kill him with the tracks of their footprints. He said, No, some of those were his too. They told him they would kill him with marrow. Deer said, No, he also had marrow. They told him they would kill him with their ears. He said they could not do that. He had ears too. They told him they would kill him with their eyes. He said, No, he had eyes too. They told him they would kill him with the skin of the deer's head and antlers worn on the head by the hunter to deceive the deer. He said, No, he had that too. They told him they would kill him with tobacco. He said, No, he had some of that too. They told him they would kill him with wood-ticks. He said, No, he had those also. They told him they would kill him with one of the big blueflies. He said, No, he had that too. Then at last he gave up when they told him they would kill him with the feathers that wing the arrows.[22]

In like manner they argued with each of the animals until the weakness of each, represented by the lack of some property, was found and each, in turn, gave up to serve the others through death. Thus was established a hierarchy of beings, although the parties involved in that hierarchy accept their plight and role somewhat unwillingly and only after a contest of rights and powers.

R. C. White addressed this aspect of Luiseño thought:

> The ecological relationships observable within the environment clearly do not exist upon a one-to-one basis. This is reflected in the cosmological stories concerning the hierarchical organization of nature. The eater is not necessarily directly responsible for having cosmologically overcome the eaten. For example, Deer is a principal food animal for the Indians, but humans are not directly responsible for the plight of Deer. . . . All the intricate ecological phenomena of nature thus becomes a matter for intensive observation upon the part of the Indians. The behavior of every "living" thing depends upon its individualistic personal "knowledge," as well as its hierarchical characteristics. The most acute observation of every detail becomes necessary if one is to have sufficient food in the face of the internecine warfare existing throughout the nature—nobody wants to be eaten; everybody strains his utmost to avoid personal power.[23]

Since this hierarchical structure is the basis of the Luiseño worldview, giving order to the myriad life-forms and their interrelationships, the accomplishment of Wiyot's death can now be more fully appreciated. It is death which is the basis for the order of life, and while the Luiseño, as their oral traditions as well as their cultural history show, do not desire death or enjoy its occurrence, they nonetheless recognize its great power for bringing order into the world.

With this understanding of the Luiseño worldview the cosmogonic acts may be considered again. An important and constant dimension of most accounts is the struggle between the brother and sister. They argued about who was the older and who was the stronger; and, in some versions, in a manner exactly like the argument between Deer and the other animals, their claim to power was demonstrated by a display of objects. The creation process itself attests to these ordering principles. In this light, incestuous rape is consistent with the process of ordering that establishes the Luiseño world. Internal evidence in the stories suggests that incest is not a culturally condoned action, yet, even as death is necessary for the world to have meaningful order—for the world to be even possible—so must such acts occur. The connection between the creative force of death and sexuality is most strongly made in the version of the story in which the female figure is first unwillingly subjected to her brother's sexual assault, the act in which the forms of the world are conceived, and then has her belly ripped open with a knife, as in a ritual sacrifice, the resulting wound permitting the forms of the world to emerge from her body.

Simply put, hierarchy, a system of dominance, is the ordering power of the created Luiseño world. Only with the dominance of brother over sister, male over female, sky (night) over earth, accomplished by such a vile act as incestuous rape, did the precreation unity, characterized as emptiness and darkness, give way to the formation of the world and all of its attributes, peoples, and powers.

Other Considerations

In order to more fully comprehend the nature of the female figures in the story traditions of the Luiseño and other cultures of the region and to understand why these have been understood as examples of earth-mother goddesses, there are other considerations that must be pursued.

First, it must be asked what the Luiseño call this female figure in their creation story and what her name means. In the story accounts she is often referred to as "earth" or as "earth who is female," and, variously, as Tai-mai-ya-wurt, Ta-no-wish, and Tomaiyowit (transformed from Harurai Chatutai). In none of the accounts is she referred to by the proper name "Mother Earth" or any of its several variants. Linguistic evidence helps reveal the meaning of her name. Sparkman's Luiseño grammar give "*tamá-yawot* (mythologically) 'the earth, first female',"[24] although in the entry for the stem indicating north, he includes: "from *tamá-yawot* the first woman, mother earth, who lay in the north."[25] DuBois was the first to refer to the figure by the proper name "Earth-mother" in her 1905 study, "Religious Ceremonies and Myths of the Mission Indians."[26] When she made the reference she was not considering the creation story, but an incidental relationship between the order of things created and ritual objects used in the *toloache* ceremony.

Another line that should be followed is the existence of world parents or earth mothers in the creation stories of other tribes in the southern California and southwestern region. Stith Thompson's *Tales of the North American Indians* (1929) indicates that we should expect to find evidence among the Diegueño (another Mission tribe), the Pima, Mohave, Yuma, and Zuni.[27] A brief review of the story traditions of these tribes is worthwhile.

The Diegueño and the Luiseño are often considered the most prominent of the Mission tribes. While they share some ceremonial practices and doubtless have long maintained close cultural contact, their conceptions of world creation are distinct. It must also be remembered that their languages and cultures stem from quite different stocks. A search through all the accounts of the Diegueño creation story reveals only one in which there is even a mention of the earth and sky as male and female creators. It is in an account collected by DuBois and published in 1901. The account begins:

> When Tu-chai-pai made the world, the earth is the woman, the sky is the man. The sky came down upon the earth. The world in the beginning was pure lake covered with tules. Tu-chai-pai and Yo-ko-mat-is, the brother, sat together, stooping far over, bowed down under the weight of the sky.[28]

The account then continues with the story of the two brothers who emerge from the ocean to model humankind and the animals out of clay. This theme of two brothers as creators is found in all other Diegueño accounts. Waterman, in an early comparative study of the accounts of several southern California cultures, concluded that "these two sentences [the first sentences in DuBois' account] came into the myths in question either from a bias on the part of the author, or from a combination of Luiseño and Diegueño story-elements by the native narrator."[29]

Among the Mohave there is but a hint of the belief in the earth and sky as mother and father of creation. There are many well-developed Mohave accounts of the creation by the two brothers, as described above. Yet, there are several brief references to the world-parent theme. In 1886, John G. Bourke visited Fort Mohave. For his tour of several Mohave villages he was assigned a guide by the name of Merryman who had served as a scout and had traveled widely. Merryman spoke, read, and wrote English. During the tour, Merryman recounted for Bourke many Mohave beliefs and practices. After a comment about Mohave hunting practices, Bourke wrote the following, apparently quoting Merryman.

> This Earth is a woman; the Sky is a man. The Earth was sterile and barren and nothing grew upon it; but, by conjunction with the Sky— (here he repeated almost the very same myth that the Apaches and Pimas have to the effect that the Earth was asleep and a drop of rain fell upon her causing conception,)—two gods were born, in the west, thousands of miles away from here. They were Ku-ku-matz and his brother, To-chi-pa. I don't know much about them: I heard they jumped down a burning mountain, what you call a volcano. They are not dead, but we do not see them any more.[30]

Merryman made another reference to the earth and sky as parents of other children, but Bourke found the evidence contradictory to what he had already been told and, while noting this peculiarity, claimed he did not question Merryman for fear he would cease giving him information.

In a couple of other accounts, there are statements which indicate the earth is female or a mother, but the bulk of evidence of Mohave belief about the creation is in contradiction to these statements.[31]

Bourke noted that Merryman told a story about the impregnation of the earth by rain and he identified this as a story he knew to exist among the Apache and Pima. I have yet to find any published evidence of such a story told by the Pima, yet it could certainly have existed. It is a well-known story among the Apache and Navajo.

The reference to a Pima belief in earth and sky parents comes in the midst of the long and complicated saga of creation recorded by Frank Russell and published in 1908.

> In the beginning there was nothing where now are earth, sun, moon, stars, and all that we see. Ages long the darkness was gathering, until it formed a great mass in which developed the spirit of Earth Doctor, who, like the fluffy wisp of cotton that floats upon the wind, drifted to and fro without support or place to fix himself. Conscious to his power, he determined to try to build an abiding place, so he took from his breast a little dust and flattened it into a cake. Then he thought to himself, "Come forth, some kind of plant," and there appeared the cresote bush.[32]

Through thought and song, the power of Earth Doctor manifested itself in the world and it was peopled. But death did not exist and the world became overcrowded, and for want of food people began eating one another. Earth Doctor became distressed and decided to destroy all that he had created.

> Earth Doctor said, "I shall unite earth and sky; the earth shall be as a female and the sky as a male, and from their union shall be born one who will be a helper to me. Let the sun be joined with the moon, also even as man is wedded to woman, and their offspring shall be a helper to me." Then he caught the hook of his staff into the sky and pulled it down, crushing to death the people and all other living things. Thrusting his stick through the earth, Earth Doctor went through the hole and came out alone on the other side. He called upon the sun and moon to come forth from the wreck of world and sky, and they obeyed him. But there was no sky for them to travel through, no stars nor milky way, so he created all these anew. Then he called for the offspring of earth and sky, but there was no response. Then he created

a race of men, as he had done before; these were the Rsasanatc. . . .
After a time the earth gave birth to one who was afterwards known as
Itany and later as Siuuhu, Elder Brother.[33]

Elder Brother then comes forth to challenge the work of Earth Doctor, threatening to destroy these things of his creation. From here a
complex saga of creation and destruction unfolds. There is no other
mention of the earth and sky as creators.

In the context of this story it seems that the conjoining of the
earth and sky is an act primarily motivated by the need to destroy the
initial world created by Earth Doctor because that world had run
amok, and thus the act is somewhat the reverse of the separation of
parents common to the world-parent type creation. While Earth
Doctor states that he will have the earth and sky serve as parents in
the manner of a man and a woman, when he calls forth their off-
spring there is no response. Only later does Elder Brother appear,
and it seems that he is born from the earth.

There is in this aspect of the story something of an enigma which
cannot be resolved, yet it seems beyond question that the union of
earth and sky is not central to Pima creation, nor does a further
examination of Pima religious culture reveal evidence that the sky
and earth are significant figures.

Despite some of the difficulties of the existing recorded accounts,
the variety of the stories of creation that exist among several tribes in
southern California and Arizona are well known. While several of
these include the female personification of the earth, she is in no
place a major creator, nor is there any extensive development in ritual or story of a female personification of the earth. What then led to
these stories being so commonly referred to as examples of world-
parent creations? Why has the figure Mother Earth been so commonly seen as present, particularly in the Luiseño stories?

The Scholarly Contribution

As indicated, in 1905 DuBois was the first to use the term "Earth-
mother" to refer to a Luiseño belief. She occasionally used the term
after that in publications on the Luiseño. In his *Handbook of Indians
of California* (1925) Kroeber includes a discussion of Luiseño creation. He is obviously dependent upon DuBois' latest account, but
he does not use the term "Earth-mother."[34] Robert Heizer's recent
summary of California mythology also presents the Luiseño story,
and this is obviously dependent upon Kroeber. Heizer does not use

any form of the Earth-mother name.[35] Åke Hultkrantz considers Luiseño creation stories in his *The Religions of the American Indians* (1979). He too is dependent upon Kroeber, and in his way of seeing the story he finds it appropriate to introduce the proper name "Mother Earth" for the Luiseño female figure. Hultkrantz writes, "In the southern California myth of the cosmic parents, . . . the spirits, human beings, and all of nature emanate from the union of the skyfather with Mother Earth."[36]

From this review of the way students of California, and in particular Luiseño, story traditions have referred to the female figure in the story, we see that only DuBois and Hultkrantz have actually referred to her by the name Earth-mother or Mother Earth, yet all have seen Luiseño concepts of creation as of the world-parent type. Perhaps most remarkable is the virtual absence of discussion of the Luiseño stories beyond identification as being of the world-parent type. It is the more remarkable in light of the common and fundamental elements of the story accounts. Every account of the story identifies the male and female figures as not only associated with sky and earth but as siblings. Every account presents their union as one of incest and as a shameful one. Every account presents their union as one of dominance and violence, that is, rape. Given these constant and central aspects of all Luiseño story accounts, it is more than surprising to find that not one of the scholarly interpreters of the story so much as mentions these salient details. There is not a single mention, not a single expressed concern, either about the incestuous nature of their relationship, the forceful nature of the sexual contact, or the violence threatened by the brother and carried out by him on his sister. Only Boscana seems to have been at all concerned with any of these factors and, according to his notes, he was only gauging the morality of the people he served. Surely this indicates that the scholarly interest in these stories has been so predisposed as to have missed their most fundamental features. Observing the presence of male and female figures whose union is associated with the creation of features of the earth, they assumed, all too quickly, the adequacy of classifying the cosmogony as being of the world-parent type. I believe that there is evidence for this predisposition in what I call "the Polynesian connection."

In Kroeber's discussion of Luiseño creation stories in his *Handbook* (1925), he focuses primarily upon demonstrating their sophistication, thus contradicting the common view that the Luiseño culture is extremely primitive. He summarizes, with considerable liberty, the last version published by DuBois (which is the most unusual and complex of all the versions). He indicates that this account is basically the same as all other accounts, with certain expected minor variations. In his tribute to the sophistication of the story, Kroeber remarks, "the beginning of the Luiseño genesis reads far more, in spirit at least, like the opening of a Polynesian cosmogonic chant than like an American Indian tradition of the world origin."[37] This point was picked up and restated by both Hultkrantz and Heizer. No one of the three indicates the specific Polynesian connection, which is quite likely the classic Polynesian text "The Children of Heaven and Earth."[38] Had this connection been developed by any of the authors who suggested it, they might have been encouraged to consider the more central issues in the Luiseño stories, for the Polynesian story begins with the statement that all beings had but one pair of ancestors, springing either from the heaven above or the earth below. It is a tale which in its full extent is focused upon the efforts of the created children to force the separation of the earth and sky so that light and life might be attained. It was a difficult and unwilling separation. The children argued and finally warred among themselves. They did much violence to their parents and, as a result of the creative separation, the price of light and life was darkness, war, death, and strife borne by siblings on a cosmic scale. Here too the order that constitutes creation is inseparable from strife, hierarchy, destruction, darkness, and despair,[39] but in the Luiseño stories the order is effected not by the separation of the world parents by the children they have created, but rather by an incestuous rape.

The investigation of the existence of a common theological belief in Mother Earth among Native Americans has directed the inquiry thus far. In the search for Mother Earth something has been learned of the religious ideas of the Luiseño and other southwestern tribes, of the Zuni and other Pueblo tribes, of the Salishan tribes of the interior plateau in the northwest United States, and of the Shawnee and their neighboring tribes in the middle United States. This search for Mother Earth among the tribal cultures of North America could be extended by many chapters. I have carefully explored a number of other tribes where female figures with some possible connection to the figure of Mother Earth can be found.[40] However, the examples presented thus far are the ones most exemplary, most noted, and most influential. To extend the search would in some manner lead farther from rather than closer to Mother Earth. The conclusion to be drawn upon consideration of all the evidence gleaned from these many tribes is that some of the tribes consider the earth to be feminine, some consider the earth to be the personification of a female variously understood as mother or as goddess, but that no common belief in an earth goddess named Mother Earth has been found. Furthermore, what has been revealed in this study is that the notion of Mother Earth as a Native American goddess has been created to meet various needs of Americans of European ancestry. In the stories told thus far, these American story-makers have come onto the stage reluctantly to claim their roles. They have had to be encouraged to come forward, as their roles in this story of Mother Earth were found to be indispensable. The motivations and needs of these persons, these Americans of European ancestry, and their European colleagues must now be considered. It is time to ask some of them to take center stage for the fuller examination of the history of their contributions to the idea and reality of Mother Earth in North America and beyond.

▲ 6 ▲

The Making of Mother Earth
The Scholars

The idea of the Earth as a mother is more simple and obvious, and no doubt for that reason more common in the world, than the idea of the Heaven as a father. Among the native races of America the Earth-mother is one of the great personages of mythology.

Edward B. Tylor made this statement in his classic work, *Primitive Culture,* published in 1873.[1] It is, I believe, the key to comprehension of the development of ideas about Mother Earth and the belief that she is one of the great figures in native North American religions. Reflection on Tylor's statement reveals some of the assumptions and the method of argumentation that underlie this development. His method of argumentation begins with the statement of principles. Tylor reasons on principle about the incidence of human ideas, arguing that the more simple and obvious the ideas are, the more widely are they found. When considering the personification of earth and sky, Tylor reasons that the idea of the earth as a mother is more simple and obvious than the idea of sky ("Heaven" is his term) as father. Rather than presenting this statement as a hypothesis to guide the investigation of Native American religions, Tylor simply demonstrates its unquestioned accuracy with another statement which asserts that the Earth-mother is one of the great personages among Native Americans. Tylor need cite but a couple of examples. Upon his principles, the Earth-mother simply must be a great personage in American mythology since he classifies the native races of America as "primitive." Underlying Tylor's argument are the principle of the evolution of culture and the assumption of the primitivity of Native Americans. With this approach, the principles are not developed in order to more fully comprehend the extant cultural data, rather highly selected data are used as exemplifying conclusions that are drawn from principle and that are never open to question. In the case of Mother Earth, it will be shown that the basic principles and assumptions of students of culture and religion absolutely required her presence among Native Americans. Thus her existence has been largely the result of these principles and assumptions. This chapter is the story of the scholarly making of Mother Earth. There is even a touch of incest in this creation story.

Tylor's evolutionist thesis was a common theoretical perspective during the rise of the modern study of culture in the last half of the nineteenth century. He was not the first to extend the thesis to the conclusion of the primacy of motherhood. J. J. Bachofen in *Das Mutterrecht* (1861) and Lewis Henry Morgan in *Ancient Society* (1877) had contemplated these issues before Tylor, and others even predated them.[2]

Tylor was the earliest to demonstrate the primacy of the Earth-mother thesis with examples from traditions in North America. While his attention to American examples was slight, Tylor's inclusion of American examples has been highly influential, and thus the story of the making of Mother Earth must begin with Tylor.

Complementing and grounding this sweeping generalization that "among the native races of America the Earth-mother is one of the great personages of mythology," Tylor provides three specific examples. This is the first:

> the Algonquins would sing medicine-songs to Mesukkummik Okwi, the Earth, the Great-Grandmother of all. In her charge (and she must be ever at home in her lodge) are left the animals whose flesh and skins are man's food and clothing, and the roots and medicines of sovereign power to heal sickness and kill game in time of hunger; therefore good Indians never dig up the roots of which their medicines are made, without depositing an offering in the earth for Mesukkummik Okwi.[3]

Tylor's source is John Tanner's captivity narrative published in 1830. The medicine songs that Tylor refers to, according to Tanner's narrative, "relate how Na-na-bush created the ground, in obedience to the commands of the Great Spirit, and how all things for the use, and to supply the wants of the uncles and aunts of Na-na-bush (by which are meant men and women), were committed to the care and keeping of the great mother."[4]

Tanner's narrative about the earth describes a figure Me-suk-kum-wik O-kwi whom he identifies as "the earth," "the great-grand-mother of all," and as the caretaker for plants and animals. But she is subordinate to "the Great Spirit," who is the creator of all and upon whose authority she was given the care of plants and animals. Na-na-boo-shoo or Na-na-bush is, in Tanner's narrative, an intermediary or "benevolent intercessor between the Supreme Being and mankind." The primacy of the Great Spirit or Supreme Being, who appears to be a sky-dwelling figure, tends to contradict Tylor's fundamental assumption about the earth mother.

Tylor's second and third examples occur in the same paragraph:

> Among the North-American Indians the Comanches call on the Earth as their mother, and the Great Spirit as their father. A story told by Gregg shows a somewhat different thought of mythic parentage. General Harrison once called the Shawnee chief Tecumseh for a talk:—"Come here, Tecumseh, and sit by your father!" he said. "You my father!" replied the chief, with a stern air. "No! yonder sun (pointing towards it) is my father, and the earth is my mother, so I will rest on her bosom," and he sat down on the ground.[5]

Tylor's source for both examples is, as he states, Josiah Gregg's *Commerce of the Prairies* (1844), critically discussed in an earlier chapter. Gregg gives no source for his Comanche reference, it being seemingly incidental. While it has been shown that the Tecumseh statement presents no valid evidence for any Native American belief in Mother Earth, it is notable that, of Tylor's three examples, the Tecumseh statement is the most extensive and most memorable.

Tylor's concerns were much broader than the Americas, and he likely had no intention to establish Mother Earth as a major figure or category in North America, but as the impact of Tylor's statements is observed, this was the effect.

By 1883, Tylor's views on the earth as mother had begun to influence studies of Native Americans. Hubert Bancroft, in his *The Native Races* (1882), wrote:

> It seems long ago and often to have come into men's mind that the over-arching heaven or something there and the all-producing earth

are, as it were a father and mother to all living creatures. The Co-
manches call on the earth as their mother, and on the Great Spirit as
their father.[6]

Though Bancroft does not cite Tylor, the wording is similar and the
examples given are so nearly identical that influence is almost certain.

The transformation of the Indian princess imagery of America in
the late eighteenth century toward a Greek goddess indicates influence from Western antiquity. This influence is commonly present in
the imagery and development of the Native American Mother Earth.
Certainly Bachofen's knowledge of Greek culture was a major factor
in his motherright hypothesis. The Greek background was highly
influential in Andrew Lang's expectations about the Native American female figures he discussed in *Myth, Ritual and Religion* (1887).
In his discussion of Demeter, Lang wrote:

> Thus conceived as the foster-mother of life, earth is worshipped in
> America by the Shawnees and Potawatomies as Me-suk-kum-mik-o-
> kwi, the "mother of earth." It will be shown that this goddess appears
> casually in a Potawatomie legend, which is merely a savage version of
> the sacred story of Eleusis.[7]

After presenting a number of non–Native American examples, Lang
returns to them.

> More remarkable still is the Pawnee version, as we may call it of El-
> eusinia. Curiously, the Red Indian myth which resembles that of De-
> meter and Persephone is *not* told about Me-suk-kum-mik-o-kwi, the
> Red Indian Mother Earth, to whom offerings are made, valuable ob-
> jects being buried in brass kettles. The American tale is attached to the
> legend of Manabozho and his brother Chibiabos, not to that of the
> Earth Mother and her daughter, if in America she had a daughter.[8]

It is not easy to trace the sources for Lang's illustrations or to sort
out his peculiar references. He cites Tanner, and it appears by his
hyphenation of the name of the female figure in the way Tanner did,
while Tylor dropped hyphens, that he actually examined Tanner.
Still, the influence of Tylor is clear. It is possible that Lang joined a
reference in Father de Smet's *Oregon Missions* (1947) to a Potawatomie practice of burying food offerings with the reference in
Tanner and Tylor to the Algonkian practice of placing offerings in
the earth. I have not been able to determine where he got the idea of
brass kettles. Obtaining the tribal names of Shawnee, Potawatomie,
and Pawnee from his various sources, Lang appears simply to have
used them with little discrimination. His confusing of tribal names

in identifying the example further attests to little comprehension of the complexity and diversity of tribal cultures in America.

In an earlier chapter, A. S. Gatschet's statements about Mother Earth were quoted from his ethnography of the Klamath published in 1890. In those statements Gatschet connected the Mother Earth figure with the Greeks and exemplified her presence in America exclusively through the examples of the statements by Smohalla and Tecumseh.

Following Gatschet in the history of Mother Earth scholarship is James Mooney, whose 1896 discussion of Smohalla in the context of Ghost Dance history has also already been presented. It does not appear that Mooney was immediately influenced by Greek expectations, nor is there evidence that he had read Tylor. He had probably read Gatschet's Klamath study, and it appears to have been an influence on his development of Mother Earth theology. Apart from Smohalla's statement, which was central to Mooney's discussion of Mother Earth, he mentions only the Tecumseh statement. Importantly, Gatschet and Mooney develop the physical identity of the earth and the Mother Earth goddess, cataloging the correspondences between earth forms and the body parts of the goddess. They also introduce the Smohalla example to this Mother Earth genesis.

Of major importance in the development of Mother Earth as a worldwide figure is Albrecht Dieterich's 1905 publication *Mutter Erde*. This work has been widely influential as has been shown by Olof Pettersson's critical study *Mother Earth: An Analysis of the Mother Earth Concepts According to Albrecht Dieterich* (1967). Pettersson traces Dieterich's influence, direct or indirect, on such eminent figures as Frederick Heiler, Joachim Wach, Gerardus van der Leeuw, E. O. James, Raffaele Pettazzoni, and Mircea Eliade.[9]

Dieterich's work deals only briefly with Mother Earth in North America for it is principally about the religions of Western antiquity. Yet his motivation for including even minor reference to North America is of much interest, and is inseparable from his method of argument. This is clearly and concisely summarized and criticized by Pettersson in a passage worth quoting at length:

> He [Dieterich] began with an analysis of a statement from St. Augustine's *De civ. Dei*. This statement gave rise to a hypothesis: The Earth is a divine Mother, a Goddess, who gives the children. He did not find any definite proofs of his hypothesis in the Roman belief. Therefore, he made an inventory of beliefs and practices among different peoples. However, these beliefs and practices were interpreted with the formulated hypothesis as a model, and thus he found many

definite proofs—as he thought—of a belief in the Mother Earth. His special interpretation, based on the same model, of the Greek records gave the same result: Ge was a Mother Earth. After this Dieterich returned to the Roman religion that was his point of departure, and now he could state that his hypothesis was correct: different practices all over the world spoke in the favour of a Mother Earth belief. It seems as if Dieterich used an argument in a circle: He formed a hypothesis of a Mother Earth belief in Rome; with this hypothesis as a model he interpreted different practices among different peoples of the world; conclusion: the practices recorded and interpreted demonstrate the correctness of the hypotheses. In this way his "Mother Earth theology" is constructed. . . . Because Dieterich is depending on his mystery-theology interpreting the goddess of the mysteries his identification of the Great Goddess with the old Mother Earth Goddess is very hypothetical, not to say gratuitous. Dieterich's model has misled him to regard the earth as a personal being even when it seems rather clear that the records deal with the earth as an *element*.[10]

Pettersson's careful review of all of the sources utilized by Dieterich led him to conclude:

We can speak of "great goddesses," but not of *one* Great Goddess, more or less identical to the Earth. In the same way we can speak of special Gods of fertility, but not of a universal fertility god.[11]

Dieterich's only North American example used to document directly the presence of Mother Earth is that of the Comanche, which he no doubt got from Tylor. Other Native American examples, such as Huron burial practices, were used to establish practices that he associated with the presence of the idea of Mother Earth in Roman religious practice.

With this brief consideration of Dieterich, who brought the Mother Earth figure fully into the arena of the worldwide study of culture and religion as well as into the twentieth century, several issues can be reviewed. There is a notable correlation in approach taken by most of those who have declared the widespread existence of Mother Earth in North America. They begin with an assumption based not on the experience of American cultures but on the assumed principles of cultural evolution or the knowledge of Western antiquity. This approach leaves no real possibility that Mother Earth is absent from North America, requiring only the demonstration of her presence through the citation of select examples. Consequently, the nature and even the presence of Mother Earth in North America have never been tested.

Another issue regarding Mother Earth emerges here. For many, the presence of an earth goddess correlates with the development of agriculture. Haeberlin upheld this correlation and added pottery-making. Many others have maintained it on the basis, in part, of the association of agricultural or other activities, such as making pottery, with women. Since agriculture developed relatively recently in human history, the correlation principle would indicate that the per-sonification of the earth as goddess or as mother would also be a relatively recent development, thus contradicting the reasoning of Tylor and others. Eliade and Hultkrantz, as will be shown, have held that her roots precede the development of agriculture, which they see as transforming her into a goddess of vegetation. This has been a hotly contested issue, gaining much more attention, sadly, than the careful examination of the multitude of female figures in North America or elsewhere. Also relevant is the importance of the hunter-cultivator distinction in the imagery of savagism and civilization that has persisted throughout American history. This distinction has been central to many theories of culture.

Finally, with Pettersson's critical review of Dieterich's study of Mother Earth, the validity of the whole category is open to question. The difficulty in documenting such a figure among the tribal cultures of North America is shown by Pettersson to be present throughout the balance of the world and even in the religions of Western antiquity. With this global issue raised, the importance of the consideration of Mother Earth in North America seems now all the greater.

In his 1907 essay "Tenure of Land Among the Indians," George B. Grinnell describes "Indians" as having no conception of the per-sonal ownership of land. We have seen this stated before in our ex-amination of Tecumseh's land policies, for example, but Grinnell gives it a negative interpretation by suggesting that the Indians are incapable of comprehending the concept of ownership. His essay seems to respond to his concern that some injustice had been done to Native Americans as a result of the Dawes Act (1887), which made individual landowners of Native Americans, yet he states, "I make no complaint here about the policy or justice of driving Indians by force from lands which we need."[12] In a footnote Grinnell describes some-thing of the native belief in the earth as mother, a belief he considers to be almost universal:

> The earth is regarded as sacred, often it is called the "mother" and it appears to rank second among the gods. A sacrifice of food is held up first to the sky and then is deposited on the earth, and perhaps rubbed

into the soil. The first smoke is directed to the sky, the second to the earth, and then those to the four directions in order. . . . Before beginning to perform any sacred office, the priest or doctor holds his hands first toward the sky and then rubs them on the ground. "It is by the earth," they say, "that we live. Without it we could not exist. It nourishes and supports us. From it grows the fruits that we eat, and the grass that sustains the animals whose flesh we live on; from it comes forth, and over its surface run, the waters which we drink. We walk on it, and unless it is firm and steadfast we cannot live."[13]

Among the most widely read and cited collections of Native American stories is that edited by Hartley Burr Alexander as volume 10 of *Mythology of All Races* (1916).[14] He presents a more widely ranging presentation of Native American religions in *The World's Rim* (1953), heavily influenced by Greek religion. In his discussion of Native American stories, Alexander wrote:

It is difficult to realize the deep veneration with which the Indian looks upon his Mother the Earth. She is omniscient; she knows all places and acts of all men; hence, she is the universal guide in all the walks of life. But she is also, and before all, the universal mother—she who brings forth all life, and into whose body all life is returned after its appointed time, to abide the day of its rebirth and rejuvenation. The conception was not limited to one part of the continent, but was general.[15]

Reminiscent of Mooney's view and very consistent with Dieterich's, Alexander's statement presents the figure of Mother Earth theologically. She knows all and directs all. She is the source of all life as well as the force of all rejuvenation and regeneration. Alexander emphasizes, as have all of the others, that this belief is universal among North Americans.

In his Gifford lectures (1924–25) published as *The Worship of Nature* (1926), James George Frazer at one point concentrated on the worship of the earth in America. He begins with the statement: "Many of the American Indians appear to have personified the Earth as their mother and to have supposed that their first ancestors issued from it as a child from the womb."[16] Frazer, in his characteristic fashion,[17] cataloged examples identified with eight different North American tribes. They are rather loosely associated, as they illustrate practices in which the earth has some association with worship. Frazer cites John Heckewelder's 1819 account of Indians living in Pennsylvania, that indicates "the Indians [Delaware] consider the earth as their universal mother. They believe that they were created within its bosom, where for a long time they had their abode, before they came to live on its surface." Heckewelder's account describes this earth indwelling as directed and intended by "the great, good, and all powerful Spirit [creator]." Heckewelder is also Frazer's source for a 1743 statement made by Rev. Christopher Pylaeus to the effect that the Mohawk, an Iroquois tribe, hold that they had dwelt in the earth where it was dark and eventually found a hole through which they came out into the world.

Frazer, as did Tylor and Lang before him, includes mention of Tanner's account of the Ottawa belief in the figure Me-suk-kum-mik O-kwi and the importance of making an offering to the earth before plants are collected. Consulting Paul Radin's work on the Winnebago, Frazer describes their belief in "the earth as goddess . . . [who appears] as Grandmother in some of their oldest myths." But here this figure is "sister of those bad spirits who are bent on destroying the human race." She is addressed in prayer for the granting of war powers.

The Cheyenne belief in Ahk tun o wihio, a god who lives underground, is mentioned as one prayed to for the growth of plants. Similarly Frazer refers to the Zuni ?awitelin citta (citing, curiously, Stevenson's Zuni ethnobotany rather than Cushing's accounts of story traditions). Frazer mentions the belief among the Klamath in the "earth as a mysterious shadowy power" and, remarkably, cites the Smohalla quotation in Gatschet rather than the one in Mooney as his evidence. Finally, using an essay on the Hopi by Walter Fewkes, Frazer indicates only that at Hopi the earth is a goddess represented by a bundle of sticks.[18]

There are correlations between Frazer's examples and the other descriptions of Mother Earth given above. Frazer's presentation of the examples shows them to be only loosely and tenuously connected and scarcely establishing the general statement with which Frazer opens his remarks on the subject.

Mircea Eliade, the influential historian of religion, has included discussions of Mother Earth in many of his major works on religion. The role of North American religions in his discussions of Mother Earth is significant.[19] In his classic *Patterns of Comparative Religion* (1958), he includes the Smohalla quotation from Mooney as a major example.

> Before becoming a mother goddess, or divinity of fertility, the earth presented itself to men as a Mother, *Tellus Mater*. The later growth of agricultural cults, forming a gradually clearer and clearer

notion of a Great Goddess of vegetation and harvesting, finally destroyed all trace of the Earth-Mother. In Greece, the place of Gaia was
taken by Demeter. However, certain ancient ethnological documents
reveal relics of the old worship of the Earth-Mother. Smohalla, an
Indian prophet of the Umatilla tribe, forbade his followers to dig the
earth, for, he said, it is a sin to wound or cut, tear or scratch our
common mother by the labours of farming. "You ask me to plough
the ground? . . . " Such a mystical devotion to the Earth-Mother is
not an isolated instance.[20]

Eliade's fuller treatment of Mother Earth is in his *Myths, Dreams
and Mysteries* (1957), in which he devotes a chapter to the figure
"Mother Earth and the Cosmic Hierogamies." The first sections of
this discussion are dependent almost entirely on examples from
native North America. The chapter opens with the Smohalla statement and proceeds to a discussion of it.

> Those words [of Smohalla] were spoken not much more than half
> a century ago. But they come to us from very distant ages. The emo-
> tion that we feel when we hear them is our response to what they
> evoke with their wonderful freshness and spontaneity—the primor-
> dial image of the Earth-Mother. It is an image that we find every-
> where in the world, in countless forms and varieties.[21]

Eliade interpreted Smohalla's statement as a demonstration of a
belief of being born from the earth but found that "the prophet
Smohalla does not tell us in what way men were born of this telluric
Mother."[22] He seeks this evidence from other Native Americans,
referring to two of the examples cited in Frazer's *The Worship of
Nature,* the Delaware and Iroquois stories that indicate humans first
existed in a region beneath the surface of the earth, a region Eliade
understands as being the womb of the Earth-Mother. For further
evidence, Eliade turns to examples of Native American stories recounting journeys of emergence from underworlds, namely, the
Navajo, Zuni, and Mandan stories, and then he presents, for fuller
discussion, a summary of the Zuni creation story. Eliade is dependent upon Cushing's "Outlines" for his account.
    Thus, Eliade's argument begins with Smohalla's statement,
which he interprets as testimony to a worldwide belief in the earth as
mother to humankind. He cites evidence of stories where human
beings or human predecessors lived in or under the earth. He considers emergence stories, emphasizing that the existence beneath the
earth's surface exemplifies a prenatal condition in the "womb of the

Earth-Mother." He sees all of this most fully exemplified in Cushing's story of Zuni creation, where the

> myth connects the ontogenetic with the phylogenetic: the condition
> of the new-born babe is homologised with a mythical pre-existence of
> the human race in the bowels of the Earth: every infant, in its pre-
> natal state, is re-living the life of that primordial humanity. The assim-
> ilation of the human mother to the Great telluric Mother is com-
> plete.[23]

His conclusions are questionable on several counts. He extends his interpretation of his evidence far beyond its facts. Eliade does not consider beliefs about childbirth and infant practices at all. He does not criticize the sources of any of his examples or place them in their cultural and historical contexts. Thus the conclusions are wholly his constructions based on the expectations of structural constituencies. A further point of contention is Eliade's identification of the Zuni place of emergence as the center of the world. Perhaps the structures of a center according to Eliade's patterns are there, but if one considers the whole of Zuni oral traditions, one finds that the great bulk of the Zuni stories tell about migration journeys that took place after the people emerged onto the earth's surface. Their journeys were in search of a place suitable to life, a place they finally found in the center of the world, a place they call ʔitiwanʔa, which means the "center place."

Depending upon Dieterich's study for documentation, Eliade asserts that the belief that "human beings were born from the Earth is a belief of universal distribution."[24] With the groundwork established, Eliade can consider the consequences of such a belief:

> The belief in a pre-existence within the bosom of the Earth has had
> considerable consequences: it has created in man a sense of cosmic
> relatedness with his local environment; one might even say that, in
> those times, man had not so much a consciousness of belonging to the
> human race as a sense of cosmo-biological participation in the life
> around him. . . . This kind of cosmo-biological experience rooted
> man in a mystical solidarity with *the place* which was intense enough
> to have survived till now in folk-lore and popular traditions.[25]

While Eliade reviews the historico-cultural hypothesis that could explain the origins of Mother Earth in the development of a matrilocal and matrilineal society in which the female dominated and agricultural activities were central, he does not feel that such a hypothesis has been firmly established. Here he parts somewhat from the position he took in *Patterns,* just quoted. His method and style are clearly revealed in his proposed alternative approach. He writes that the problem of the explanation of Mother Earth

> belongs to the history of religions. And the history of religions is concerned not only with the *historical becoming* of a religious form, but also with its *structure*. For religious forms are nontemporal; they are not necessarily bound to time. We have no proof that religious structures are created by certain types of civilisation or by certain historic moments....religious reality is more complex: it transcends the plane of history.[26]

Eliade's examination of the structure of the Earth-Mother divinity allows him to place her both historically and in terms of her relationship with other basic divinities. He concludes that

> the Earth Mother is a very old divinity, known since paleolithic times. But we cannot say that she was ever the *sole* primordial divinity, and this for the simple reason that "femininity" does not seem to have been thought of as a primordial mode of being.[27]

Here he counters, in part, Tylor's fundamental assumption, but he does not contend that a masculine conception would precede a feminine one, rather that the "primordial situation," as he calls it, would be a "neuter and creative wholeness." This explains, he says, why hierogamy appears to be absent in the oldest religions. Rather than tell the history of Mother Earth, Eliade outlines various forms that she has taken, considering varieties of examples ranging from shamanic recollections to labyrinths, grottoes, and caves; to laying the child on the ground (one of Dieterich's principal concerns); to death and human sacrifice. Of the examples that Eliade is able to bring together as forms of Mother Earth, he concludes,

> one might say that the Earth-Mother constitutes a form that is "open" to, or susceptible of, indefinite enrichment, and that is why it takes in all the myths dealing with Life and Death, with Creation and generation, with sexuality and voluntary sacrifice.[28]

More must be said of Eliade's study, but it can be said more effectively once we have introduced another major scholar.

The noted Swedish authority on Native American religions, Åke Hultkrantz, has written much on Mother Earth in North America. In *The Religions of the American Indians* (1979), he wrote:

> The cosmic dualism of agrarian tribes places the powers of heaven and ·atmosphere in more or less clear opposition to the chthonic

powers, especially to the deities of earth and water. . . . [This confrontation] is expressed, perhaps most fundamentally, in the sexual distance between the celestial male and the chthonic female elements. Attention is then focused on the sky god and the earth goddess. According to the myth, the universe and mankind arose from the union of the heavenly father and Mother Earth.

The earth goddess or mother goddess is accordingly the foremost representative of the chthonic powers. In cultures where cultivation of the soil is among the foremost societal concerns her cult is of paramount importance. In many such communities she is the all-powerful divinity. In daily existence her role corresponds to that of the woman-mother, the cultivator and keeper of domestic plants and the bearer of children to the world, just as the earth is the producer of plants and verdure.[29]

Hultkrantz seems to refer to a general class of religious belief and worldview and a general class of deities through which this religious worldview is expressed. Yet, despite this, he tends to hold to a unitary view among Native Americans when he refers to "the myth" and uses the proper name "Mother Earth." With this general introduction he focuses on major geographic areas. For North America he gives two tribal examples where the earth is associated with femininity or is considered a goddess, then concludes:

It is an indisputable fact that the concept of the earth goddess has grown strongest among the cultivating peoples. . . . Her origins may have been in the old hunting culture which ranged all through America until about 2000 B.C. and was maintained by many tribes until the last decades of the nineteenth century. Far away from agricultural peoples lived, in the state of Washington, those Shahaptin Indians whose chief in the 1880s was the dreamer Smohalla.[30]

Then after quoting the famous statement of Smohalla, whom Hultkrantz apparently considers as representative of hunters who were replaced by agriculturalists beginning four thousand years ago, he comments on the statement in a manner reminiscent of Mooney.

As elsewhere, the earth deity is here represented as animatistic, at one with her substratum and yet an intimately experienced personal being. Many hunting tribes in North America manifest the same primitive belief in "our mother," "Mother Earth."[31]

Shifting back to the agricultural tribes, Hultkrantz continues:

From a mythological point of view it is true that the agrarian peoples see the mother goddess as only one of the two primordial procreative beings. This idea of the emanation of life and the world through a

sacred union seems to fade in practical faith, where the performance of
the goddess is often enough emphasized at the expense of the sky god.
She is mentioned, as we have seen, as the one who alone brings forth
the earth and the plants, giving birth to them from herself. In some
areas this belief has stimulated the thought that the world was created
from the dead body of the goddess.[32]

Hultkrantz then turns to the associated beliefs in vegetation goddesses, especially the corn goddesses.

Hultkrantz's most extensive and recent essay on Mother Earth,
"The Religion of the Goddess in North America" (1983), will be
discussed fully below, but first several summary comments are in
order.

From Tylor (1873) to Hultkrantz (1983), the position with respect to Mother Earth in North America has, in one important respect, remained unchanged. All have, without question, considered
her as well established in the region since great antiquity. Tylor proclaimed that "among the native races of America the Earth-mother is
one of the great personages of mythology." Eliade held that "the
primordial image of the Earth-mother . . . [is found] everywhere in
the world." Hultkrantz wrote that "Mother Earth is a common idea
among Indians over large parts of North America."[33]

Yet, during this century, the more than dozen major scholars I
have considered have depended upon a remarkably small number of
specific tribal examples to document Mother Earth in North America. When the sources are carefully examined, it is found that, apart
from a few casually mentioned incidental examples, all of these discussions have depended upon only five sources. John Tanner's captivity narrative published in 1830 provided a scant reference to an
Algonkian female figure associated with the earth and the depositing
in the earth of offerings to her before roots were dug. Josiah Gregg's
1844 travel narrative provided a single incidental statement about
the Comanche belief in the earth as mother and tells an anecdote,
related by an unnamed person, about Tecumseh. James Mooney presented to a wide readership the statements of Smohalla made to
Huggins and MacMurray, though A. S. Gatschet actually published
a comment on Smohalla prior to Mooney. Frank Hamilton Cushing
published outlines of Zuni stories in 1884 and 1896. Finally,
Kroeber's *Handbook of California Indians* (1925) made more widely
known the Luiseño stories collected by DuBois and interpreted
them as evidence of a world-parent type of creation. A number of
other specific tribes are occasionally named as representing belief in

Mother Earth, especially in discussions of cosmic dualism, tribes such as Navajo, Pawnee, Sioux, Huron, Hopi, Shoshoni, and Comanche. But none of these were carefully examined or interpreted.

Given that there are hundreds of tribes in North America and hundreds of thousands of pages of ethnographic documentation of the history, oral traditions, and religious practices of these tribes, it is highly peculiar that the documentation for the nature and existence of Mother Earth, held to be a major figure throughout North America, rests almost wholly upon a scant reference to an earth-related goddess told in a captivity narrative, a statement attributed to Tecumseh during negotiation with the U.S. government revealed in an anecdote, the statement of a leader of a small and hopeless millenarian movement in which the leader defended his relationship with the land against the overwhelming forces of American settlement, the outlines of Zuni creation conceptions formulated into story form by a romantic ethnologist, and the stories of an incestuous, rapacious world creation told by persons of a culture at the brink of extinction.

Given the above analysis, it would not be inaccurate to criticize or even to dismiss a century of scholarship on Mother Earth in North America as inadequate, even irresponsible, and certainly inconclusive. But this is not my purpose, for a great deal may be learned from the story that has been told. If it had made any difference whether or not Mother Earth could be firmly established throughout the ethnographic materials of native North America, these sources would have been rigorously examined for evidence of Mother Earth's presence. Since such a study has never been done, it is important to ask why. One likelihood is that the existence of Mother Earth has never been set forth in the form of a hypothesis, but rather her existence has been accepted without question. Mother Earth has seemed so primordial, so archetypical, so fundamental as to be herself a key element in the demonstration of a variety of theories concerning the nature and development of religion and culture. Consequently, on nothing but the scant evidence of a few sentences attributed to Smohalla, as spoken in 1885, Hultkrantz can see evidence of "the old hunting culture which ranged all through America until about 2000 B.C." and Eliade can see evidence in the same sentences for "relics of the old worship of the Earth-Mother" that was replaced millennia ago by a "Great Goddess of vegetation and harvesting" who developed with the growth of agriculture. Tylor argues that the idea of the earth as mother is more simple and obvious than the idea of heaven as father, a principle he sees exemplified by Tecumseh's

1810 statement. Eliade argues that "femininity does not seem to have been thought of as a primordial mode of being, though the Earth Mother is a very old divinity."

I believe that there is no possibility whatsoever of beginning with the data of North America and drawing the same conclusions that have been so commonly made, that is, that Mother Earth is a major American goddess, or even more strongly put, that she is the goddess of the native races of America. The only explanation for such conclusions is that, for scholars who have studied her, Mother Earth must exist before they even consider the North American evidence. This may also imply that they understand her to have existed even before the formation of North American cultures. Such a relationship may be logical or structural as well as historical, as Eliade has argued.

To use terms consistent with much of this book, it is proposed that, for these scholars, Mother Earth is a figure in a story they are telling, a story in which the world in its multifarious forms makes sense and coheres. It is their story of human culture, their story of religion in human history. I would want to suggest that this story is part of a creative enterprise reflecting the needs of the storytellers even more than it does the concrete realities of at least some of the subjects around which they have created the story. The story reflects a view of the world and serves also to shape the world according to that view.

I believe that the process of this story-making is fully evident in one of the most recent and certainly the most comprehensive studies of Mother Earth in North America, Åke Hultkrantz's recent essay, "The Religion of the Goddess in North America" (1983).[34] I would like to consider in some detail the structure of the argument (more appropriately "story") as well as the extent and nature of the evidence on which it is built.

In the opening two pages of the article, Hultkrantz constructs the "general concept of a mother goddess" that is pervasive in North America. His initial point is "that the belief in a goddess, usually identified with Mother Earth, is found almost everywhere in North America."[35] One could have no contention with the basic statement, for it is well known that female figures or goddesses occur among tribes all over North America. But the statement, while not directly saying so, implies much more than that Native Americans have goddesses, and that is that they recognize *a* goddess and that this goddess is "Mother Earth."

Hultkrantz soon sets to the task of describing and identifying this goddess. He begins by declaring that "her first appearance dates back to the days of the Paleolithic hunters in the Old World."[36] He describes the hunters who ranged across the ice-free steppes in Europe, northern Asia, and northern North America during the ice age some twenty-five thousand years ago. He believes that their religion included a belief in a goddess. His evidence for the belief in the goddess is the presence of "figurines in ivory, bone, and stone of such deities" found "from France to Lake Baikal."[37] There has been much controversy about the nature of these figurines, yet Hultkrantz has no difficulty in seeing them as deities, and from there it is an easy step for him to conclude to the character of the deity that the figurines represent. In the space of three sentences he leaps with her to the present.

> The crude figurines of Europe and Siberia emphasized the sexual, procreative parts of the goddess. In a hunting milieu this meant that she was supposed to be a birth goddess, a mother goddess—perhaps not for humanity alone, but also for the animals necessary to human existence. All the evidence shows that this goddess has survived up to our own time.[38]

Crude female figurines with emphasized breasts and buttocks, identified by physical and temporal proximity with ice-age hunters, are seen as unquestionable evidence of a hunter religion centering on a goddess of birth who is mother to humans and animals and whose religion has survived over twenty-five millennia to the present. The evidence for the present Eurasian presence of the religion of the goddess is found in recent Siberian ethnology. Here Hultkrantz notes that "these peoples, who were then hunters, fishermen, and reindeer nomads, believed in birth goddesses that protected women during pregnancy and childbirth." He says that such goddesses are known all over Eurasia. He continues by describing another Siberian belief. "The Siberian tribes also believed in a mother of the wild animals, a spirit who gave her children to the hunter if he conformed to the hunting ritual."[39] In other words, a goddess was present who played the same role as a master of animals. Putting the birth goddess and the protector of women goddesses, whom Hultkrantz has identified as the survivor of the goddess of the ancient ice-age hunters evidenced by the figurines, together with this mistress of animals, he can achieve a great synthesis. "As the producer of most living things, the great goddess might also . . . become the mistress of the wild animals."[40]

The general concept of the "great goddess," usually identified in

North America as Mother Earth, is thus formed. The "general concept" is that the goddess is a great mother who is a birth goddess, who protects women during pregnancy and birth, who herself gives birth to humans and to animals, and who serves as mistress to the animals. She came into existence some twenty-five thousand years ago in the formation of the religion of ice-age hunters. She is present all over Eurasia down to the present. Thus equipped, Hultkrantz is ready to consider this goddess in North America. "It is this general concept of a mother goddess that penetrated North America with the arrival of the first Siberian hunters, who became the ancestors of the American Indians."[41]

Hultkrantz's next sentence is most telling and requires some reflection. He says, "Of course we have no sources on the goddess from those early days."[42] Most certainly what he was referring to immediately is the absence of prehistoric documentation for the goddess in North America, for he has noted that no figurines have been found in North America, but we must note that the only prehistoric evidence he has for the goddess in Eurasia is the controversial figurines. The balance of his argument is constructed from Siberian ethnology collected no earlier than the nineteenth century. What, in fact, has taken place is not the careful documentation of the history of a goddess over twenty-five thousand years but the *making* of a goddess from precious little hard evidence. While the general concept is constructed on interpretations of evidence with an appropriate number of qualifying "perhapses" and "likelies," once the general concept is formed these phrases are dropped and "the goddess" steps forth. She gains existence. Existence that the author attests to by his own experience, another aspect of the argument that is important to discuss.

After Hultkrantz makes his first declaration of the existence of Mother Earth in North America, he turns to his personal experience of her. "I made the acquaintance of this goddess during my fieldwork among the Shoshoni Indians of Wyoming in the 1940s and 1950s."[43] He says that she does not exist in the hunting-related religious practices of the Shoshoni, or among vision-questing practices, or in oral tradition. But the Shoshoni have a name for her, and near the end of their sun dance a medicine man offers a prayer to "Our Mother" and concludes by letting tobacco fall from his pipe onto the ground, an act that Hultkrantz interprets as "a smoke sacrifice to the progenitor of all living things."[44]

Beginning his article with his personal experience of Mother Earth in North America, Hultkrantz concludes his essay with another personal experience of her, thus framing his study in the evidence of his own experience. Upon suggesting that Peyote Woman, a figure in the origin stories of Peyote religion in North America, is "a divinity probably created after the pattern of Mother Earth," Hultkrantz concludes the article with his own experience of her in this guise. "Those who take peyote during a peyote ritual may hear her sing, as I did once when I attended a peyote ceremony. Certainly, Indian goddesses also appear to white people."[45] I believe that framing the story of Mother Earth in personal experience has much persuasive power. What can be stronger evidence than the personal testimony of one who has met and heard the goddess whose story he is telling?

Within this frame, Hultkrantz is ready to tell the balance of the story of Mother Earth in North America. It requires only the description of what is all too obvious, that during the twenty-four and a half millennia since her origin and during her thousands of years of existence in North America, she has undergone some transformations. Hultkrantz writes, "By this time [that is, by the time of the ethnographic documentation of tribes in North America] the old goddess has developed into multifarious forms, some of them retaining her original symbolism and others giving her entirely new meanings."[46] Thus a principle for interpreting the ethnographies of Native American female figures is set: if she has characteristics of the motherhood of humans or animals; if she is mistress of animals; if she is a creator, nurturer, or protector, then she is the old goddess in her original symbolism; if not (which is rare enough), then one must trace her features by associations back to the traits of the old goddess.

Upon these interpretive principles, Hultkrantz then turns to the discussion of the following manifestations of the old goddess, whom he has said in North America is most usually identified as Mother Earth.

1. The Mother Earth concept "has had a natural anchoring in the areas where collecting of plant foods by women constituted the main economic pursuit—among the tribes of the Great Basin and the Southwest that since 8000 B.C.E. belonged to the so-called desert culture."[47]

2. Corn goddesses from Mexico throughout North America are seen as transformations of the goddess. This connection opens numerous possibilities to see the various forms of the goddess. She is present in the sacrificial rites of some plains tribes, an identification made in the story of the killing of the corn woman in the creation of

corn cultivation. She is a goddess of the netherworld, an identification made in the story of the corn woman leaving the human world.
By association she is goddess of the dead as found among hunting
and collecting tribes in northern California and Oregon. Hultkrantz
writes that in these tribes "The lunar mythological affiliations of this
goddess may indicate that here we are dealing with quite a different
type of goddess, the original birth goddess connected with woman's
menstrual cycle. The moon dies and regains life and, during its dead
period, is presumably the mistress of the dead in [the] underworld."[48]

3. The old goddess is seen as taking the form of the Virgin Mary.
Hultkrantz cites the example of the Virgin of Guadalupe, whose
identity with the goddess is based on the observation that "her first
revelation occurred at a place that was formerly dedicated to a Mex-
ican goddess."[49]

4. Eskimo Sea Women (Sedna, in particular, is discussed) are
obviously manifestations of the goddess, for they are mistresses of
game (sea animals). And through a discussion of Sedna, Hultkrantz
can conclude that "we could say that Sedna is the prototype of the
woman who is ritually unclean. She is, in other words, like her Paleolithic progenitor, still the goddess of women."[50]

5. White Buffalo Calf Woman of the Dakota is also seen as the old
goddess by associating her with the role of mistress of the game. The
argument here runs:

> The buffalo is the symbol of animal food . . . it "contains" the earth
> and dwells inside the earth when it disappears. Such beliefs point to
> the buffalo's close association with Mother Earth. . . . The white buf-
> falo is the master of the game. . . . From all this we can conclude that
> the Buffalo Calf Woman is the mistress of the buffalo, related to
> Mother Earth.[51]

6. The Shawnee goddess "Our Grandmother," whose origins
have been documented as occurring in the mid-nineteenth century,
supplanting a male creator figure, provides a curious case. Hultkrantz identifies her house as "a typical Proterozoic bard house (wig-
wam) in the sky," suggesting a continuity of form since the
Proterozoic. He suggests, although he is probably simply projecting,
that she was operative in the visions of Tenskwatawa and the revelation of a Buffalo dance to Tecumseh in the early nineteenth century,
yet he acknowledges that she did not supplant the male figure until
later.

7. Considering the corn goddesses of the Iroquois, Hultkrantz
notes that the assumption that the corn goddesses are Mother Earth

would be wrong here, for there is "a mother-daughter relation between the great goddess and the corn spirit, just as in ancient Greece Demeter (possibly originally *gē meter*, 'earth mother') was the mother of Kore, 'the girl'." And upon examining another story from the region he notes "that the corn plant sprang from the bosom of the great primeval female divinity who obviously functioned as Mother Earth."[52]

8. The Hopi Spider Woman is also seen as Mother Earth:

> The world was created by command of the sun god. There was also Spider Woman, who gave life to the world, creating plants, birds, animals, and finally human beings out of the earth and out of herself. So, although human beings have human parents, the real parents are Mother Earth (Spider Woman), from whose flesh all are born, and Father Sun. It is apparent that Mother Earth is symbolized by Spider Woman, Sand Altar Woman, and other female spirits conceived to be the mothers of all living things. This mother is represented in the cult by the *sipapuni*, the opening in the floor of the underground ceremonial chamber, or *kiva*, for the *sipapuni* is the Womb of Mother Earth, just as is the hole through which humankind originally emerged from the underworld.[53]

And of the Hopi corn women, Hultkrantz says, "The corn goddess is obviously mostly identical with Mother Earth."[54]

Hultkrantz identifies an astounding array of Native American female figures and goddesses with "the old goddess," "the goddess," "Mother Earth," all of whom are for him, more or less synonymous. She is the earth and the moon; she lives in the earth, the sky, and the sea; she is goddess of hunters, cultivators, and gatherers; she is goddess of birth and nurturance and of sacrifice and the dead; she is mistress of the game and she is the corn maiden; she is peyote woman and the Virgin Mary. In such an approach, any figure, even a male one, could somehow be assimilated into the goddess by one attribute or another.

Hultkrantz does here more fully what has been as aspect of nearly every other scholarly discussion of Mother Earth in North America. Eliade, rather than document her history, outlined her forms and meanings. In this way he found her "form" in "all myths dealing with Life and Death, with Creation and generation, with sexuality and voluntary sacrifice." Hultkrantz has, as have most others, presented the character and history of Mother Earth as a key character in a story of the history and meaning of culture and religion. She is the necessary product of various theories of culture and religion.

If one is not drawn to this story of the goddess and her existence outside of North America and if one is not persuaded that she exists because of Hultkrantz's personal experience of her, I believe that there is no basis for accepting the means by which she is found to exist all over North America. The collapsing of all of these figures into a single goddess, or even the view of all of them as emanating from a single goddess, distracts from the richness and complexity of all of these figures. We cannot see and understand the depths and sophistication of these many very different figures, even their specific and important histories, when we are motivated to discern only some aspect of "the goddess" as adequate explanation and interpretation. We will find only what we expect to find, and it will always be an aspect of the goddess who is our own creation.

While I do not accept the story, because there is too little evidence for it, and, to be quite clear, because it does not meet my personal and intellectual needs or correspond with my understanding of the nature of culture and religion, I still recognize it as a very powerful story. It is a story that not only reflects, but effects, an understanding of the world and its many peoples. It is a story of the oneness of humankind, but a story in which the many peoples of the world are hierarchically interrelated with one another. It is a story that makes Native Americans primitives when compared with European-Americans. It is a story that supports a range of social, economic, and political relationships, very likely oppressive, among peoples in America.

But I also recognize the story as powerful in another way, a way perhaps not so commonly expected, especially by scholars who tend to comprehend their role as somewhat removed from history and reality. It is the story of the creation of a goddess, the making of Mother Earth in North America. And stories, especially creation stories, have power. With the persuasion and authority of the written and spoken word that created Mother Earth in North America, I believe it can be shown that Mother Earth has literally stepped forth from the word to become a major Native American goddess. It is to this part of the story that I now turn.

▲ 7 ▲

The Making of Mother Earth
The Indians

All European tradition, Marxism included, has conspired to defy the natural order of all things. Mother Earth has been abused, the powers have been abused, and this cannot go on forever. No theory can alter that simple fact. Mother Earth will retaliate, the whole environment will retaliate, and the abusers will be eliminated. Things will come full circle, back to where they started.

Russell Means, 1980

In light of a survey of female figures in the ethnographic documentation for the tribal traditions of native North America, it is not surprising that the scholars who have considered her have tended to depend upon the evidence cited by other scholars for their examples of Mother Earth. It is not peculiar that the same few examples were used again and again. While I have been able to find a number of tribal traditions that make references to the earth in personal and kinship terms, there is an absence in the vast literature on North American tribes of any identification of the earth or the spiritual personification of the earth as a major goddess. Not until the twentieth century and then for the most part not until mid-century is there any extent of clear reference to Mother Earth made by native peoples.

The many factors thus far considered suggest a set of hypotheses.

129

It seems that Mother Earth as a major goddess of the Indians of North America is a reality, but that she has become so only during the twentieth century. And furthermore, it seems that her historical origin, although she is primordial, occurred within this century, but with roots running through the entire history of the Native American and European-American encounter. From a historical perspective, before Mother-Earth emerged as a major figure to Indians, she was a goddess important to Americans' views of themselves, and in this self-definitional process Mother Earth was identified both as Indian and as Indian goddess; all of this being apart from Native Americans and their tribal religious traditions. In this view, it seems beyond serious doubt that the origin of Mother Earth as a goddess to Native Americans was, in some respects, inspired by, dependent upon, or transformed from the figure as she existed for Americans of European ancestry. Thus, knowledge of European-American expectations, acquired through encounter, through reading the literature, or in some indirect way, was central to this development. Finally, it seems that the origins of Mother Earth as a Native American goddess were in some measure encouraged by the exigencies of the emergence of an "Indian" identity that has complemented and often supplanted tribal identities. It will be the subject of this chapter to document and to examine the impact and implications of this set of hypotheses.

Indian Statements on Mother Earth

The record of statements made by individual Native Americans that include some reference to Mother Earth or to the earth as mother begins at least as early as 1855, with the treaty negotiations in Walla Walla Valley. As we keep in mind the statements that were made in the interior plateau between 1855 and 1885, other Native American statements on Mother Earth will now be surveyed. They date from the early decades of this century up to the present.

There are dozens of such statements. When one looks for them they begin to appear everywhere. The following is a selection intended not only to show the historical incidence and pattern of these statements but also the common forms these statements have taken and the historical contexts in which they have been made.

Until after the middle of this century, there is scant evidence that any Native American spoke of the earth as mother in any manner that could be understood as attesting to a major figure or a great goddess. The first half of the twentieth century is practically mute in this respect, though some few examples can be found.

One notable example dates from early in the century. During decades of the late nineteenth and early twentieth centuries, a number of Native Americans began to make transitions from their native cultures and lifeways into majority American culture. These notable individuals obtained schooled educations, often earning university degrees, and many established themselves as professional leaders. Charles A. Eastman, also known throughout his life by his Sioux name, Ohiyesa, is exemplary among this group.

Eastman was born into a Santee Sioux family in 1858. Even then his family had long been influenced by European-American culture and Christianity. At a time of personal crisis during the winter of 1828–29, his great-grandfather, Cloud Man, had converted to Christianity. As a child Eastman was reared as a hunter and warrior and distinguished himself as such among his people. The killing of five settlers by a group of Santee Sioux in 1862 led to retaliatory measures by the non-Indian people in the area. More than three hundred Indians received a death sentence for the action, though later President Lincoln intervened and reduced the number to thirty-eight. Because it was thought that his father, Many Lightning, was among those executed, Charles was taken by his father's brother, Mysterious Medicine, to Canada along with many Santees who fled the white counterhostilities. Here he was reared according to the old tribal ways.

Many Lightning was, however, not executed, he was imprisoned for several years. During this time, he came under the influence of two European-Americans who encouraged him to accept Christianity. They persuaded him that the future was open for him and his children only upon his acceptance and advancement of white ways. Consequently, he took the name Jacob Eastman, became Christian, and began to bring his family back together so that they could follow his new way of life. Jacob's reunion with his fifteen-year-old son in Canada marked a moment of radical transformation in the young man's life.

Taken back to Flandreau, South Dakota, Charles was immediately told of his father's wishes and sent off to school. After a difficult start, Charles adapted to school and soon began to do well. Once started on this course, he was to go on and on. He attended Beloit College for three years, then spent several years at Knox College in Galesburg, Illinois. He attended Dartmouth College, beginning in

January 1882, and graduated in 1887. While at Dartmouth he was a distinguished scholar, studying Latin, Greek, French, and German, as well as zoology, botany, chemistry, physics, natural history, philosophy, geometry, political science, and history. He was an athlete, active in football, baseball, tennis, and boxing, and he held the school record for long-distance running for several years. He was a member of a fraternity and was highly popular among his classmates.

Following his education at Dartmouth, Charles attended Boston University School of Medicine where he graduated high in his class in 1890 and, as class orator, delivered a paper at his graduation exercises.

At this time Charles Eastman was the most highly educated Native American in the country. He had not become simply acculturated into majority American culture, he had become a distinguished and successful American, who was also a Native American. He returned to his people and began to practice as a physician at Pine Ridge.

Quite in contrast with Eastman's success, Native Americans from the northern plains across to the Northwest were losing their lands and their lifeways. Unlike Eastman, they did not have schooled educations; they had no way of entering the European-American world; they had no way of maintaining their way of tribal life without the land that was being so rapidly taken from them. The Ghost Dance was one response to this experience of deprivation, this crisis of being. Ghost Dance rituals were performed throughout the plains and Northwest in 1890, the year Eastman returned home. The millenarian expectations expressed by the Ghost Dance movement led non-native peoples in the area to become increasingly fearful that militant action was forthcoming. This ultimately led to a tragic massacre of native people at Wounded Knee on December 29, 1890. Eastman attended to the wounded as they arrived in nearby Pine Ridge, working to the point of exhaustion in the Episcopal church that had been turned into a hospital. On January 1, 1891, he led a party to the site of the massacre, seeking other survivors in a mission that had been delayed until then by a blizzard. Remarkably, some survivors were found and taken to Pine Ridge. But Eastman also found the grizzly remains of the massacre and was himself thrust into experiencing as he never had before the gulf that separated the two cultures he knew and in which he lived.

Eastman spent the balance of his long life making his way along the narrow path that bridged his two cultures. He was extremely influential and became a major model for the way of resolving the tensions that existed between cultures. He was proof that Indians could leave their old ways and do well in the new American world. While never abandoning his tribal roots and while remaining proud of his heritage, Eastman nonetheless promoted this approach throughout his life. He attempted through government service, through lecturing and writing, through participation—often in founding and formative roles—in many organizations such as the YMCA and the Boy Scouts of America, to build bridges of understanding between cultures.[1]

The background of Charles Eastman's life is important not only for the consideration of his statements about Mother Earth; he also represents the attitude of a number of influential Indians during the late nineteenth and early twentieth centuries in their response to the crises so widely suffered by Native Americans. One major way taken by many important Indian leaders such as Eastman, was to develop a ground for cooperation, understanding, and sympathy that would permit Native Americans to adjust to the way of life of majority culture, and to find meaningful places within it.

Eastman wrote several books and many articles. A portion of these writings is about the Indian way of life as he knew and remembered it from his childhood. They were written for non-native Christian readers, with the expressed intent of presenting Indian ways in a light that could be appreciated and understood by Christian Americans. Eastman described "Indian religion" in his book *The Soul of the Indian* published in 1911, in order, in his words, "to paint the religious life of the typical American Indian as it was before he knew the white man." His source was his memory of his childhood and his style was personal. "It is as true as I can make it to my childhood teaching and ancestral ideals, but from the human, not the ethnological standpoint." With this setting we can consider Eastman's statements on Mother Earth, though they are but two. He first wrote:

> The Indian no more worshipped the Sun than the Christian adores the Cross. The Sun and the Earth, by an obvious parable, holding scarcely more of poetic metaphor than of scientific truth, were in his view the parents of all organic life. From the Sun, as the universal father, proceeds the quickening principle in nature, and in the patient and fruitful womb of our mother, the Earth, are hidden embryos of plants and men. Therefore our reverence and love for them was really an imaginative extension of our love for our immediate parents, and

with this sentiment of filial piety was joined a willingness to appeal to them, as to a father, for such good gifts as we may desire. This is the material or physical prayer.[2]

Eastman's statement is important in several respects. It serves as evidence that there was a widespread belief among non-Indian Americans that the religious beliefs of Indians center on the sun and, secondarily, on the earth as deities. His statement is motivated by the need to counter this view, which he sees is as misplaced as declaring that Christians worship the cross. He explains the apparent deification of sun and earth by poetic metaphor, that is, the sun and earth are thought of metaphorically through the extension of the piety one feels for natural parents. As such, appeal to the sun and earth is a form of prayer. His explanation is precisely the interpretation I have made of the many statements uttered by individuals in the interior plateau, including Smohalla. Eastman's explanation confirms key portions of my hypotheses.

Eastman's writing on "Indian religion" may be seen as evidence of a major transitional phase in the development of Native American religions. Eastman uses here the metaphorical language of sun and earth that in various forms communicates the sentiments commonly felt by many native peoples during the nineteenth and twentieth centuries. As Eastman uses this language, it can be observed in a transitional moment. While he proclaims that the intentions of Native Americans in their identification of the sun and earth as father and mother are correctly understood as metaphorical, his presentation of the sun and earth as having a role in prayer is transformative. That is, with a role in prayer they move beyond simply metaphorical figures to take on a spiritual and theological reality.

The transitional features are even clearer in the second statement Eastman made about the sun and earth later in the same book.

> In the Sioux story of creation, the great Mysterious One is not brought directly upon the scene or conceived in anthropomorphic fashion, but remains sublimely in the background. The Sun and the Earth, representing the male and female principles, are the main elements in his creation, the other planets being subsidiary. The enkindling warmth of the Sun entered into the bosom of our mother, the Earth, and forwith she conceived and brought forth life, both vegetable and animal.[3]

Eastman says that he draws this statement about the sun and earth from the Sioux creation stories, but it corresponds with other known Sioux creation stories only in the most general way. In light of Eastman's earlier statement about the sun and earth being aspects of "an obvious parable," here Eastman renders the parable as creation story and identifies it with the tradition of Sioux creation stories. This brief passage is evidence, I believe, of very early stages of a transformative and reformative process, a process that did not flower until the 1970s. At fifty years of age, with knowledge of Sioux tribal traditions gained primarily in his early childhood and knowledge of the literature and attitudes about Indians acquired in formal education and in his career in Indian service, Eastman makes a happy union of these elements in his version of Sioux creation. He uses a language almost biblical in style, suggesting theological as well as poetical intent. The sentiment and respect for the earth as presented in this statement is in continuity with traditional Sioux ethos and most certainly it expresses the importance of the lost and threatened lands deeply felt by Indian peoples nearly everywhere. The language Eastman used, for example, the phrasing "the enkindling warmth of the Sun entered into the bosom of our mother, the Earth," is new to Native American expressions, yet it aligns remarkably with the style of statements about Indian religiousness made widely by Americans of European ancestry for, by then, nearly a century. In earlier chapters these statements were traced through nineteenth-century American literature and ethnography. The similarities of style and sentiment are too great not to strongly suggest influence, particularly when Eastman's background is known.

These Eastman statements about Mother Earth and Father Sun, though they are brief, are, I believe, very important to this study, for they stand at a point of convergence of some of the stories that have been recounted. First consider Eastman's statement in light of the story of the statement attributed to Tecumseh. As it has been shown, this statement about the Indian belief in Father Sky and Mother Earth was part of an American story and was not an Indian statement at all. Eastman's statements mark the moment when the sentiment expressed in the statement attributed to Tecumseh finally becomes an Indian story. While Eastman denies that Indians worship the sun and the earth, he nonetheless presents a poetic parable representing Sioux (and thereby, in his categories, the Indian) belief that "life, both vegetable and animal" was brought forth when the "enkindling warmth of the Sun entered into the bosom of our mother, the Earth." Eastman is true to his use of poetic metaphor, for he says that the sun and the earth represent the male and female principles, but his choice of language to describe the engendering act is so poetic and powerful and also so familiar in American literature

that the metaphor seems overwhelmed. Eastman's statements serve
to transform the Tecumseh statement into a truly Indian story. The
story of Smohalla's statement is also relevant here. Eastman says
expressly that to refer to the sun and earth as mother and father is an
extension by metaphor of the filial piety felt for one's natural parents.
This is in direct continuity with the strategies of Smohalla and the
others in his region. But in Eastman's presentation the metaphor is
diminished as the Indian story begins to take shape.

I believe that these brief statements that Charles Eastman wrote
about Mother Earth are very important to acquiring an understanding of this branch of the story. They represent a pivotal moment in
the Indian making of Mother Earth. The role that story and language play here is no surprise. It is in Eastman's appropriation of
European-American language and imagery and his incorporation of
it into story that Mother Earth begins to emerge as a real goddess of
major importance to the Indians.

While Eastman was interested in communicating aspects of his
native heritage to non-native peoples, few individual Native Americans who had attempted to gain standing in the non–Native American world wished to do the same, at least in the early decades of this
century. They wanted principally to set examples for other native
peoples to follow, thereby leading them out of the old tribal ways
into new non-native ways. Thus such examples as the Eastman statements are not common during this time, and those that exist are
characterized by a mood of accommodation between Native American tribal traditions and the traditions of European-Americans. The
motivation was at once to show a sympathy and basic level of similarity between Native Americans and European-Americans, thus
creating a road on which native peoples could move from their
cultures into the rapidly expanding majority culture.

Few other statements by Native Americans about the earth as
mother can be found until well after the middle of this century. Then
they begin to emerge with great abundance. Remarkably, most of
these are characterized by a tone much in contrast with that of Eastman's, although they still address the same issues.

For example, in the early 1970s Grace Black Elk, granddaughter
to the famous Black Elk, said,

> One day soon, the white man will come to us, and say: Help us!
> We have used up the energy of Mother Earth! We have wasted the
> energy of Father Sun! . . .
>   Now, what is this "energy crisis" the white man has? It is *his* "ener-
> gy crisis." The white man created it, because he does not respect

Mother Earth; he has to consume the energy of his Mother the Earth, for his electric toothbrushes. . . .

Mother Earth has no "energy crisis." Father Sun has no "energy crisis." The People, the Indian People, they have no "energy crisis."
Who does:
It is the white man, who has broken the Sacred Circle of Life.[4]

Here we see a conception of the earth in continuity with that described by Eastman. Furthermore, the statement about Mother Earth is made in the context of cultural confrontation, that is, in the history of contact, the history of oppression of Native Americans. What is new here is the tone and motivation of the statement. Unlike those in the interior plateau who so desperately wanted their attachment to their lands to be understood, and unlike Eastman who wanted to accommodate and to emphasize the similarities among cultures, Grace Black Elk wants to emphasize the differences between cultures. Further, she clearly wants to demonstrate the superiority of Indian culture over white European-American culture. Mother Earth, now formally characterized as an entity with a proper name, along with Father Sun, is the language around which Black Elk centers her discussion of differences.

A hint of millennial expectation is present in the statements of Grace Black Elk. Certainly she has the expectation of a major crisis. She does not envision a mysterious or spiritual intervention, nor does she see the crisis to be one suffered by the Indian people. Rather she sees that it will be a crisis, an energy crisis, caused and suffered by "the white man," and that it will be the Indians who will hold the solution to this crisis, a solution inherent in their relationship with Mother Earth.

While Grace Black Elk speaks of Mother Earth as a person, it seems that she does not imagine her as a willful person intervening in human affairs. But this conception of her, as portrayed earlier by Mooney, appears strongly in other instances. For example, Sun Bear, a Chippewa, reportedly said,

The people who really want to survive the destruction of the System and the Great Purification and who really want to live to find real brotherhood on the Earth Mother again will move away from these situations. . . . The Earth Mother is about to declare her complete rebellion.[5]

Such statements develop the theme of Mother Earth as a willful being who oversees the way human beings treat the physical earth. When they mistreat the earth, she rises to punish them.

By the mid 1970s and after, Native Americans' consciousness of their Indian identity was well developed. They had begun to see that their distinctiveness, their very identity as Indians, provides an alternative to the materialistic and ecologically unconscionable ways that distinguish for them Americans of European descent. Indians thus took up the theme of Mother Earth as retaliator, and saw that her exaction of retribution would surely not be directed toward them, so long as they nurtured their "Indian" identity.

Russell Means, instrumental in the development of a politically powerful organization of American Indians, the American Indian Movement, is perhaps unsurpassed in his ability to formulate this argument. In his statement that refers to Mother Earth quoted at the head of this chapter, Means angrily indicts "all European tradition" in the presentation of his "Indian manifesto," as the editors of *Mother Jones* termed it.

Means is knowledgeable about American and Western history, and he rejects wholesale the features that characterize this history. He detests writing which to him "epitomizes the European concept of 'legitimate' thinking." He rejects the whole Western intellectual heritage: philosophies, histories, mental processes, and cultures. Means speaks harshly of the immorality fostered by capitalism, the lack of responsibility taken for the earth's resources, the meaningless accumulation of material objects by capitalism, and on and on. He, of course, posits American Indian ways as alternative to all that he finds wrong with Western and American ways, declaring that

> it is the role of American Indian peoples, the role of all natural beings, to survive. A part of our survival is to resist. We resist not to overthrow a government or to take political power, but because it is natural to resist extermination, to survive. We don't want power over white institutions; we want white institutions to disappear. *That's* revolution.[6]

Mean's statements may seem novel, perhaps even revolutionary, but when seen in light of American history they are not. In rejecting what he sees as distinctive aspects of majority American culture, the culture that he rightly sees as oppressive and threatening to all Native Americans and their heritages, Means proposes a strategy that has been chosen often since at least the time of the Delaware prophet, Neolin, in 1762, a strategy that anthropologists have identified worldwide by the term "nativism." Nativism indicates the rejection of the oppressing culture and the assertion of native or indigenous values and ways in response to the experience of cultural deprivation. The broad intentions of the American Indian Move-ment correspond with those of Tecumseh and his brother Tensk-watawa in their efforts to establish an alliance among Indian peoples to resist the persistent desires of white Americans for land. Tensk-watawa's prophetic message encouraged the rejection of any "white" influences, yet it also rejected the old tribal religious practices.

Means also has a millennial expectation. He believes in an im-pending worldwide catastrophe and expects that American Indians will endure into the postcataclysmic future.

> When the catastrophe is over, we American Indian peoples will still be here to inhabit the hemisphere. I don't care is it's only a handful living high in the Andes. American Indian people will survive: harmony will be reestablished. *That's* revolution.[7]

The references Means makes to Mother Earth, quoted at the be-ginning of this chapter, emphasize her role as retaliator against wrongful treatment of the earth. While this aspect of the future role of Mother Earth has been emphasized in recent decades by Native Americans, the same aspect of her character was also well developed in James Mooney's construction of Mother Earth theology in 1896.

In a variety of Native American tribes, individuals in recent dec-ades have devoted themselves to the presentation of their philosophy to the world outside of their tribes. Their messages are spoken to or written for an English-speaking audience, and one invariably sym-pathetic to Native Americans. Here especially Mother Earth is com-monly presented as central to these Indian philosophies, as for example in a public presentation made by the Hopi, Thomas Banyacya, in Seattle in March 1983. His remarks, published in *The Northern Light,* were received as "ancient Hopi prophecies."

Banyacya opened his remarks by saying,

> Hopi prophecy is the spiritual side of our lives, our knowledge of things pertaining to the Mother Earth, and to the sun, moon and stars as the elements that help to keep nature in balance. Hopi know that there was a life before this one and even one before that one. Both were destroyed—the last one by a great flood—because mankind had gone too far away from love, nature, and the Great Spirit's plan of life.[8]

Rather than presenting Hopi beliefs and practices in Hopi terms, a task that most certainly would not be condoned by the Hopi, he speaks primarily of "the Great Spirit's plan of life." This phrase, "the Great Spirit," renders for Banyacya the name of the utterly complex

Hopi figure Masau'u, but Banyacya quickly makes another connection: "surprisingly, in the Bible he is called the Messiah."

Banyacya's presentation centers upon a story revealed to Hopi people and represented in graphic form on two stone tablets now kept in a shrine at Hopi. The story begins with the separation of two brothers. Originally they had the same knowledge, but the older brother was given a set of stone tablets (a reference to the ten commandments?) and sent to the east to "develop, record, and invent things." It was known that "someday he would come back and look for his younger brother, who would still be holding on to his land and living in a spiritual way."

After many years the older brother's skin changed color, becoming white. In this story, the people of the younger brother were warned of the time when the older brother would return.

> When your white brother comes with another symbol [i.e. other than that of the sacred circle] you had better watch out. He's going to have a sweet tongue, many inventions, and he will say, "Let your ways go. Come follow me."

The Great Spirit charted out the future, appointing three nations to "watch other races of mankind to see if they follow the religious instructions and do things the way the Great Spirit told them." When they observed a departure from the appointed way, they were to warn those who had gone astray.

> Our skin is the color of the great Mother Earth. We[the Hopi] were given the duty to take care of the North American continent so that this life will go on in a natural way with everything in balance.

Banyacya, attending to this duty, proceeds to make his warning to his white brothers by describing his observations of white aberrancy.

> It is told in your history books that you came to this land for religious freedom, a good, free life. But what are you doing to your brothers who are holding to this land in a simple, spiritual, and humble way?...
>
> When our white brothers came to our homeland from across the waters, we welcomed them and did everything a brother would do for a brother who had been away for a long time. We gave you food, let you live on our land, we even let you live in our tipis [the Hopi live in adobe houses]. We did everything so that you could have this kind of life.
>
> But today we find this life has been broken down because our white brother has come with different inventions and religious beliefs.

The prophecy predicted numerous European-American inventions and introductions and the accompanying prophesied negative effects. Banyacya documents these in some detail. Almost nothing of the way set forth by "the Great Spirit" is described, though it seems to be identified with "the Hopi way."

The inclusion of Mother Earth in Thomas Banyacya's presentation is done in two ways. Banyacya's first reference to the earth follows a Hopi pattern of seeing the earth, sun, moon, and stars, along with many other elements of the world, as essential to health and survival. But Banyacya, or *The Northern Light* editor, chose to set the earth apart from the rest with the more formal designation, "Mother Earth." If it is Banyacya's term, it is most surely selected because of his familiarity with the expectations of his white audience, a factor that motivates his translation of Masau'u to "the Great Spirit" and his identification of Masau'u as the Christian "messiah."

Banyacya's second way is one that is the same as that used in the nineteenth century by native peoples negotiating with the U.S. government. As shown earlier, they commonly made the connection between their skin color and the color of the earth as the basis of kinship, or a relationship of responsibility, what they termed "chieftainship."

Banyacya's inclusion of the term "Mother Earth" appears to be motivated by his interest in communicating with non-Hopi, non-native people. Throughout his presentation, he utilizes a terminology and a history that is familiar to his audience. His intent is to demonstrate the error of the ways of the culture and history of his audience over against the rightness of the ways of his own culture. He does not describe his ways but rather encompasses the errors of others within the prophecy of his people.

Banyacya's presentation includes the modern feature of criticizing European-American history and lifeways while holding native ways to be superior and the future to be ultimately dependent upon them. But, like Charles Eastman, Banyacya is interested in showing similarities between cultures, even to the point of establishing original kinship and a guardianship role for the Hopi over their brother peoples. Thus much of the history of encounter, including the elements of Mother Earth, is reflected in Banyacya's presentation.

Even the protection of lands by the establishment of reservations was not successful, as in the case of the further shrinking of the Nez Perce reservation when gold was discovered on it. A long conflict has taken place on the Navajo reservation over the removal of minerals from the soils on the reservation. In a document submitted to an

Arizona court, an eighty-four-year-old Navajo woman protested the mining activities of Peabody Coal Company on her homelands on Black Mesa. Her statement is highly interesting for the various reasons she gives for her disapproval, one of them being that the earth is mother to the people.

"In English they call me 'Kee Shelton's Mother.' In Navajo my name is Asa Bazhonoodah, 'Woman who had squaw dance.' "[9] With this introduction of herself, Asa Bazhonoodah traces her long life-history and that of her immediate ancestors upon the lands affected by the mining operation in progress. She says that her family died on the land and their bodies are buried on the land. She was born on this land and has lived her whole life upon it. She protests the many adverse effects of the mining operation that she has observed. The mine workers drink and influence the young Navajos. The pollution from the mining causes the deaths of the cows and sheep belonging to her children. The explosions scare her horses. The healing herbs, the trees, and grasses are scorched and are dying.

But beyond these observations, Asa Bazhonoodah speaks of the earth in language intended to demonstrate the importance of the earth to her and her people. Here she uses the terminology of Mother Earth.

> A long time ago the earth was placed here for us, the people, the Navajo. It gives us corn and we consider her our mother.
>
> When Mother Earth needs rain we give pollen and use the prayers that were given us when we came from the earth. That brings rain. Black Mesa area is used to ask for rain. And afterward (after the mining) we don't know what it will be like. We make prayers for all blessings for Mother Earth, asking that we may use her legs, her body and her spirit to make ourselves more powerful and durable. After this the pollen is thrown into the water. . . .
>
> The Earth is our mother. The white man is ruining our mother. I don't know the white man's ways, but to us the Mesa, the air, the water, are Holy Elements. We pray to these Holy Elements in order for our people to flourish and perpetuate the well-being of each generation.
>
> Even when we were small, our cradle is made from the things given to us from Mother Earth. We use these elements all of our lives and when we die we go back to Mother Earth.

Asa Bozhonoodah thinks that the result of the disturbance of the earth by the mining company will destroy the Navajo, making them like the Anasazi, the ancient ones whose remains are scattered about the land. She believes this to be the will and intention of "the white men." She goes on to describe how the Navajos are dependent upon the earth and how they interrelate with it. She uses an interesting metaphor.

> Mother Earth is like a horse. We put out hay and grain to bring in the horse. So it is when we put out pollen to bring life from Mother Earth. We pray to Mother Earth to ask blessings from the water, the sun, and the moon. Why are they going up there (to the moon)? I'm also against this. This fooling around with the sacred elements.

Speaking futher about her sensitivities to all sorts of mining pollutions, she concludes in a style that is reminiscent of that of Smohalla.

> How can we give something of value to Mother Earth to repay the damages that the mining has done to her. We still ask her for blessings and healing, even when she is hurt.
> They are taking water and the other Holy Elements from her veins.
> I don't want highways built because stock will be run over and the children hurt.
> I see the cedar trees next to the ponds they build have turned red. The grasses are dying.
> I want to see them stop taking water from inside the Mesa. The water underground, which works with that water that falls to the surface of Mother Earth, will wash away.
> I want to see the burial grounds left alone. All of my relatives' graves are being disturbed.
> How much would you ask if your mother had been harmed? There is no way that we can be repaid for the damages to our Mother. No amount of money we repay, money cannot give birth to anything. I want to see the mining stopped.

Many of the old themes and issues are present here in a situation that seems never to change. Native Americans are asked to give up their land or to permit the exploitation of their lands by mining. Asa Bozhonoodah makes the most rational and obvious conclusions from the observations of the mining activities that are everywhere around her. She persuasively describes the value of the earth by presenting the earth as mother. She is clearly within direct and immediate continuity with Navajo religious traditions in her comments, though here the emphasis is drawn in a way to give earth the special distinction of the proper name Mother Earth. She goes on to ask those same impossible kinds of questions that Smohalla had asked.

Her·question, "How much would you ask if your mother had been harmed?" is powerful, as is her observation that "money cannot give birth to anything."

Yet the mining still goes on.[10]

A final example to be examined occurred during a meeting convened by the Institute for Resource Management, an organization serving the interests of the actor Robert Redford. Redford met with representatives of the Navajo people in Canyon de Chelly along with representatives of energy production concerns. Seated at a table on the sandy floor of Canyon de Chelly, the Navajo tribal chairman, Peterson Zah, spoke of the issue of mining the resources on Navajo lands.

> The earth is our Mother. When we talk about development of our land which involves mining, we ask ourselves: "How can we take from her face? How can we squeeze out what we want for money? For other people's use and other people's energy? Can we do this much to our Mother?"[11]

There is a notable similarity between the statement made by Chairman Zah and the statement made by Smohalla a century earlier. The context is the same: white Americans seeking to persuade Native Americans that they should engage in harvesting the mineral resources of their land. Zah, as did Smohalla before him, responded by presenting a series of questions, questions asked, it seems, more introspectively than in the earlier case. Still, the structure of the statement is the same. The earth is considered to be mother to the people. To engage in mining would be to alter their relationship with the land, an alteration they describe in the metaphorical terms of marring the body of their mother.

One difference that is notable in the two statements is that in Smohalla's case it is quite clear what he intended as the answer to each of his questions. In Zah's statement, the questions are less rhetorical, and thus are to be taken as more practical. And answers were offered. As reported, the Navajo woman Annie Wauneka, who has been instrumental in bringing Western medicine to Navajo people, pursued answers to Zah's questions. She said,

> Let's do it together. Let's develop for our children, but let's not forget that this is our Mother. There are precious things inside here. It's got to go out. Our new Indian friends, our non-Indian friends have the knowledge.[12]

The Indian Mother Earth

There are several lines of development in the Indian making of Mother Earth. Perhaps most important is that the earth was not formally referred to as a mother figure or goddess until the twentieth century. Before that the earth was referred to as a mother in metaphorical terms and in the manner of identifying the elements of the world by personal and kinship terms. It is also important to recognize that the various lines of development are not at all separate ones, rather they were interwoven throughout the last century. Considering them separately will aid in gaining a fuller understanding.

Perhaps most significant in the Indian making of Mother Earth is that the great majority of references to Mother Earth or to the earth as mother are in the context of communication with European-Americans and the subject is invariably land or land usage. The history of these references, from the nineteenth-century statements in the interior plateau region through the statements made by Charles A. Eastman to the many statements by Indians since 1970, reveals a fairly clear line of development. In the nineteenth century, the statements were basically metaphorical in character, made by Native Americans to communicate to non-natives the value and importance of their land and the continuity of their relationship to the land. These statements were all made in the face of threats to the lands and to Native Americans' relationships to their land. There was confirmation of the metaphor, yet a transformation of it in the early twentieth century in the statements written by Charles Eastman. While Eastman stated that Indians no more worship the sun and earth than Christians worship the cross, explaining the misconception by the discussion of the personification of sun and earth through metaphor, he nonetheless employed the figures Father Sun and Mother Earth in his telling of the Sioux creation story. The metaphor was extended to the point of giving a kind of poetic existence to these figures as creators. It is beyond question that Eastman was responding to the widely held views by non-Native Americans that Indians worship sun and earth as father and as mother. His intention to accommodate, while also gently to correct, these views was prominent in his many writings about Indians.

By the 1970s, Mother Earth is commonly referred to by Indians, especially to demonstrate a contrast between themselves and non-Native American peoples. Here Mother Earth has become a major figure central to the distinctions between peoples. The shift since the time of Eastman has been away from accommodation to an emphasis on differences. Mother Earth, the figure erroneously identified by European-Americans for a century as the central goddess of Native Americans, has now been appropriated by Native Americans. But the point they make is that their special relationship with her distinguishes their identity and destiny in opposition to Americans of European ancestry. The acceptance of Mother Earth as a major figure gives a primordial and spiritual foundation to the history, culture, morality, and values of Native Americans, especially when considered over against Americans of European ancestry. She is part of their story, even the base of their story, and as such she is given existence.

This development may be viewed from another vantage point. Several aspects of the story being told reveal the development of multi- or pan-tribal associations since at least the time of Tecumseh. Tecumseh traveled among tribes throughout the eastern United States attempting to form an alliance among them by which to stem the tide of American expansion into Indian lands. Even in this early movement there was a religious dimension to the alliance. This was offered by Tenskwatawa, the prophet brother to Tecumseh, whose prophecies established a religious base for the alliance. It was a move from the tribal traditions practiced separately by the various peoples involved in the alliance to a common religious practice. Tenskwatawa recognized the importance of this religious aspect in establishing a commonality of purpose and identity among these peoples. In a speech he made to William H. Harrison in 1808 he said,

> The religion which I have established for the last three years, has been attended to by the different tribes of Indians in this part of the world. Those Indians were once different people; they are now but one: they are all determined to practice what I have communicated to them, that has come immediately from the Great Spirit through me.[13]

Tenskwatawa's prophetic religion was nativistic in calling for the rejection of many accoutrements of American culture, and reformative in calling for the abandonment of old tribal medicine practices, but it was not a religion of Mother Earth. The spirit of alliance that these Shawnee brothers fostered has been an important inspiration and model to twentieth-century Indian leaders who have endeavored to do the same task. I believe that, however circuitous the route through history, Tecumseh's alleged statement about Mother Earth has served to encourage the appropriation of Mother Earth as a major figure in the pan-Indian movement in the twentieth century.

The greatest motivation for the development of a multitribal alliance in the nineteenth century was the threat to land and consequently the threat to lifeways and cultural existence felt in common among Native American peoples. As early as Tenskwatawa this was seen as the essential feature of the common identity. By the twentieth century the motivations remained the same, and the consciousness of a common identity began to emerge more strongly. It has been identified by the term "Indian," a term used by European-Americans since the days of Columbus to give a common identity to peoples native to the Americas. In the twentieth century the term has been appropriated by the native peoples to describe the identity they share among themselves, an identity fostered and distinguished largely by the unavoidable encounter with European-Americans, invariably over the subject of land. Interestingly, the use of the term "Indian" by Native Americans is commonly distinguished by a special pronunciation. Rather than the three-syllable pronunciation "iṅdēən" common to European-Americans, the Native American pronunciation is closer to two syllables, "iṅdin."

There is a line of development from the statement attributed to Tecumseh that the earth is a mother, through those statements of the Native Americans of the interior plateau during negotiations, to Eastman's statements where Father Sun and Mother Earth begin to take on real existence as "Indian" deities. Given this much of the story, the importance of the erroneous allegations and interpretations that introduced the theology of the figure Mother Earth so strongly into the literature about Native Americans must be appreciated. Eastman was responding to these widely held views, yet in his reponse he initiated the process by which Mother Earth was appropriated and given full existence as a Sioux creator goddess; but since Eastman spoke as an exemplary Indian, both to native and to nonnative peoples, he served, as did his writings, to establish a model for an emerging "Indian identity."

This identity is much more fully developed in the statements of Grace Black Elk, Sun Bear, and Russell Means. While they do not abandon or deny their individual tribal identities, they speak for and as Indians, and very consciously they strongly contrast their Indian identity to that of the "white men."

As evident in these statements, Mother Earth serves as mother to this common Indian identity. She may be recognized as being in continuity with a land ethos relatively common among Native American tribes, the conception of many elements of nature in personal, even kinship, terms. Mother Earth is identified with the most fundamental concerns of all Indian peoples, the retention of lands. She also nurtures and gives identity to peoples who have lost their lands, yet who retain as central to their identity a respect and reverence for land and nature. Mother Earth as an Indian goddess serves a need for the alliance of peoples whose cultural identities have faced enormous crises and transformations, often due to loss of land or the forced revision of their ancestral relationships with land. Mother Earth gives a primordial and spiritual base, and thus religious authority and responsibility, to the Indian identity. She is the basis on which Indians articulate the superiority of their way of life over against "white Americans" and from which they derive their responsibility to maintain their Indian identity.

One aspect of this line of development is an appeal to the recurrent popularity of primitivism among white Americans. Throughout American history there have been periods when European-Americans, in criticism of their own ways, have upheld the advantages of Native American ways. These criticisms are commonly expressed through popular literature about Indians written by sympathetic whites. These are often whites who somehow consider themselves Indians—they have Indian mentors or they have been initiated into Indian tribes. They might be called White Indians in that they have European ancestry, yet they seem to have gained identity with Native Americans on whose behalf they often speak. In recent decades the literature of White Indians is very popular and contains extensive references to "our Mother Earth." The impact such non-Indian writers have on Indian spirituality and even on tribal traditions must be considerable.[14] At base these writings are more criticisms of isolated tendencies of European-American lifeways than they are balanced and informed presentations of Native American cultures and their religions.[15]

Aware of certain advantages a primitivist mode may hold for Native Americans, individuals like Thomas Banyacya have exploited it. They direct themselves to the primitivist sensitivities of those who historically have oppressed Native Americans. These individuals thereby gain support while directly voicing their criticisms of, and their superiority to, the old adversary.[16]

A third line of development can be described. In the examination of the various tribal and historical examples, there was to be found no documentation of Mother Earth as a distinct divinity in any Native American tribal culture. Yet, two instances have been documented in which there is a transition in tribal cultures that suggests the incorporation and development of Mother Earth. One of these is found in the writings of Charles Eastman. Eastman identified Mother Earth, along with Father Sun, as a creator figure in Sioux cosmogony. The other example is the story of Okanagon creation recorded at a time almost coincident with Eastman's writing of Mother Earth. While this story had obvious and extensive Christian influence, and while it probably incorporated the Mother Earth elements from widely held non-native expectations, it nonetheless is a story that speaks to specifically tribal needs and is in immediate and direct continuity with a specific tribal story tradition. Thus while the Okanagon story addresses a situation of crisis and challenge widely felt among tribal peoples, it is a tribal, rather than a pan-Indian, response to the situation. It is a development of Okanagon religious tradition.

With these examples appearing early in this century, and with the wide acceptance of Mother Earth during the last twenty years as an important facet of the development of an Indian identity, the development of Mother Earth features might be expected to have occurred widely in recent years among tribal traditions. There is general evidence of this, but scant documentation.

From my personal contact with Navajo traditions I know of two indications of such development. There is a Navajo sandpainting of the Shootingway ceremonial complex that depicts earth and sky as personified beings. Gladys Reichard tended to identify earth with other Navajo female figures, including Changing Woman, and an aspect of the Navajo principle *sq'ah naagháii bik'eh hózhǫ́ǫ́* (Long Life and Happiness).[17] I believe that at the present time many Navajo people would identify the figures in this earth-sky sandpainting by the English terms "Father Sky" and "Mother Earth." Navajos have told me an interpretation of the significance of the design features of the Navajo wedding basket that includes reference to Father Sky and Mother Earth.

I believe that presently among tribal practices throughout North America, Mother Earth—and also Great Spirit, Creator, Father Sky, and Father Sun—is commonly addressed or named in prayers, especially in traditions where English is the language now used. Still, I am unaware of any extensive story or ritual development of Mother Earth in any tribal tradition in North America.

These three lines of the development of Mother Earth among Native Americans are often inseparable and intertwined. Together they describe the making of Mother Earth among and by "the Indians." These lines of development are based upon documentation showing that Mother Earth is a major goddess of the Indians. But all of these lines show that Mother Earth has come to be a major goddess to the Indians within this century and that her development has been necessarily dependent not only upon the crises caused by Americans of European ancestry but also upon European-American interpretations and expectations of Indians and their religions. Despite this influence the emergence of Mother Earth is testimony to the vitality and flexibility of Native American religious traditions, particularly in the construction of an Indian tradition out of a huge variety of tribal traditions and, in turn, in the reflection of aspects of this common tradition in the respective tribal traditions. Mother Earth has been instrumental in this creative process.

▲ 8 ▲

Mother Earth
The Mother of Us All

No matter how carefully and positively I have tried to consider Mother Earth in North America, to tell her American story, I believe that there will remain among some readers a strong reluctance to accept what may appear to be a certain discrediting of Mother Earth among the Indians and an attribution of a kind of creative role to scholars and other Indian observers. If taken only this way, what I have said will surely not be popular to many readers. Some will want to cite certain tribal examples of an earth-connected goddess known to them that I have not mentioned. Some will want to say that obviously one so sacred to the Indians will not be documentable in the ethnographic literature and other writings of "white men." Others will want to appeal to mother goddesses in the religions of Western antiquity or in cultures in other parts of the world. The emotion bound up with Mother Earth is deep. She is seen as unquestionably primordial, as fundamentally archetypal.

I do not disagree that there are many important goddess figures throughout the tribal cultures of North America and throughout human history. I do not disagree with the structural evaluations of the primacy of a goddess identified with the earth, as mother to the earth, or as mother to all of the fruits of the earth enjoyed by humankind. What I am arguing on the one hand is that it is unproductive to collapse the many goddesses and other figures of feminine identity into a single goddess and that, at least for native North America, it would seem to be historically and ethnographically in error to do so. On the other hand, I am arguing that though the structure of Mother Earth may be primordial and archetypal, historically this structure was not formally identified nor did it take on importance until recently, that is, within the last hundred years. However, when it did take on this importance, it soon became widespread and important for Europeans, for Americans of European ancestry, and finally for Native Americans, and pretty much in that order historically.

For those who remain dissatisfied that the several cultures I have examined are adequate to make my case, who know of a Mother Earth–like goddess in some Native American culture that I have not considered and feel that this example would negate my argument, let me try one last time for clarification. While it is far from universal in North America, I believe that there is evidence of a relatively widespread practice among Native Americans to see and to relate to the world in personal, and often kinship, terms. Beyond Native Americans there is a marked human tendency to relate to the world in this way. The natural and physical world may be divided and identified in complex categorizations that include, among many other attributes, those of sex and kinship. Thus, for example, the Zuni may address the earth, clay, cotton, eagle, and so on in personal terms that have sexual and kinship elements. At times these personal terms may be included as references in prayer. Still, wanting evidence of the development of these personal categories in oral tradition, in ritual personification, or in other ways of indicating them as spiritual or theological entities, and with evidence such as Eastman's statement that these prayer references are the extension of poetic metaphor, there is no reason to conclude that they are spiritual or theological to any degree more than all other aspects of reality so designated. There is no evidence, from this form of designation, of an animistic form of belief.

Furthermore, suppose for the moment that one may find one or more Native American cultures where a figure exists precisely as scholars have described Mother Earth. Or even more dramatically let us suppose that such a figure exists among most or all Native American peoples as a secret belief yet undocumented and unknown by non-native peoples. Given the diversity of Native American cultures, I find either of these propositions to be highly unlikely. But for the sake of a clarifying discussion, I am quite willing to suppose that such a figure may exist. From the perspective of the study of Mother Earth, in these supposed circumstances the existence of the figure could only be structurally or historically hypothesized (for little if any documentable evidence exists) or her existence in scores of cultures would have to be based on the evidence of a very few examples (scarcely adequate by any academic standards). What is most important is the need to comprehend the fact that a century of scholarship has made such claims, based on a small set of examples, inadequate to support such a hypothesis. At the very best, as I see it, every one of these alternatives produces an undocumented hypothetic construct, a construct generated by and necessary to certain theories of religion and culture. But, as I have shown, Mother Earth has never been considered either as hypothetical or as a construct.

Let me pursue this point by means of a historical comparison. As shown, it was common for European and American conceptions of America, as land and as idea, to take a female form. From early identifications as an Indian queen and Indian princess, this personified conception of America metamorphosed by the early nineteenth century into a form more like that of a Greek goddess; later it shifted to Brother Jonathan and finally to Uncle Sam and Lady Liberty. These figures have been commonly and widely recognized in Europe and America, and they are connected to one another historically. It is not farfetched to think that one could find any of these figures named or mentioned in prayers uttered by Americans. While some would want to see religious dimensions to these figures, I think that no one who knows even the most simple and obvious facts about American religious history would argue that these conceptions of America attest to belief in a goddess known widely in European-American mythology, and that since the goddess is identified with America as a land that she is therefore a representative of the old goddess of ancient hunters, and that since she is all of these, that the religion of Americans of European ancestry includes a central belief in Mother Earth. Upon this reasoning one might easily see Brother Jonathan and Uncle Sam as major divinities who supplant Mother Earth or are perhaps her later male forms. With but a little imagination one could develop a most interesting history of American theology upon these figures.

The sort of leap that would make a principal divinity of Mother Earth or Uncle Sam to all American people, a leap over American Christianity and Judaism, a leap over Afro-American and Native American religious traditions, is even less of a leap than the one that scholars have taken to declare Mother Earth as a major goddess of Native Americans.

Simple reflection upon the richness, distinctiveness, and complexity of figures such as Sedna and Selu (Eskimo), White Buffalo

Calf Woman (Sioux), Changing Woman (Navajo and Apache), the
many corn women, Spider Woman (various tribes), Thought Woman (Acoma and Laguna), the Woman-who-fell-from-the-sky (Iroquoian), Atakvish (Luiseño), among hundreds more, demonstrates
the distinctiveness of traditions native to North America. I believe
that there is no more basis for assuming a commonality among
Native American religious beliefs from tribe to tribe, from region to
region, where as many as seven distinct language stocks exist, than
can be assumed between Protestant and Catholic Christians in
America; or between Christians, Jews, and Moslems in the Middle
East; or between any of the Western religious traditions and any of
the Eastern religious traditions. Language differences are commonly
held to be key to cultural and historical differences. I have been told
that the degree of relatedness between Navajo and Hopi languages,
the languages of peoples living for at least half a millennium geographically contiguous, is no greater than that between English and
Chinese.

My argument here is extraordinarily simple. In attempts to comprehend and understand Native American tribal traditions, if any
weight is placed upon the descriptions of particular cultures and
their religious traditions and practices, Mother Earth, as most have
described her, will not be found, yet a rich variety of female figures
whose stories and characters are often complex and sophisticated will
be found. Some of these figures may be associated with fertility and
growth, but many of them with evil and death; some of them are
treated with reverence and respect, but many of them are not; some
of them are associated with the earth or with the earth's life and
productivity, but many of them are not. Some of these figures can
be interrelated structurally, historically, or theologically, but it is our
own views that will create these interrelations.

If, on the other hand, there is an interest in finding Mother Earth
in North America, most of these many Native American female figures will be seen as manifestations of her, though but a very few
common examples illustrate the distinctive character that has been
assigned to her.

But all of this is the critical or negative side of the consideration of
Mother Earth in North America. And above all I have wanted to
place this negative side in the most productive and positive light,
though I have seen no way to gain new insights without first making
clearer the historical background. Without this perspective new
questions do not arise, there is no motivation to construct new hy-

potheses; without it one cannot see that there are stories that have yet to be told. Since I believe so firmly in the creative power of telling stories, and since stories are almost always stimulating, I have sought to tell the story of Mother Earth in North America, but it is a story composed of other stories, stories that must be told from the perspectives of the Americans, the scholars, and the Indians.

First, I believe that Mother Earth is a central figure in that long saga in which Americans of European ancestry have attempted to define and to create themselves as Americans. They have needed to do so over against Europeans and European landscapes that most had left and they also needed to do so over against the native peoples who had occupied for so much longer the lands called America. There is a line of development leading to Mother Earth that began as early as 1575. There is much revealed in this history of American imagery. America, the nation, the land, depicted as a dark-skinned woman, as an Indian, as a mother, is rich and complex. The imagery embraces the expression of the potentiality, the fruition, the bounty, the productivity of the landscape and the people. It alludes to the mystery and enticing character of America. The imagery expresses the civilizing, building, transforming aspects of Americans. Yet it also permits expression of the male, conquering, destructive, defiling aspects of the American character.

For me, a peculiar aspect of this study has been the second story, the story of the scholars. This story, of all of them, has often irritated me (and for the obvious reason that I am by profession a part of this story as this book is a part of it). Many have been the times that I have been unable to comprehend how so little hard evidence has satisfied scholars much my superior. While relatively unfounded constructions often occur in scholarship and are to some extent inevitable, I, for one, have not been able to accept, without fuller understanding, that this is simply part of the nature of scholarship. I value fiction as much as academic writing, and I believe that neither has a greater claim to the truth or responsibility for telling the truth. I nonetheless believe that academic writers are distinguished from writers of fiction by their agreement to ground their writings, their stories, in certain kinds of evidence and to proceed toward their conclusions in terms of the conventions of academe. When I found this evidence wanting, and the conventions skewed, the distinction between academic writing and fiction was greatly blurred, and I believe that in some respects this has raised the questions most problematic for me.

One way that I have wanted to think about the scholarly story of Mother Earth is in the discussion of a term so common to many of the scholars I have considered. This is the term "myth." In recent years I have found the term "myth" to be sufficiently confused in its usage, not only in a technical sense among scholars, but also in its contrast with common public usage, to make it a term worth avoiding. Still, there is an element of myth, one that correlates with the scholarly discussion of the term, in what I have learned about Mother Earth and the scholarly acceptance of the figure Mother Earth.

It is common to hear "myth" referred to, in a relatively non-technical way, as "a true story," though the term is defined in many other ways. I think that to focus the definition of myth on "truth" is important, but I prefer to think of myth as the story on which truth is based. This is a logical definition of myth, positing that in questions of truth there must logically be some base on which truth-judgments are made. If one could isolate that base, it would necessarily not be subject to the question of truth, for if it were, there would logically have to be some other base on which the judgment could be made. If this base for truth is called "myth," it would then not be correct to say that myth is a true story, but rather that myth is the story on which truth is based. This makes sense to me in a number of other respects as well. First, it helps us to be free of the tangle of myth with history, for we can see that the common setting proclaimed in myths by such a phrase as "in the beginning," is not a historical statement at all. It is not even intended to establish a temporal setting. It is rather a declaration of a logical sort. It declares that this is the first story upon which all other stories are based or from which they derive. It tells of that upon which all else is measured. This is why myth is usually a narrative of creation.

In terms of the story of the scholars and their studies of Mother Earth, the judgments they have made and the truths they have claimed make sense when placed within the parameters of a myth which they themselves have largely constructed. For the scholars, Mother Earth is not a hypothesis, she is a figure whose existence, whose structure, whose character is the basis on which many of the disparate and complexly diffuse cultures from throughout human history and geography cohere meaningfully. She is of their myth, she is primordial, and is therefore not subject to questions of truth. Thus the questions I have raised and considered herein are not just unacceptable, they are practically unthinkable. They are heretical.

We may see that while the scholars have themselves played a very creative role in the making of Mother Earth, she has in turn served metaphorically as mother to them, for their observations and conclusions (their stories) are based upon her existence.

The view of scholars as mythmakers is a very attractive one. But for me it has raised many questions that I cannot easily resolve. I do not think that I would like to take on the responsibility for such mythmaking, particularly in light of the story of Mother Earth in North America and the impact of mythmaking on it; nor do I think that I like the conclusion that seems necessary, which is that in receiving academic training (a phrase I have never liked), one is essentially receiving the myths to be perpetuated.

At the very least, I think that for me personally this study has led to much skepticism about what might be termed "top-down" scholarship, at least when it is directed toward particular cultures and particular people. And, though I realize that my view may be peculiar, I find it hard to think of religion and culture in ways that are not rather firmly grounded in the particular. This does not mean that I would prefer an exclusively "bottom-up" style of scholarship. I doubt that purely "bottom-up" scholarship is even possible. Surely in the most healthy circumstances, constructed "top-down" categories must be engaged constantly in a process that challenges them and thereby enriches them with the experience of "bottom-up" data. In this approach the scholars must accept the role of being responsible human beings performing this process motivated by a need to understand something. They must also see this need as most likely peculiar and skewed by a variety of personal, cultural, and historical factors that somehow intersect in the seeker of knowledge.

Finally, in the third story, Mother Earth is also mother to the Indians. This study has shown that she has become so only recently and then not without influence from Americans, with their thirst for land and their need to define themselves in terms of likeness and contrast with those they imagined to be "the Indians." These historical factors neither dilute nor denigrate Mother Earth or the Indians who believe in her. In times of enormous crisis, the very identity of the Indians has in some ways depended upon her, as much so as their existence once depended upon the physical land with which she is identified. In thinking of the Indian story of Mother Earth, I have had almost constantly on my mind a statement made known to me by N. Scott Momaday, a statement he attributes to Isak Dinesen. It is this: "All sorrows can be borne if you put them into a story or tell a story about them." While Mother Earth has not become a very prominent subject of Native American story traditions, she has become a central figure of *the* Native American story. Native Americans have embraced her as mother, and she has returned their embrace by giving them identity, purpose, responsibility, and even a sense of superiority over very powerful adversaries.

These various tales have now all come together. The story of Mother Earth as told herein is an American story. It is a story in which for Americans, whatever their heritage, Mother Earth is the mother of us all.

Notes

Chapter One

1. James Mooney, "The Ghost Dance Religion and the Sioux Outbreak of 1890," *Fourteenth Annual Report of the Bureau of Ethnology, 1892–1893* (Washington, D.C.: Government Printing Office, 1896), p. 716.

2. Thomas W. Pew, Jr., "Summit Powwow at Canyon de Chelly," *American West* (November/December 1984), p. 42.

3. Russell Means, "Fighting Words on the Future of the Earth," *Mother Jones,* December 1980, p. 31.

4. Edward B. Tylor, *Primitive Culture: Researches into The Development of Mythology, Philosophy, Religion, Language, Art and Custom* (London: John Murray, 1873), 1:326.

5. Åke Hultkrantz, "The Religion of the Goddess in North America," in Carl Olson, ed., *The Book of the Goddess Past and Present: An Introduction to Her Religion* (New York: Crossroads, 1983), p. 202.

6. "A Scholar's Sacred Quest," *Newsweek,* July 15, 1985, p. 63.

7. Albrecht Dieterich, *Mutter Erde: Ein Versuch über Volksreligion* (Berlin-Leipzig, 1905).

8. See my books, *Native American Religions: An Introduction* (Belmont, Calif.: Wadsworth, 1982), *Native American Traditions: Sources and Interpretations* (Belmont, Calif.: Wadsworth, 1983), and *Native American Religious Action: A Performance Approach to Religion* (Columbia: University of South Carolina Press, 1987).

Chapter Two

1. There are many sources for the general historical background to this meeting. Among those that were consulted are: Moses Dawson, *Historical Narrative of the Civil and Military Services of Major General William H. Harrison...* (Cincinnati: The Cincinnati Advertiser, 1824); Benjamin Drake, *Life of Tecumseh, and of His Brother The Prophet; with a Historical Sketch of the Shawanoe Indians* (Cincinnati: E. Morgan & Co., 1841); Samuel G. Drake, *The Book of the Indians; or Biography and History of the Indians of North America, From Its First Discovery to the Year 1841* (Boston: Benjamin B. Mussey, 9th ed., 1845); James Hall, *A Memoir of the Public Services of William Henry Harrison, of Ohio* (Philadelphia: Key & Biddle, 1836); Logan Esarey, ed., *Governors Messages and Letters: Messages and Letters of William Henry Harrison*, Vol. 1, *1800–1811* (Indianapolis: Indiana Historical Commission, 1922); Logan Esarey, *A History of Indiana from Its Exploration to 1850* (Indianapolis: W. K. Stewart Co., 1915); *William Henry Harrison: A Political Biography*, Indiana Historical Collections, vol. 14, (Indianapolis: W. K. Stewart Co., 1926); Benson J. Lossing, *The Pictorial Field Book of the War of 1812* (New York: Harper & Brothers, 1869); H. Montgomery, *The Life of Major-General William H. Harrison, Ninth President of the United States* (New York: C. M. Saxton, Barker & Co., 1860); John M. Oskinson, *Tecumseh and His Times: The Story of a Great Indian* (New York: G. P. Putnam's Sons, 1938); and Glenn Tucker, *Tecumseh: Vision of Glory* (Indianapolis: Bobbs-Merrill, 1956).

2. John Dillon, *A History of Indiana* (Indianapolis: Bingham & Doughty, 1859), pp. 441f.

3. Esarey, *Messages and Letters*, 1:460; Tecumseh's speech referred to in the letter is on pp. 463–69.

4. For accounts of Tecumseh's involvement in the War of 1812, see R. David Edmunds, *Tecumseh and the Quest for Indian Leadership* (Boston: Little, Brown, 1984), and other biographies of Tecumseh.

5. *Indiana Centinel*, December 2, 1820. Newspaper of Vincennes, Indiana.

6. Glenn Tucker, *Tecumseh* p. 325.

7. The recent biography by Edmunds, *Tecumseh*, deals clearly with the events of Tecumseh's life and the transformations following it. See also the studies by Herbert Goltz, "Tecumseh: The Man and the Myth" (M.A. thesis, University of Wisconsin, Milwaukee, 1966) and "Tecumseh, the Prophet and the Rise of the Northwest Indian Confederation" (Ph.D. diss., University of Western Ontario, 1973).

8. The *National Recorder* was published in Philadelphia from July 1819 to June 1821 and was succeeded by the *Saturday Magazine*, which was published until June 1822.

9. Henry Rowe Schoolcraft, *Travels in the Central Portions of the Mississippi Valley: Comprising Observations on its Mineral Geography, Internal Re-*

sources, *Aboriginal Population* (New York: Collins & Hanney, 1825), pp. 144–45.

10. Dawson, *Historical Narrative* p. 156.

11. Ibid., p. 157.

12. Ibid., p. 159.

13. See Constance Rourke, "The Indian Background of American Theatricals," in Abraham Chapman, eds., *Literature of the American Indians: Views and Interpretations* (New York: New American Library, 1975), pp. 256–65, and Roy Harvey Pearce, *Savagism and Civilization: A Study of the Indian and the American Mind* (Baltimore: The Johns Hopkins Press, 1953, 1965).

14. Alexander Malcomb, "Pontiac; or the Siege of Detroit" (Boston: Samuel Colman, 1835).

15. See Albert Keiser, *The Indian in American Literature* (New York: Oxford University Press, 1933), pp. 64–70.

16. James S. French, *Elkswatawa or, The Prophet of the West. A Tale of the Frontier* (New York: Harper & Brothers, 1836), p. vii.

17. William Emmons, *Tecumseh: or, The Battle of the Thames, a National Drama in Five Acts* (New York: Elton & Harrison, 1836), p. 9.

18. Hall, *A Memoir,* pp. 10–11.

19. Drake, *Life of Tecumseh,* pp. 125–26.

20. See, for example, Henry Harvey, *History of the Shawnee Indians, From the Year 1681 to 1854, Inclusive* (Cincinnati: Ephraim Morgan & Sons, 1855), p. 155; O. H. Smith, *Early Indiana Trials and Sketches* (Cincinnati: Moore, Wilstach, Keys & Co., 1858), p. 228; Lossing, *The Pictorial Field-Book,* p. 192; and Elizabeth Eggleston Seelye, *Tecumseh and the Shawnee Prophet* (New York: Dodd, Mead, 1878), p. 182.

21. *Southern Literary Messenger,* May 1840, p. 335.

22. Drake, *The Book of the Indians,* pp. 123–24.

23. *Ladies Wreath,* May 1850.

24. G. Walter Barr, "Grouseland," *Chicago Tribune,* March 6, 1886.

25. Ethel T. Raymond, *Tecumseh: The Last Great Leader of His People* (Toronto: Glasgow, Brook, 1915), pp. 71–72.

26. William E. Wilson, *The Wabash* (New York: Farrar and Rinehart, 1940), p. 85.

27. Edward B. Tylor, *Primitive Culture,* 1:326.

28. Josiah Gregg, *Commerce of the Prairies* (1844) in 2 vols. (reprint ed., New York: J. B. Lippincott, 1962 ed.), 2:305.

29. The Draper Manuscripts are microfilmed and a guide to their use is available, *Guide to the Draper Manuscripts* (Madison: State Historical Society of Wisconsin, 1983). The Tecumseh papers are a series within the Draper manuscripts.

30. Draper Manuscripts, 3yy, 106–7. Draper appears to have written back to Jones. He formulated a series of questions in the margins of Jones's letter, but there is no record of this letter or a reply.

31. Ibid., 3yy, 109.

32. Ibid., 3yy, 103.

33. "Harrison's letter to Secretary of War, August 22, 1810," in Esarey, *Messages and Letters,* 1:460.

34. Homer J. Webster, *William Henry Harrison's Administration of Indiana Territory.* (Indianapolis: Sentinel Printing Company, 1907), p. 268.

35. C. C. Trowbridge, *Shawnese Traditions,* ed. Vernon Kinietz and Erminie W. Voegelin, Occasional Contributions from the Museum of Anthropology of the University of Michigan, no. 9 (Ann Arbor: University of Michigan Press, 1939), p. 40.

36. Lewis Henry Morgan, *The Indian Journals, 1859–62* (Ann Arbor: University of Michigan Press, 1959), p. 77.

37. See C. F. and E. W. Voegelin, "The Shawnee Female Deity in Historical Perspective," *American Anthropologist* n.s. 46 (1944): 370–75.

38. Trowbridge, *Shawnese Traditions,* p. 37.

39. C. F. and E. W. Voegelin, "The Shawnee Female Deity," *Yale University Publications in Anthropology,* no. 10 (1936): 6–7.

40. Ibid., pp. 13–14.

41. W. A. Galloway, "A Sacred Slab of the Shawnee Prophet," *Cranbrook Institute of Science News Letter* (1943): 6–7.

42. See Pearce, *Savagism and Civilization.*

43. Pearce, *Savagism and Civilization,* pp. 215–16.

44. Esarey, *Messages and Letters,* pp. 460, 471.

45. See Edward D. Seeber, "Critical Views on Logan's Speech," *Journal of American Folk-lore* 60 (1947): 130–46.

46. See Cooper Union Museum for the Arts of Decoration, *The Four Continents from the Collection of James Hazen Hyde* (New York: Cooper Union Museum, 1961), Clare Le Corbeiller, "Miss America and Her Sisters: Personifications of the Four Parts of the World," *Bulletin of the Metropolitan Museum of Art,* n.s., 19 (1961): 209–23, and Bernadette Bucher, *Icon and Conquest: A Structural Analysis of the Illustrations of de Bry's "Great Voyages,"* trans. Basia Gulati (Chicago: The University of Chicago Press, 1981).

47. E. McClung Fleming, "The American Image as Indian Princess," *Winterthur Portfolio* 2 (1968):74. See also Fleming, "Symbols of the United States; From Indian Queen to Uncle Sam," in Ray Browne et al., eds., *The Frontier in American Culture* (Lafayette, Ind.: Purdue University Press, 1967), pp. 1–24.

48. Fleming, "The American Image," p. 81.

49. Philip Young, "The Mother of Us All: Pocahontas Reconsidered," *Kenyon Review* 24 (Summer 1962): 391–441. See also Wynette L. Hamilton, "The Correlation between Societal Attitudes and Those of American Authors in the Depiction of American Indians, 1607–1860," *American Indian Quarterly,* 1, no. 1 (1974): 1–26.

50. In Young, "The Mother of Us All," p. 395.

51. In ibid., p. 401.

52. Ibid., p. 401.

53. Ibid., p. 409.

54. Ibid., p. 413.

55. In ibid., p. 407.

56. In ibid., p. 408.

57. Ibid., p. 415. For the impact of this imagery on Native American women, see Rayna Green, "The Pocahontas Perplex: The Image of Indian Women in American Culture," *The Massachusetts Review* 16, no. 4 (1976): 698–714.

58. There is a delightful example of this Pocahontas-in-reverse story in John Barth's *The Sot-Weed Factor*. An Indian prince, Cohunkowprets, leaves his barbaric ways to take up life as a gentleman farmer in Maryland. He is remarkably and instantly successful. But when he takes a wife, a prim, civilized British lady, she as quickly becomes a savage squaw, the lowliest primitive. The inversion is righted however by appealing to the Indian, whose English name is Billy Rumbly, "the case of humankind, of Civilization *versus* the Abyss of savagery." And, of course, Billy Rumbly becomes once again Cohunkowprets and returns to his people, and the English lady is retransformed.

59. William Albert Galloway, *Old Chillicothe: Shawnee and Pioneer History* (Xenia, Ohio: The Buckeye Press, 1934). There is no reason to believe that any aspect of the story is historically based (see Edmunds, *Tecumseh*, pp. 217–18). For a recent version of the story, see Allan W. Eckert, *The Frontiersmen: A Narrative* (Boston: Little, Brown, 1967), pp. 485–93.

60. Annette Kolodny has traced the American need to experience the land as feminine, documented through expressions she sees as a uniquely American pastoral impulse, in her book *The Lay of the Land: Metaphor as Experience and History in American Life and Letters* (Chapel Hill: University of North Carolina Press, 1975). Canadian literature pertaining to themes we have considered has been surveyed and interpreted by Margaret Atwood in *Survival: A Thematic Guide to Canadian Literature* (Toronto: Anansi, 1972); see especially chap. 4.

Chapter Three

1. James Mooney, "The Ghost Dance Religion and the Sioux Outbreak of 1890," *Fourteenth Annual Report of the Bureau of Ethnology, 1892–1893*, (Washington, D.C., 1896), p. 716.

2. See David F. Aberle, "The Prophet Dance and Reaction to White Contact," *Southwestern Journal of Anthropology* 15, no. 1 (1959): 74–83, and Deward E. Walker, Jr., "New Light on the Prophet Dance Controversy," *Ethnohistory* 16, no. 3 (1969): 245–55.

3. See Leslie Spier, *The Prophet Dance of the Northwest and Its Deriva-*

tives: The Source of the Ghost Dance, General Series in Anthropology, no. 1 (Menasha, Wisc.: George Banta, 1935), p. 30.

4. See Clifford M. Drury, *Henry Harmon Spaulding* (Caldwell, Idaho: Caxton Printers, 1936).

5. See Clifford M. Drury, *Marcus Whitman, M.D., Pioneer and Martyr* (Caldwell, Idaho: Caxton Printers, 1937), and Clifford M. Drury, *Marcus and Narcissa Whitman, and the Opening of Old Oregon* (Glendale, Calif.: A. H. Clark, 1973).

6. The official record of the 1855 treaty negotiations is published in Allen P. Slickpoo, Sr., and Deward E. Walker, Jr., *Noon Nee-me-poo (We, The Nez Perces)* (Lapwai, Idaho: Nez Perce Tribe, 1973), pp. 83–144.

7. Lawrence Kip, *The Indian Council at Walla Walla* (San Francisco, 1855).

8. Ibid., p. 15.

9. Ibid., p. 24.

10. Slickpoo and Walker, *Noon Nee-me-poo,* pp. 118–19.

11. Ibid., p. 116.

12. Ibid., p. 119.

13. Kip, *The Indian Council,* p. 19.

14. Slickpoo and Walker, *Noon Nee-me-poo,* pp. 120–21.

15. Ibid., p. 78.

16. Mooney, "The Ghost Dance," p. 710.

17. U.S. Department of Interior, "Report of Civil and Military Commission to Nez Perce Indians, Washington Territory and the Northwest," *Annual Report 1877, Indian Affairs* (Washington, D.C., 1877), pp. 608–9.

18. Oliver O. Howard, *Nez Perce Joseph* (Boston: 1881; reprint ed., New York: Da Capo Press, 1972), p. 64.

19. Ibid., p. 66.

20. Chief Joseph, "An Indian's View of Indian Affairs," *North American Review,* 182 (April 1879): 421, 432.

21. The only extended study of "the Dreamers" is Click Relander, *Drummers and Dreamers* (Caldwell, Idaho: Caxton Printers, 1956).

22. E. L. Huggins, "Smohalla, The Prophet of Priest Rapids," *Overland Monthly,* 2nd ser., 17 (1891), p. 212.

23. Ibid., p. 213.

24. J. W. MacMurray, "The 'Dreamers' of the Columbia River Valley, in Washington Territory," *Transactions of the Albany Institute* (Albany, 1887), pp. 247–48.

25. See Deward E. Walker, Jr., *Conflict and Schism in Nez Perce Acculturation: A Study of Religion and Politics* (Pullman: Washington State University Press, 1968).

26. Spier, *The Prophet Dance.*

27. Aberle, "The Prophet Dance."

28. Deward E. Walker, Jr., "Prophet Dance Controversy."

29. Ibid., p. 252.

30. Spier, *The Prophet Dance,* p. 11.

31. As quoted in Spier, *The Prophet Dance,* p. 11.

32. Franz Boas, ed., *Folk-Tales of Salishan and Sahaptin Tribes,* Memoirs of the American Folk-Lore Society, vol. 11 (1917):80–83.

33. Albert S. Gatschet, "The Klamath Indians of Southwest Oregon," *Contributions to North American Ethnology,* vol. 2, pts. 1 and 2 (Washington, D.C., 1890), p. xcii.

34. Ibid., p. xcii.

35. Ibid., p. xci.

36. Mooney, "The Ghost Dance," p. 721.

37. Gatschet's statement is actually preceded by one in Hubert H. Bancroft, *Native Races,* vol. 3, *Myths and Languages* (1874–75), p. 121, and Edward B. Tylor, *Primitive Culture* (London: John Murray, 1873), 1:326–27. These will be discussed more fully in a later chapter.

Chapter Four

1. H. K. Haeberlin, "The Idea of Fertilization in the Culture of the Pueblo Indians," *Memoirs of the American Anthropological Association,* vol. 3, no. 1 (1916): 1–55.

2. Ibid., p. 12.

3. Ibid., p. 14.

4. Ibid., p. 15.

5. Ibid., p. 16.

6. Ibid., p. 23.

7. Ibid., pp. 50–51.

8. See Jesse Green, *Zuñi: Selected Writings of Frank Hamilton Cushing* (Lincoln: University of Nebraska Press, 1979), especially the Foreword by Fred Eggan and the Introduction by Green.

9. Frank H. Cushing, "Zuñi Breadstuff," *Millstone* 9 (1884), nos. 1–12, and 10 nos. 1–4, 6–8, (1885). Portions also published in Green, *Zuñi,* pp. 246–331 (for this passage, see pp. 246–47).

10. Frank H. Cushing, "Outlines of Zuñi Creation Myths," *Thirteenth Annual Report of the Bureau of American Ethnology, 1891–1892* (Washington, D.C., 1896), p. 379.

11. Matilda Cox Stevenson, "The Zuñi Indians," *Twenty-third Annual Report of the Bureau of American Ethnology, 1901–1902* (Washington, D.C., 1902), pp. 23–24.

12. Ruth L. Bunzel, "Introduction to Zuñi Ceremonialism," *Forty-seventh Annual Report of the Bureau of American Ethnology, 1929–1930* (Washington, D.C., 1932), p. 488.

13. Ibid., p. 486, n. 12.

14. This is of course the etic-emic controversy on which much has been written by anthropologists. See also the discussion in Green, *Zuñi,* pp. 16–20.

15. Cushing, "Outlines," p. 375.

16. Green, *Zuñi*, p. 19.

17. Anthropologists such as Laura Bohannan and Hortense Powder-maker have written anthropological novels and short stories.

18. Bunzel, "Zuñi Ceremonialism," p. 483.,

19. See Dennis Tedlock, "Zuni Religion and World View," in *South-west: Handbook of North American Indians*, vol. 9, William C. Sturtevant, gen. ed. (Washington, D.C.: Smithsonian Institution, 1979), pp. 499–508, and Dillard Walker, "Zuni Semantic Categories" in the same volume, pp. 509–13.

20. Stevenson, "Zuñi Indians," p. 20.

21. See Tedlock, "Zuni Religion and World View," p. 499.

22. Bunzel, "Zuñi Ceremonialism," p. 484.

23. For a description of the Zuni cosmology, see Tedlock. "Zuni Religion and World View," pp. 499–501.

24. Bunzel, "Zuñi Ceremonialism," pp. 483–84.

25. Ibid., p. 484.

26. Ibid.

27. Ibid. Evidence of a similar prayer is found in Matilda Cox Stevenson, "Ethnobotany of the Zuñi Indians," *Thirtieth Annual Report of the Bureau of American Ethnology* (Washington, D.C., 1915), p. 37.

28. Bunzel, "Žuñi Ceremonialism," p. 485.

Chapter Five

1. Alfred L. Kroeber, *Handbook of Indians of California* Bureau of American Ethnology Bulletin 78 (Washington, D.C., 1925), p. 677.

2. Basic sources for Luiseño culture follow: Lowell J. Bean and Florence C. Shipek, "Luiseño," in *California: Handbook of North American Indians*, vol. 8, ed. William C. Sturtevant (Washington, D.C.: Smithsonian Institution, 1978), pp. 550–63; Bernice E. Johnston, *California's Gabrieliño Indians* (Los Angeles: Southwest Museum, 1962); Florence C. Shipek, "History of Southern California Mission Indians," in *California: Handbook of North American Indians*, vol. 8, ed. William C. Sturtevant (Washington, D.C: Smithsonian Institution, 1978), pp. 610–18; and Raymond C. White, "Luiseño Social Organization," *University of California Publications in American Archaeology and Ethnology* 48: 2 (1963): 91–194.

3. R. C. White, "Luiseño Social Organization," p. 92.

4. See John P. Harrington, *A New Original Version of Boscana's Historical Account of the San Juan Capistrano Indians of Southern California*, Smithsonian Miscellaneous Collections 92, no. 4 (Washington, D.C.), pp. 1–62.

5. Harrington, *Boscana's Historical Account*, p. 5.

6. Ibid., p. 10.

7. Henry W. Henshaw, "The Luiseño Creation Myth," Robert F. Heizer, ed., *Masterkey* 46: 3 (1972): 93–100.

8. Constance G. DuBois, "Mythology of the Mission Indians," *Journal of American Folk-Lore* 19 (1906): 145. This essay does not contain any of DuBois's accounts of the creation story. These accounts may be found in the following articles by DuBois: "Mythology of the Mission Indians," *Journal of American Folk-Lore* 17 (1904): 185–88; "Religious Ceremonies and Myths of the Mission Indians," *American Anthropologist*, n.s. 7 (1905): 620–29; and "The Religion of the Luiseño and Diegueño Indians of Southern California," *University of California Publications in American Archaeology and Ethnology* 8 (1908): 69–186.

9. Alfred L. Kroeber, "Two Myths of the Mission Indians of California," *Journal of American Folk-Lore* 19 (1906): 309–321.

10. Harrington, *Boscana's Historical Account*, pp. 10–11.

11. Henshaw, "Luiseño Creation Myth," pp. 93–94.

12. DuBois, "Mythology of the Mission Indians" (1904), p. 185.

13. Ibid., (1906), p. 52.

14. DuBois, "Religion of the Luiseño," pp. 129–30.

15. Ibid., pp. 138–40.

16. Another figure in Luiseño oral traditions and ritual, similar in many ways to Wiyot, is Chungichnish. There is an extensive cycle of stories centered on this figure. Many scholars believe that the origins of this figure and the accompanying ritual practices are of relatively recent date. See R. C. White, "Luiseño Social Organization," p. 136.

17. DuBois, "Mythology of the Mission Indians" (1906), p. 55.

18. For the stories related to Wiyot, see Harrington, *Boscana's Historical Account*, pp. 12–15; DuBois, "Religion of the Luiseño," pp. 145–48; DuBois, "Mythology of the Mission Indians" (1906), pp. 55–60.

19. See DuBois, "Religion of the Luiseño," pp. 93–97, for a description of the girls' initiation rites.

20. See ibid., pp. 77–87, for a description of the Toloache and Milky Way rituals.

21. Kroeber, *Handbook of Indians of California*, p. 790.

22. DuBois, "Religion of the Luiseño," p. 147.

23. White, "Luiseño Social Organization," pp. 142, 143.

24. Alfred L. Kroeber and George W. Grace, "The Sparkman Grammar of Luiseño," *University of California Publications in Linguistics,* 16 (Berkeley and Los Angeles: University of California Press, 1960), p. 80.

25. Ibid., p. 122.

26. DuBois, "Religious Ceremonies," p. 629.

27. Stith Thompson, *Tales of the North American Indians* (Bloomington: University of Indiana Press, 1929), p. 280, n. 37.

28. Constance G. DuBois, "The Mythology of the Diegueños," *Journal of American Folk-Lore* 14 (1901): 181.

29. Thomas Waterman, "Analysis of the Mission Indian Creation Story," *American Anthropologist* n.s. 2 (1909): 46.

30. John G. Bourke, "Notes on the Cosmogony and Theogony of the Mojave Indians," *Journal of American Folk-Lore* 2 (1889): 178.

31. Edward S. Curtis, *The North American Indian* Frederick W. Hodge, ed. 20 vols. Norwood, Mass.: Plimpton Press, 1907–30. (Reprinted: Johnson Reprint, New York, 1970), vol. 2, pp. 56–57, and p. 86, attributes creation to the earth and sky, as mother and father, for the Mohave and the Maricopa tribes. Alfred L. Kroeber, "More Mohave Myths," *Anthropological Records*, 27 (1972): 5, notes the Mohave belief in the earth as woman and mother. The search of other records on these tribes has failed to produce any corroborative evidence and has suggested these ideas to be inconsistent with the arguing-brother creation theme which is well developed and dominant. Cyril Forde discusses mythic themes of the various southern California tribes, with some suggestions about their relatedness and history, in his "Ethnography of the Yuma Indians," *University of California Publications in American Archaeology and Ethnography* 28 (1931): 178. I do not find evidence to confirm the presence of the general theme of sky-earth cosmogony among the Luiseño and Mohave.

32. Frank Russell, "The Pima Indians," *Twenty-sixth Annual Report of the Bureau of American Ethnology, 1904–1905,* (Washington, D.C.: Government Printing Office, 1908), p. 206.

33. Ibid., pp. 208–9.

34. Kroeber, *Handbook of Indians of California,* p. 677.

35. Robert F. Heizer, "Mythology: Regional Patterns and History of Research," in *California: Handbook of North American Indians,* vol. 8, ed. William C. Sturtevant (Washington, D.C.: Smithsonian Institution, 1978), p. 656.

36. Åke Hultkrantz, *The Religions of the American Indians* (Berkeley: University of California Press, 1979), p. 31.

37. Kroeber, *Handbook of Indians of California,* p. 677.

38. Sir George Grey, *Polynesian Mythology and Ancient Traditional History* (Auckland: H. Brett, 1885), pp. 1–8.

39. The importance of the separation of the world parents as part of the cosmic creation process is discussed by Charles H. Long, *Alpha: The Myths of Creation* (New York: George Braziller, 1963), pp. 66–80.

40. See the Bibliographic Supplement.

Chapter Six

1. Edward B. Tylor, *Primitive Culture,* 1:326.

2. See Åke Hultkrantz, "Bachofen and the Mother Goddess: An Appraisal after One Hundred Years," *Ethnos* 1 and 2 (1961): 75–85.

3. Tylor, *Primitive Culture,* 2:270.

4. John Tanner, *A Narrative of the Captivity & Adventures of John Tanner During 30 Years' Residence Among the Indians of the Interior of North America,* ed. Edwin James (New York: G. & C. & H. Corvill, 1830), pp. 192–93.

5. Tylor, *Primitive Culture,* 1:326–27.

6. Hubert Howe Bancroft, *The Native Races [of the Pacific States]* (San Francisco: A. L. Bancroft, 1882), 3:121.

7. Andrew Lang, *Myth, Ritual and Religion* (London: Longmans, Green, 1887), p. 281.

8. Ibid., p. 295.

9. Olof Pettersson, *Mother Earth: An Analysis of the Mother Earth Concepts According to Albrecht Dieterich,* Scripta Minora, Regiae Societatis Humanorum Litterum Lundensis, 1965–1966, 3 (Lund, CWK Gleerup, 1967), pp. 7–15.

10. Ibid., pp. 88–89.

11. Ibid., p. 88.

12. George B. Grinnell, "Tenure of Land among the Indians," *American Anthropologist,* n.s., 9 (1907): 11.

13. Ibid., p. 3, n. 1.

14. Hartley B. Alexander, *Mythology of All Races,* vol. 10: *North American Mythology* (Boston: Marshall Jones, 1916).

15. Ibid., p. 91.

16. James G. Frazer, *The Worship of Nature* (New York: Macmillan 1926), p. 427.

17. For a critical evaluation of Frazer, see Jonathan Z. Smith, "The Glory, Jest and Riddle: James George Frazer and *"The Golden Bough"* (Ph.D. dissertation, Yale Divinity School, 1969) and "When the Bough Breaks," *History of Religions* 12 (1973): 342–71.

18. Frazer, *Worship of Nature,* pp. 427–440.

19. Apart from those references to Eliade's discussion of Mother Earth presented below, see his *The Sacred and the Profane* (New York: Harper and Row, 1957), pp. 17, 122, 141–45.

20. Mircea Eliade, *Patterns of Comparative Religion* (Cleveland and New York: World, 1958, 1963), pp. 245–246.

21. Mircea Eliade, *Myths, Dreams, and Mysteries* (New York: Harper & Row, 1957), p. 155.

22. Ibid., p. 156.

23. Ibid., p. 158.

24. Ibid., p. 163.

25. Ibid., pp. 163, 165.

26. Ibid., p. 178.

27. Ibid., p. 179.

28. Ibid., p. 185.

29. Åke Hultkrantz, *The Religions of the American Indians* (Berkeley: University of California Press, 1979; originally published as *De Amerikanska Indianernas Religioner,* 1967), p. 53.

30. Ibid., p. 54.

31. Ibid.

32. Ibid., p. 55.

33. Åke Hultkrantz, *Belief and Worship in Native North America* (Syracuse: Syracuse University Press, 1981), p. 128.

34. Åke Hultkrantz, "The Religion of the Goddess in North America," in Carl Olson, ed., *The Book of the Goddess Past and Present: An Introduction to Her Religion* (New York: Crossroads, 1983), pp. 202–16.

35. Ibid., p. 202.
36. Ibid., p. 203.
37. Ibid.
38. Ibid.
39. Ibid.
40. Ibid.
41. Ibid.
42. Ibid.
43. Ibid., p. 202.
44. Ibid. Hultkrantz discusses the Shoshoni and their sun dance in several articles in his *Belief and Worship in Native North America*; see particularly, "Configurations of Religions Belief among the Wind River Shoshoni" (pp. 28–47), "Tribal and Christian Elements in the Religious Syncretism among the Shoshoni Indians of Wyoming" (pp. 212–34), and "The Changing Meaning of the Ghost Dance as Evidenced by the Wind River Shoshoni" (pp. 264–81). The latter two essays make it clear that the Shoshoni have been very much in contact with and influenced by tribes in the interior plateau and Great Basin areas, areas where the millenarian movements developed most extensively and where tribes developed the earth-as-mother metaphor and later, by the early twentieth century, a Mother Earth concept in their literature. These articles also document the extensive Christian influence on the Shoshoni sun dance. Hultkrantz presents plenty of evidence in these essays to show that "Our Mother" is certainly not a major figure in Shoshoni religion, that her identity as Mother Earth is not clearly established, and that any presence of Mother Earth could very likely be due to major influences and transformations in this century stemming from the nineteenth-century contact experience in the greater region. Furthermore, in Fred W. Voget's extensive study *The Shoshoni-Crow Sun Dance* (Norman: University of Oklahoma Press, 1984), there is no mention of Mother Earth in the Crow sun dance, which was revitalized and redeveloped with major Shoshoni influence during the 1940s.
45. Hultkrantz, "The Religion of the Goddess," p. 215.
46. Ibid., p. 204.
47. Ibid.
48. Ibid., p. 206.
49. Ibid.
50. Ibid., p. 209.
51. Ibid., p. 210.
52. Ibid., p. 212.
53. Ibid., pp. 213–14.
54. Ibid., p. 214.

Chapter Seven

1. For a recent biography of Eastman, see Raymond Wilson, *Ohiyesa: Charles Eastman, Santee Sioux* (Urbana: University of Illinois Press, 1983).

2. Charles Alexander Eastman, *The Soul of the Indian: An Interpretation* (New York: Johnson Reprint Company, 1971; originally published in 1911), pp. 13–14.

3. Ibid., pp. 122–23.

4. Stan Steiner, *The Vanishing White Man* (New York: Harper & Row, 1976), pp. 129–30.

5. Brad Steiger, *Medicine Talk: A Guide to Walking in Balance and Surviving on the Earth Mother* (Garden City: Doubleday, 1975), p. 162.

6. Russell Means, "Fighting Words on the Future of the Earth," *Mother Jones,* December 1980, p. 31.

7. Ibid.

8. This and the following references are from "Hopi Messenger Speaks," *The Northern Light* 2, no. 2 (March 23, 1983). My thanks to Peter Nabokov for giving me this article.

9. This and the following references are from Asa Bazhonoodah, "They Are Taking the Holy Elements from Mother Earth," in Jay David, ed., *The American Indian: The First Victim* (New York: William Morrow, 1972), pp. 160–64.

10. In a suit filed by the Navajo Medicineman's Association (*Navajo Medicineman's Association v. Block*) to prevent expansion of a ski area in the San Francisco Peaks area near Flagstaff, Arizona, the testimony of ten Navajo medicine persons addressed the religious significance of this mountain. Morris Nez said that "the mountains are in the form of a man sitting there." Several medicine persons described the mountain as a house in which holy people dwell. Several described the role of the mountain in grand cosmological terms in which the mountain stands as a main support pillar for the house which is the whole world. Three medicine persons—Fred Stevens, Frank Blue Horse, and Tony Trujillo—testified in identical words: "The San Francisco Peak is a body just like a human body and the Snow Bowl Skiing facility is a cancer to the Peak and to my religion and culture." Only one person, Faye B. Tso, a female herbalist, described the mountain in terms similar to descriptions associated with Mother Earth:

> The San Francisco Peaks are also a sacred body. The various peaks form a head, two shoulders, and the knees of a body reclining and facing to the east. The trees and plants and rocks and earth form this body's skin. If it is cut or dug or cleared, the body can lose its power the same as a human. The Navajo people have a sacred duty to protect this sacred body.

While the body is not described sexually or named, this description is reminiscent of the Smohalla statements. In the presentation of facts for this suit, this language was emphasized.

In other court cases such as *Sequoyah v. TVA* in which the proposed use of land was opposed by Native Americans on religious grounds, in part, there was no identification of the land with a goddess of any kind or with any named Mother Earth. The Lakota and Cheyenne (*Fools Crow v. Gullet*) did identify Bear Butte in South Dakota as a bear.

11. Thomas W. Pew, Jr., "Summit Powwow at Canyon de Chelly," *American West* (November/December 1984), p. 42. My thanks to Chas Clifton for bringing this to my attention.

12. Ibid.

13. Quoted in Benjamin Drake, *Life of Tecumseh, and of His Brother the Prophet* (Cincinnati: E. Morgan & Co., 1841), pp. 107–9.

14. For a major recent example of this literature, see Peter Matthiessen, *Indian Country* (New York: Viking, 1984). See also Peter Nabokov's review of the book in *The New York Review of Books,* September 27, 1984, pp. 44–45.

15. A comparative valuative motivation is a distinctive characteristic of primitivism, as shown in the worldwide studies of Arthur O. Lovejoy and George Boas, *Primitivism and Related Ideas in Antiquity* (New York: Octagon Books, 1965).

16. A full study of Native Americans who use this primitivist tendency to their advantage has yet to be done. Yet in recent decades this way of managing cultural interrelations has been extensive.

17. For the sandpainting, see Franc J. Newcomb and Gladys A. Reichard, *Sandpaintings of the Navajo Shooting Chant* (New York: Dover Publications, 1975; originally published by J. J. Augustin, New York, 1937). For Reichard's discussion of earth woman, see her *Navaho Religion: A Study of Symbolism* (Tucson: University of Arizona Press, 1983; originally published by Princeton University Press, 1950), p. 431.

Bibliography

Abbott, Rev. John S. C. "Tecumseh," *Ladies Wreath,* May 1850. From Draper Manuscripts, series yy, vol. 3, Tecumseh Papers.

Aberle, David F. "The Prophet Dance and Reaction to White Contact." *Southwestern Journal of Anthropology* 15,1 (1959):74–83.

Alexander, Hartley B. *Mythology of All Races.* Vol. 10: *North American Mythology.* Boston: Marshall Jones, 1916.

Atwood, Margaret. *Survival: A Thematic Guide to Canadian Literature.* Toronto: Anansi, 1972.

Bancroft, Hubert Howe. *The Native Races [of the Pacific States].* 5 vols. San Francisco: A. L. Bancroft, 1882; first published 1874–75.

Barr, G. Walter. "Grouseland." *Chicago Tribune,* March 6, 1886. From Draper Manuscripts, vol. 3, series yy, Tecumseh Papers. See entry for Draper, Lyman D.

Barth, John. *The Sot-Weed Factor.* Garden City: Doubleday, 1960; revised edition, 1967.

Bazhonoodah, Asa. "They are Taking the Holy Elements from Mother Earth." In *The American Indian: The First Victim,* pp. 160–64. Edited by Jay David. New York: William Morrow, 1972.

Bean, Lowell J., and Florence C. Shipek. "Luiseño." In *California: Handbook of North American Indians,* vol. 8, pp. 550–63. Edited by William C. Sturtevant. Washington D.C.: Smithsonian Institution, 1978.

Boas, Franz, ed. *Folk-tales of Salishan and Sahaptin Tribes.* Collected by James A. Teit, Livingstone Farrand, Marian K. Gould, and Herbert J. Spinden. Memoirs of the American Folk-Lore Society, vol. 11. Lancaster, Penn: American Folklore Society, 1917.

173

Bourke, John G. "Notes on the Cosmogony and Theogony of the Mojave Indians of the Rio Colorado, Arizona." *Journal of American Folk-Lore* 2 (1889): 169–89.

Bucher, Bernadette. *Icon and Conquest: A Structural Analysis of the Illustrations of de Bry's "Great Voyages,"* trans. Basia Gulati. Chicago: University of Chicago Press, 1981.

Bunzel, Ruth L. "Introduction to Zuñi Ceremonialism." In *Forty-seventh Annual Report of the Bureau of American Ethnology, 1929–1930.* Washington, D.C.: Government Printing Office, 1932.

Chief Joseph. "An Indian's View of Indian Affairs." Introduced by Wm. H. Hare. *North American Review* 182 (April 1879): 412–33.

Cooper Union Museum for the Arts of Decoration. *The Four Continents from the Collection of James Hazen Hyde.* New York: Cooper Union Museum, 1961.

Curtis, Edward S. *The North American Indian.* Frederick W. Hodge, ed. 20 vols. Norwood, Mass.: Plimpton Press, 1907–30. (Reprinted: Johnson Reprint, New York, 1970.)

Cushing, Frank H. "Outlines of Zuñi Creation Myths." *Thirteenth Annual Report of the Bureau of American Ethnology, 1891–1892.* Washington, D.C.: Government Printing Office, 1896.

———. "Zuñi Breadstuff." *Millstone* 9, nos. 1–12 (1884), and 10, nos. 1–4, 6–8 (1885).

Dawson, Moses. *Historical Narrative of the Civil and Military Services of Major General William H. Harrison....* Cincinnati: The Cincinnati Advertiser, 1824.

Dieterich, Albrecht. *Mutter Erde: Ein Versuch über Volksreligion.* Berlin-Leipzig, 1905.

Dillon, John B. *A History of Indiana, from Its Earliest Exploration by Europeans to the Close of the Territorial Government in 1816.* Indianapolis: Bingham & Doughty, 1859.

Drake, Benjamin. *Life of Tecumseh, and of His Brother The Prophet; with a Historial Sketch of the Shawanoe Indians.* Cincinnati: E. Morgan & Co., 1841.

Drake, Samuel G. *The Book of the Indians; or Biography and History of the Indians of North America, from Its First Discovery to the Year 1841.* Boston: Benjamin B. Mussey, 9th ed., 1845.

Draper Manuscripts, The Lyman D. Draper Manuscripts are available on microfilm from Microfilming Corporation of America. See also *Guide to the Draper Manuscripts.* Madison: State Historical Society of Wisconsin, 1983. The Tecumseh papers are in volume 3, series yy.

Drury, Clifford M. *Henry Harmon Spaulding.* Caldwell, Idaho: Caxton Printers, 1936.

———. *Marcus and Narcissa Whitman, and the Opening of Old Oregon.* Glendale, Calif: A. H. Clark, 1973.

———. *Marcus Whitman, M.D. Pioneer and Martyr.* Caldwell, Idaho: Caxton Printers, 1937.

DuBois, Constance G. "The Mythology of the Diegueños." *Journal of American Folk-Lore* 14 (1901):181–85.

⸻. "Mythology of the Mission Indians." *Journal of American Folk-Lore* 17 (1904):185–88; 19(1906):52–60, 145–64.

⸻. "Religious Ceremonies and Myths of the Mission Indians." *American Anthropologist*, n.s. 7 (1905):620–29.

⸻. "The Religion of the Luiseño and Diegueño Indians of Southern California." *University of California Publications in American Archaeology and Ethnology* 8 (1908):69–186.

Eastman, Charles Alexander. *The Soul of the Indian: An Interpretation.* Reprint ed., New York: Johnson Reprint Company, 1971; originally published in 1911.

Eckert, Allan W. *The Frontiersmen: A Narrative* Boston: Little, Brown, 1967.

Edmunds, R. David. *Tecumseh and the Quest for Indian Leadership.* Boston: Little, Brown, 1984.

Eliade, Mircea. *Myths, Dreams, and Mysteries.* New York: Harper & Row, 1957.

⸻. *Patterns of Comparative Religion.* Cleveland and New York: World, 1958, 1963.

⸻. *The Sacred and the Profane.* New York: Harper and Row, 1957.

Emmons, William. *Tecumseh: or, The Battle of the Thames, a National Drama in Five Acts.* New York: Elton & Harrison, 1836.

Esarey, Logan. *A History of Indiana from Its Exploration to 1850.* Indianapolis: W. K. Stewart Co., 1915.

Esarey, Logan, ed. *Governors Messages and Letters: Messages and Letters of William Henry Harrison.* Vol. 1, *1800–1811.* Indianapolis: Indiana Historical Commission, 1922.

Fleming, E. McClung. "The American Image as Indian Princess." *Winterthur Portfolio* 2, (1968):65–81.

⸻. "Symbols of the United States; From Indian Queen to Uncle Sam." In *The Frontier in American Culture,* pp. 1–24. Edited by Ray Browne et al. Lafayette, Ind.: Purdue University Press, 1967.

Fools Crow v. Gullet, 82–1852 (8th Cir.) May 10, 1983.

Forde, Cyril D. "Ethnography of the Yuma Indians." *University of California Publications in American Archaeology and Ethnography* 28 (1931):83–278.

Frazer, James G. *The Worship of Nature.* New York: Macmillan, 1926.

French, James Strange. *Elkswatawa or, The Prophet of the West. A Tale of the Frontier.* New York: Harper & Brothers, 1836.

Galloway, William Albert. *Old Chillicothe: Shawnee and Pioneer History.* Xenia, Ohio: The Buckeye Press, 1934.

⸻. "A Sacred Slab of the Shawnee Prophet." *Cranbrook Institute of Science News Letter* (1943):6–7.

Gatschet, Albert S. "The Klamath Indians of Southwest Oregon." *Contri-*

butions to North American Ethnology, vol. 2, pts. 1 and 2 (Washington, D.C.: Government Printing Office, 1890).

Gill, Sam. *Native American Religions: An Introduction.* Belmont, Calif.: Wadsworth, 1982.

————. *Native American Religious Action: A Performance Approach to Religion.* Columbia: University of South Carolina Press, 1987.

————. *Native American Traditions: Sources and Interpretations.* Belmont, Calif.: Wadsworth, 1983.

Goltz, Herbert. "Tecumseh, the Prophet and the Rise of the Northwest Indian Confederation." Ph.D. dissertation, University of Western Ontario, 1973.

————. "Tecumseh: The Man and the Myth." M.A. thesis, University of Wisconsin, Milwaukee, 1966.

Green, Jesse. *Zuñi: Selected Writings of Frank Hamilton Cushing.* Lincoln: University of Nebraska Press, 1979.

Green, Rayna. "The Pocahontas Perplex: The Image of Indian Women in American Culture." *The Massachusetts Review* 16 (1976):698–714.

Gregg, Josiah. *Commerce of the Prairies or, The Journal of a Santa Fe Trader, 1831–1839.* Cleveland: 1844, 2 vols.; reprint ed., New York: J. B. Lippincott, 1962.

Grey, Sir George. *Polynesian Mythology and Ancient Traditional History.* Auckland: H. Brett, 1885.

Grinnell, George B. "Tenure of Land among the Indians." *American Anthropologist,* n.s. 9 (1907):1–11.

Haeberlin, H. K. "The Idea of Fertilization in the Culture of the Pueblo Indians." *Memoirs of the American Anthropological Association,* vol. 3, no. 1 (1916):1–55.

Hall, James. *A Memoir of the Public Services of William Henry Harrison, of Ohio.* Philadelphia: Key & Biddle, 1836.

Hamilton, Wynette L. "The Correlation between Societal Attitudes and Those of American Authors in the Depiction of American Indians, 1607–1860." *American Indian Quarterly* 1, no. 1 (1974):1–26.

Harrington, John P. *A New Original Version of Boscana's Historical Account of the San Juan Capistrano Indians of Southern California.* Smithsonian Miscellaneous Collections 92, no. 4 (Washington, D.C., 1934), pp. 1–62.

Harvey, Henry. *History of the Shawnee Indians, from the Year 1681 to 1854, Inclusive.* Cincinnati: Ephraim Morgan & Sons, 1855.

Heizer, Robert F. "Mythology: Regional Patterns and History of Research." In *California: Handbook of North American Indians,* 8:654–57. William C. Sturtevant, general editor. Washington, D.C.: Smithsonian Institution, 1978.

Henshaw, Henry W. "The Luiseño Creation Myth." Robert F. Heizer, ed., *Masterkey* 46 (1972):93–100.

"Hopi Messenger Speaks." *The Northern Light* 2, no. 2 (March 23, 1983):1–2, 5–6.

Howard, Oliver O. *Nez Perce Joseph*. Boston: 1881; reprint ed., New York: Da Capo Press, 1972.

Huggins, E. L. "Smohalla, the Prophet of Priest Rapids." *Overland Monthly*, 2d ser., 17 (1891):208–15.

Hultkrantz, Åke. "Bachofen and the Mother Goddess: An Appraisal after One Hundred Years." *Ethnos* 1 and 2 (1961):75–85.

———. *Belief and Worship in Native North America*. Syracuse: Syracuse University Press, 1981.

———. "The Religion of the Goddess in North America." In *The Book of the Goddess Past and Present: An Introduction to Her Religion*, pp. 202–16. Edited by Carl Olson. New York: Crossroads, 1983.

———. *The Religions of the American Indians*. Berkeley: University of California Press, 1979. Originally published as *De Amerikanska Indianernas Religioner*, 1967.

The Indiana Centinel (newspaper of Vincennes, Indiana), 2 December 1820.

Johnston, Bernice E. *California's Gabrieliño Indians*. Los Angeles: Southwest Museum, 1962.

Keiser, Albert. *The Indian in American Literature*. New York: Oxford University Press, 1933.

Kip, Lawrence. *The Indian Council at Walla Walla*. San Francisco: 1855; reprint ed., Eugene, Ore.: Star Job Office, 1897.

Kroeber, Alfred L. *Handbook of Indians of California*. Bureau of American Ethnology Bulletin 78. Washington, D.C.: Government Printing Office, 1925.

———. "More Mohave Myths." *Anthropological Records*, 27 (1972).

———. "Two Myths of the Mission Indians of California." *Journal of American Folk-Lore* 19 (1906):309–21.

Kroeber, Alfred L., and George W. Grace. "The Sparkman Grammar of Luiseño." *University of California Publications in Linguistics*, 16. Berkeley and Los Angeles: University of California Press, 1960.

Kolodny, Annette. *The Lay of the Land: Metaphor as Experience and History in American Life and Letters*. Chapel Hill: The University of North Carolina Press, 1975.

Lang, Andrew. *Myth, Ritual and Religion*. London: Longmans, Green, 1887.

Le Corbeiller, Clare. "Miss America and Her Sisters: Personifications of the Four Parts of the World." *Bulletin of the Metropolitan Museum of Art*, n.s., 19 (1961):209–23.

Long, Charles H. *Alpha: The Myths of Creation*. New York: George Braziller, 1963.

Lossing, Benson J. *The Pictorial Field Book of the War of 1812*. New York: Harper & Brothers, 1869.

Lovejoy, Arthur O., and George Boas. *Primitivism and Related Ideas in Antiquity*. New York: Octagon Books, 1965.

MacMurray, J. W. "The 'Dreamers' of the Columbia River Valley, in Washington Territory." *Transactions of the Albany Institute*. Albany, 1887, pp. 241–48.

Malcomb, Alexander. *Pontiac; or the Siege of Detroit*. Boston: Samuel Colman, 1835.

Matthiessen, Peter. *Indian Country*. New York: Viking, 1984.

Means, Russell. "Fighting Words on the Future of the Earth." *Mother Jones,* December 1980, pp. 24–38.

Montgomery, H. *The Life of Major-General William H. Harrison, Ninth President of the United States*. New York: C. M. Saxton, Barker & Co., 1860.

Mooney, James. "The Ghost Dance Religion and the Sioux Outbreak of 1890." *Fourteenth Annual Report of the Bureau of Ethnology, 1892–1893*. Washington, D.C.: Government Printing Office, 1896.

Morgan, Lewis Henry. *The Indian Journals, 1859–62*. Ann Arbor: University of Michigan Press, 1959.

Nabokov, Peter. "Return to the Native." *The New York Review of Books,* September 27, 1984, pp. 44–45.

Navajo Medicineman's Association v. Block, 81-0493 (D.D.C.). June 15, 1981.

Newcomb, Franc J., and Gladys A. Reichard. *Sandpaintings of the Navajo Shooting Chant*. New York: J. J. Augustin, 1937; reprint ed., New York: Dover Publications, 1975.

Oskinson, John M. *Tecumseh and His Times: The Story of a Great Indian*. New York: G. P. Putnam's Sons, 1938.

Pearce, Roy Harvey. *Savagism and Civilization: A Study of the Indian and the American Mind*. Baltimore: The Johns Hopkins Press, 1953, 1965.

Pettersson, Olof. *Mother Earth: An Analysis of the Mother Earth Concepts According to Albrecht Dieterich*. Scripta Minora, Regiae Societatis Humanorum Litterum Lundensis, 1965–66, 3. Lund, CWK Gleerup, 1967.

Pew, Thomas W., Jr. "Summit Powwow at Canyon de Chelly." *American West* (November/December 1984):38–44.

Raymond, Ethel T. *Tecumseh: The Last Great Leader of His People*. Toronto: Glasgow, Brook, 1915.

Reichard, Gladys A. *Navaho Religion: A Study of Symbolism*. Princeton, N.J.: Princeton University Press, 1950; reprint ed., Tucson: University of Arizona Press, 1983.

Relander, Click. *Drummers and Dreamers*. Caldwell, Idaho: Caxton Publishers, 1956.

Rourke, Constance. "The Indian Background of American Theatricals." In *Literature of the American Indians: Views and Interpretations*, pp. 256–65. Edited by Abraham Chapman. New York: New American Library, 1975.

Russell, Frank. "The Pima Indians." *Twenty-sixth Annual Report of the Bureau of American Ethnology, 1904–1905*. Washington, D.C.: Government Printing Office, 1908.

"A Scholar's Sacred Quest." *Newsweek,* July 15, 1985, p. 63.

Schoolcraft, Henry Rowe. *Travels in the Central Portions of the Mississippi*

Valley: Comprising Observations on Its Mineral Geography, Internal Resources, Aboriginal Population. New York: Collins & Hanney, 1825.

Seeber, Edward D. "Critical Views on Logan's Speech." *Journal of American Folk-Lore* 60 (1947):130–46.

Seelye, Elizabeth Eggleston. *Tecumseh and the Shawnee Prophet.* New York: Dodd, Mead, 1878.

Sequoyah v. TVA, 79–1633. (6th cir.). April 15, 1980.

Shipek, Florence D. "History of Southern California Mission Indians." In *California: Handbook of North American Indians,* vol. 8, pp. 610–18. William C. Sturtevant, general editor. Washington, D.C.: Smithsonian Institution, 1978.

Slickpoo, Allen P., Sr., and Deward E. Walker, Jr. *Noon Nee-me-poo (We, The Nez Perces).* Lapwai, Idaho: Nez Perce Tribe, 1973.

Smith, Jonathan Z. "The Glory Jest and Riddle: James George Frazer and 'The Golden Bough.'" Ph.D. dissertation, Yale Divinity School, 1969.

———. "When the Bough Breaks." *History of Religions* 12 (1973):342–71.

Smith, O. H. *Early Indiana Trials and Sketches.* Cincinnati: Moore, Wilstach, Keys & Co., 1858.

Southern Literary Messenger, May 1840. See Draper Manuscripts, vol. 3, series yy, Tecumseh Papers, p. 335.

Spier, Leslie. *The Prophet Dance of the Northwest and Its Derivatives: The Source of the Ghost Dance.* General Series in Anthropology, no. 1. Menasha, Wisc.: George Banta, 1935.

Steiger, Brad. *Medicine Talk: A Guide to Walking in Balance and Surviving on the Earth Mother.* Garden City,: Doubleday, 1975.

Steiner, Stan. *The Vanishing White Man.* New York: Harper & Row, 1976.

Stevenson, Matilda Cox. "Ethnobotany of the Zuñi Indians. *30th Annual Report of the Bureau of American Ethnology.* Washington, D.C.: Government Printing Office, 1915.

———. "The Zuñi Indians." *Twenty-third Annual Report of the Bureau of American Ethnology, 1901–1902.* Washington, D.C.: Government Printing Office, 1904.

Tanner, John. *A Narrative of the Captivity and Adventures of John Tanner During 30 Years' Residence Among the Indians of the Interior of North America.* Edited by Edwin James. New York: G. & C. & H. Corvill, 1830.

"Tecumseh." *The National Recorder,* May 12, 1821, p. 299. From Draper Manuscripts, vol. 2, series yy, Tecumseh Papers, p. 160.

Tedlock, Dennis. "Zuni Religion and World View." In *Southwest: Handbook of North American Indians,* vol. 9, pp. 499–508. William C. Sturtevant, general editor. Washington, D.C.: Smithsonian Institution, 1979.

Teit, James A. "Okanagon Tales." In *Folk-Tales of Salishan and Sahaptin Tribes,* pp. 65–97. Edited by Franz Boas. Memoirs of the American Folk-Lore Society, vol. 11, 1917.

Thompson, Stith. *Tales of the North American Indians.* Bloomington: University of Indiana Press, 1929.

Trowbridge, C. C. *Shawnese Traditions*. Edited by Vernon Kinietz and Erminie W. Voegelin. Occasional Contributions from the Museum of Anthropology of the University of Michigan, no. 9. Ann Arbor: University of Michigan Press, 1939.

Tucker, Glenn. *Tecumseh: Vision of Glory*. Indianapolis: Bobbs-Merrill, 1956.

Tylor, Edward B. *Primitive Culture: Researches into the Development of Mythology, Philosophy, Religion, Language, Art and Custom*. 2 vols. London: John Murray, 1873.

U.S. Department of Interior. "Report of Civil and Military Commission to Nez Perce Indians, Washington Territory and the Northwest." *Annual Report of 1877, Indian Affairs*. Washington, D.C., 1877.

Voegelin, C. F. and E. W. "The Shawnee Female Deity." *Yale University Publications in Anthropology*, no. 10 (1936):3–21.

———. "The Shawnee Female Deity in Historical Perspective." *American Anthropologist* n.s. 46 (1944):370–75.

Voget, Fred W. *The Shoshoni-Crow Sun Dance*. Norman: University of Oklahoma Press, 1984.

Walker, Deward E., Jr. *Conflict and Schism in Nez Perce Acculturation: A Study of Religion and Politics*. Pullman: Washington State University Press, 1968.

———. "New Light on the Prophet Dance Controversy." *Ethnohistory* 16, 3 (1969):245–55.

Walker, Dillard. "Zuni Semantic Categories." In *Southwest: Handbook of North American Indians*, vol. 9, pp. 509–13. William C. Sturtevant, general editor. Washington, D.C.: Smithsonian Institution, 1979.

Waterman, Thomas. "Analysis of the Mission Indian Creation Story." *American Anthropologist* n.s. 2 (1909):41–55.

Webster, Homer J. *William Henry Harrison's Administration of Indiana Territory*. Indianapolis: Sentinel Printing Company, 1907.

White, Raymond C. "Luiseño Social Organization." *University of California Publications in American Archaeology and Ethnology* 48 (1963):91–194.

William Henry Harrison: A Political Biography. Indiana Historical Collections, vol. 14. Indianapolis: W. K. Stewart Co., 1926.

Wilson, Raymond. *Ohiyesa: Charles Eastman, Santee Sioux*. Urbana: University of Illinois Press, 1983.

Wilson, William E. *The Wabash*. New York: Farrar and Rinehart, 1940.

Young, Philip. "The Mother of Us All: Pocahontas Reconsidered." *Kenyon Review* 24 (Summer 1962):391–441.

Bibliographic Supplement

The research conducted on the several areas within this study of Mother Earth included hundreds of documents that were not cited in the book. This supplement is intended to make available some of these references and an indication of the relevant content. None of the citations in the notes and bibliography, with a couple of exceptions, has been included herein, thus this should be used to supplement the notes and bibliography. The organization of this section corresponds roughly with the organization of *Mother Earth*.

Tecumseh, Shawnee, and Related History

There are many references that have been used but not cited. Among them are histories of Indiana and surrounding states, and the War of 1812; biographies and studies of William Henry Harrison; the presidential papers of Harrison, Henry Adams, and James Monroe; and biographies and biographical notes on Tecumseh and his prophet brother. Many of these are helpful, yet few need be cited even in a supplement.

Howard, James H. *Shawnee! The Ceremonialism of a Native American Indian Tribe and Its Cultural Background*. Athens: Ohio University Press, 1981. This book offers excellent background for the Shawnee, their history and religious traditions, including much on Tecumseh.

Hunter, John D. *Memoirs of a Captivity among the Indians of North America from Childhood to the Age of Nineteen* . . . . London: Longman, Hurst, Orme, Brown, and Green, 1823. Hunter recalled in his memoirs a speech

181

that Tecumseh made to the Osages around 1812. Hunter quotes Tecumseh as saying, *"Brothers*—My people wish for peace; the red men all wish for peace: but where the white people are, there is no peace for them, except it be on the bosom of our mother" (p. 46).

Smohalla and the Washington Territory

Works consulted that do not appear in the bibliography include:

Bancroft, Hubert H. *The Works of Bancroft.* Vol. 30, *History of Oregon.* Vol. 31, *History of Washington.* San Francisco: The History Co., 1886–88.

Clark, Elle E. "George Gibb's Account of Indian Mythology in Oregon and Washington Territories." *Oregon Historical Society Quarterly* 56 (1955):293–324 and 57 (1956):125–67.

Curtis, Edward S. *The North American Indian.* Vol. 8, *The Nez Perces.* Frederick W. Hodge, ed. Norwood, Mass.: Plimpton Press, 1907–1930. (Reprinted: Johnson Reprint, New York, 1970).

Garth, Thomas R. "Early Nineteenth Century Tribal Relations in the Columbia Plateau." *Southwest Journal of Anthropology* 20 (1964):43–57.

Gunther, Erna. "The Indian Background of Washington History." *Pacific Northwest Quarterly* 41 (1950):189–202.

Howard, Helen Addison. "Isaac Ingalls Stevens: First Governor of Washington Territory." *Journal of the West* 2 (1963):336–46.

Howard, Oliver O. *My Life and Experiences Among Our Hostile Indians.* Hartford, Conn.: A. T. Worthington, 1907.

Josephy, Alvin M., Jr. *The Nez Perce Indians and the Opening of the Northwest.* New Haven: Yale University Press, 1969.

———. *The Patriot Chiefs; A Chronicle of American Indian Leadership.* New York: Penguin Books, 1976.

Kappler, Charles J., ed. *Indian Affairs: Laws and Treaties.* Washington, D.C.: U.S. Government Printing Office, 1904. See "Treaty with the Walla Walla, Cayuse, etc., 1855," vol. 2, *Treaties,* pp. 694–706.

Kip, Lawrence. *Army Life on the Pacific Coast, A Journal of the Expedition against the Northern Indians in the Summer of 1858.* New York: Redfield, 1859.

Letters Received by the Office of Indian Affairs, 1824–81. National Archives, Washington, D.C., Microcopy No. 234, 1958. Includes letters and communications regarding treaties and negotiations in the Washington Territory.

Murdock, George P. "Tenino Shamanism." *Ethnology* 4, no. 2 (1965):165–71.

Ray, Verne F., et al. "Tribal Distributions in Eastern Oregon and Adjacent Regions." *American Anthropologist,* n.s. 40 (1938):384–415.

Spier, Leslie, and Edward Sapir. *Wishram Ethnography.* University of Washington Publications in Anthropology, vol. 3. Seattle, Wash.: 1930. See "The Smohallah Cult," pp. 251–54.

Spinden, Herbert Joseph. *The Nez Perce Indians*. Memoirs of the American Anthropological Association, vol. 2, pt. 3. Lancaster, Penn.: 1908.

Stern, Theodore. "The Klamath Indians and the Treaty of 1864." *Oregon Historical Society Quarterly* 57 (1956):229–73.

Teit, James A. "Tahltan Tales." *Journal of American Folk-Lore* 32 (1919):198–250.

U.S. Congress, House of Representatives. *Indian Disturbances in Oregon and Washington*. Ex. Doc. No. 48, 34th Cong., 1st Sess., 1856. See statements by George W. Maypenny and Isaac I. Stevens.

U.S. Congress. Senate. *Special Message of Gov. Isaac I. Stevens to Joint Session of Council and House of Representatives, Washington Territory, Monday, January 21, 1856*. Ex. Doc. No. 66, 34th Cong., 1st Sess., 1856.

Walen, Sue. "The Nez Perces' Relationship to Their Land." *The Indian Historian* 4, no. 3 (Fall 1971):30–33.

Luiseño and Other Southern California and Southwest Tribes

A large number of documents pertaining to the many tribes in southern California and Arizona have been examined for evidence of Mother Earth or the presence of other goddesses. The following are those of most significance; however, as indicated in Chapter 4, no evidence of Mother Earth, an earth goddess, or a female earth creator was found.

Curtis, Edward S. *The North American Indian*. 20 volumes. Frederick W. Hodge, ed. Norwood, Mass.: Plimpton Press, 1907–30. (Reprinted: Johnson Reprint, New York, 1970). See vol. 2 for Mohave creation story, pp. 56–67, vol. 2 for Maricopa creation story, p. 86, and vol. 15 for Diegueño creation story, pp. 121–24.

Densmore, Frances. *Yuman and Yaqui Music*. Bureau of American Ethnology, Bulletin 110. Washington, D.C.: Government Printing Office, 1932. See reference to earth-sky parentage, p. 5.

Devereux, George. "The Social and Cultural Implications of Incest Among Mohave Indians." *Psychoanalytic Quarterly* 8 (1939):510–33.

DuBois, Constance G. "Ceremonies and Traditions of the Diegueño Indians." *Journal of American Folk-Lore* 21 (1908):228–36.

————. "Diegueño Myths and Their Connection with the Mohave." *International Congress of Americanists, Proceedings*, vol. 2 (1906):129–33.

Harrington, John P. "Yuma Account of Origins." *Journal of American Folk-Lore* 21 (1908):324–48.

Hooper, Lucile. "The Cahuilla Indians." *University of California Publications in American Archaeology and Ethnography* 16, no. 6 (1920:316–80. See "Origin Beliefs," pp. 317–21.

Johnston, Bernice Eastman. *California's Gabrielino Indians*. Los Angeles: Southwest Museum, 1962. First published in series in *Masterkey* 1955–58.

Kroeber, Albert L. "The Religion of the Indians of California." *University of California Publications in American Archaeology and Ethnology* 4, no. 6 (1907):320–56. See "Mythology and Beliefs," pp. 342–46.

———. "The Mission Indians." *Journal of American Folk-Lore* 19 (1906):312–14.

Kroeber, Henriette R. "Traditions of Papago Indians." *Journal of American Folk-Lore* 25 (1912):95–105.

Sparkman, Philip S. "Culture of Luiseño Indians." *University of California Publications in American Archaeology and Ethnography* 8, no. 4 (1908):187–234.

Spier, Leslie. "Southern Diegueño Customs." *University of California Publications in American Archaeology and Ethnology* 20, no. 16 (1923):295–358

Waterman, T. T. "The Religious Practices of the Diegueño." *University of California Publications in American Archaeology and Ethnography* 8, no. 6 (1910):271–358.

White, Raymond C. "The Luiseño Theory of 'Knowledge'." *American Anthropologist* 59 (1957): 1–19.

Woodward, John A. "The Anniversary: A Contemporary Diegueño Complex." *Ethnology* 7 (1968):86–94.

Zuni and Other Pueblos

The literature for the Pueblo tribes in the southwestern United States is enormous. Of this literature, the following items are helpful in ascertaining the many story and ritual figures that are relevant to a study of Mother Earth.

Benedict, Ruth. *Zuni Mythology.* Columbia University Contributions to Anthropology, no. 21. New York, 1935.

———. "Tales of the Cochiti Indians." *Bureau of American Ethnology, Bulletin* 98. Washington, D.C.: Government Printing Office, 1931.

Boas, Franz. *Keresan Texts.* American Ethnological Society, vol. 8, pt. 1. New York: G. E. Stechert, 1928.

Bradfield, Richard M., Jr. *A Natural History of Associations: A Study in the Meaning of Community.* Tiptree, Great Britain: Gerald Duckworth: 1973. See vol. 2, pp. 426 and 441, for reference to Tü'wa-poñya-tümsi as mother of all living things.

Bunzel, Ruth L. "Zuni Origin Myth" and "Ritual Poetry." *Forty-seventh Annual Report of the Bureau of American Ethnology, 1929–1930.* Washington, D.C.: Government Printing Office, 1932.

———. *Zuni Texts. Publications of American Ethnological Society,* no. 15. New York, 1933.

Cushing, Frank Hamilton. "Zuni Fetishes." *Second Annual Report of the Bureau of American Ethnology, 1880–1881.* Washington, D.C.: Government Printing Office, 1883.

———. *Zuni Tales*. New York: G. P. Putnam's Sons, 1901.

Densmore, Frances. "Music of Santo Domingo Pueblo, New Mexico." *Southwest Museum Papers,* no. 12. Los Angeles, Calif., 1938. See "Song Concerning the Corn Harvest," pp. 110–11.

Dozier, Edward P. *Pueblo Indians of North America.* New York: Holt, Rinehart & Winston, 1970.

Fewkes, J. Walter. "Hopi Katcinas Drawn by Native Artists." *Twenty-first Annual Report of the Bureau of American Ethnology, 1899–1900.* Washington, D.C.: The Government Printing Office, 1903. See Earth-goddess reference, p. 55.

———. "Hopi Shrines Near the East Mesa, Arizona." *American Anthropologist,* n.s. 8 (1906):346–75. See especially pp. 350–51.

———. "An Interpretation of Katcina Worship." *Journal of American Folk-Lore* 14 (1901):81–94.

———. "The Lesser New Fire Ceremony at Walpi." *American Anthropologist,* n.s. 3 (1901):438–53. See names associated with Earth-Mother, p. 449.

———. "The Tusayan Ritual; A Study of the Influence of Environment on Aboriginal Cults." *Smithsonian Institution Annual Report for the Year Ending June 30, 1895.* Washington, D.C.: Government Printing Office, 1896. See Mother-Earth-related reference, p. 688.

Fox, Robin. *Encounter with Anthropology.* New York: Harcourt Brace Jovanovich, 1968; rev. ed., 1975. See reference to absence of Pueblo belief in Mother Earth, pp. 258 and 260.

Newmann, Stanley. *Zuni Grammar.* University of New Mexico Publications in Anthropology, no. 15 (1965).

Parsons, Elsie Clews. *Pueblo Indian Religion.* Chicago: University of Chicago Press, 1939.

———. "The Religion of the Pueblo Indians." *International Congress of Americanists, Proceedings,* vol. 21 (1924):140–61.

———. "Taos Pueblo." *General Series in Anthropology,* vol. 2. Menasha, Wisc., 1936. See "our tender prostrate Earth Mother," p. 108.

Purley, Anthony F. "Keres Pueblo Concepts of Deity." *American Indian Culture and Research Journal* 1 (1974):29–32.

Stevenson, Matilda Cox. "Zuni Ancestral Gods and Masks." *American Anthropologist,* o.s. 11 (1898):33–40. See Shi wano-ʇka identified as Earth-mother, pp. 33–34.

———. "The Religious Life of the Zuni Child." *Fifth Annual Report of the Bureau of American Ethnology, 1883–1884.* Washington, D.C.: Government Printing Office, 1887.

Stirling, Matthew W. "Origin Myth of Acoma." *Bureau of American Ethnology, Bulletin* 135. Washington, D.C.: Government Printing Office, 1942.

Tedlock, Dennis. *Finding the Center: Narrative Poetry of the Zuni Indians.* New York: Dial Press, 1972.

White, Leslie A. "The Pueblo of Sia, New Mexico." *Bureau of American*

Ethnology, Bulletin 184. Washington, D.C.: Government Printing Office, 1962.

―――. "The Pueblo of Santa Ana." *Memoirs of the American Association of Anthropology* 60. Menasha, Wisc., 1942.

―――. "The World of the Keresan Pueblo Indians." In Stanley Diamond, ed. *Primitive Views of the World*. New York: Columbia University Press, 1969, pp. 53–64. See reference to burial as return to the mother and to the four-fold womb of earth, pp. 56, 58.

Other Tribes in North America

The identification of figures as Mother Earth, or some permutation of that name, can be found here and there in the ethnographic literature for North America. In most cases the names given these figures amount to an interpretive gloss rather than to a careful translation of the tribal name. Nonetheless, as I found these references during my search for Mother Earth among tribal cultures, I analyzed their sources for a fuller consideration of the cultures in which the references appeared. No one of the references led to the establishment of a figure named Mother Earth or one having her characteristics. While they do not contribute significantly to the story of Mother Earth, quotation and citation of these statements suggest how many other chapters to the Mother Earth story might be told. The list demonstrates the range of references I have found but is likely not exhaustive for the full ethnographic literature.

Converse, Harriet Maxwell. "Myths and Legends of the New York State Iroquois." *New York State Museum Bulletin* 125. Albany, 1908.

> "Hah-gweh-di-ya [Converse renders this 'Spirit of Evil'] then drew forth from the breast of his Mother, the Moon and the Stars, and led them to the Sun as his sisters who would guard his night sky. He gave the Earth her body, its Great Mother, from whom was to spring all life" (p. 35). See also pp. 48–49.

Dorsey, George A. *The Pawnee: Mythology.* part I. Washington, D.C.: Carnegie Institution, 1906.

> " . . . at the sound of his [Tirawa's, the creator] voice a woman appeared upon the earth. . . . Tirawa made a man and sent him to the woman; then he said: 'Now I will speak to both of you. I give you the earth. You shall call the earth "mother." The heavens you shall call "father." You shall also call the moon "mother," for she rises in the east; and you shall call the sun "father," for he rises in the east. . . . The earth I give you, and you are to call her "mother," for she gives birth to all things. . . . Never forget to call the earth "mother," for you are to live upon her. You must love her, for you must walk upon her" (pp. 13–14).
>
> "Tirawa then spoke and said: 'I told you to call the earth "mother." The lodge represents the mother's breast. The smoke that escapes from the opening is like milk that flows from the mother's breast. . .'" (pp. 15–16).

Dorsey, George A. *Mythology of the Wichita*. Washington, D.C.: Carnegie Institute, vol. 21, 1904.

"When the Wind first got the child, on the fourth visit, there was the child and no woman, so he called the woman the Earth, the mother of the first woman born after the deluge, and this is why we call the Earth 'mother'" (p. 29).

Dorsey, J. O. "Study of Siouan Cults." *Eleventh Annual Report of the Bureau of American Ethnology, 1889–1890*. Washington, D.C.: Government Printing Office, 1894. See Mother-Earth reference, p. 513.

Frisbie, Charlotte. *Kinaaldá: A Study of the Navajo Girls' Puberty Ceremony*. Middleton, Conn.: Wesleyan University Press, 1967.

"She [Changing Woman] also told the people to make a round cake, representing Mother Earth during the Kinaaldá" (p. 12).

Fletcher, Alice C., and Francis LaFlesche. "The Omaha Tribe." *Twenty-seventh Annual Report of the Bureau of American Ethnology, 1905–1906*. Washington, D.C.: Government Printing Office, 1911.

"The Above was regarded as masculine, the Below feminine; so the sky was father, the earth, mother" (p. 134).

Franciscan Fathers. *An Ethnologic Dictionary of the Navajo Language*. St. Michaels, Ariz.: The Franciscan Fathers, 1910.

"The sky is considered male, the earth female, and both are in the relation of man and wife to each other. The earth may also be considered the mother of all living, insomuch as it provides vegetable life, and harbors many insects and animals in addition to being the abode of man" (p. 35).

Grinnell, George. B. *The Cheyenne Indians, Their History and Ways of Life*. New Haven: Yale University Press, 1923.

" . . . the power of the earth is named in prayer. It is implored to make everything grow which we eat, so that we may live; to make the water flow, that we may drink; to keep the ground firm, that we may walk on it; to make grow those plants and herbs that we use to heal ourselves when we are sick; and to cause to grow also the grass on which the animals feed" (vol. 2, pp. 88–89).

_____. "Pawnee Mythology." *Journal of American Folk-Lore* 6 (1893):113–30.

"Next in importance to Atius [father, Tirawa] comes the Earth, which is greatly reverenced. The Pawnee came out of the earth and return to it again. . . . Not very much is said by the Pawnees about the reverence which they feel for the earth, but much is told about the power of Mother Corn" (p 114).

Hatt, Gudmund. "The Corn Mother in American and in Indonesia." *Anthropos* 46 (1951):853–914. This article contains many references to corn women and corn mothers in America.

Heckewelder, Rev. John. "An Account of the History, Manners, and Customs of the Indian Nations who once inhabited Pennsylvania and the Neighboring States." *Transactions of the Historical and Literary Committee of the American Philosophical Society*. Philadelphia, 1819.

"The Indians consider the earth as their universal mother. They believe that they were created within its bosom, where for a long time they had their abode, before they came to its surface" (p. 241).

Jones, William. "Ethnography of the Fox Indians." *Bureau of American Ethnology, Bulletin* 125. Washington, D.C.: Government Printing Office, 1939.

"The earth on which we live is a woman. . . . She provides us with all the food we eat and lets us live and dwell upon her" (p. 20).

McClintock, Walter, *The Old North Trail; or Life, Legends and Religion of the Blackfeet Indians.* London: Macmillan, 1910.

"Great Sun Power! I am praying for my people that they may be happy in the summer and that they may live through the cold winter. . . . Help us, Mother Earth! for we depend on your goodness. Let there be rain to water the prairies, that the grass may grow long and the berries be abundant. O Morning Star! . . . Great Spirit! . . . " (p. 297).

Melody, Michael. "Maka's Story: A Study of a Lakota Cosmogony." *Journal of American Folk-Lore* 90 (1977):149–67.

According to Melody, Maka is Earth. Inyan, who is the rock, gave Maka a spirit which is Maka-akan or Earth-goddess. Melody's essay is a study of Maka.

Radin, Paul. "The Winnebago Tribe." *Thirty-seventh Annual Report of the Bureau of American Ethnology, 1915–1916.* Washington, D.C.: Government Printing Office, 1923.

"[The Winnebago] look upon earth as a goddess. She is indeed one of the most ancient deities of the tribe, and appears as the Grandmother in some of their oldest myths. Offerings are made to her at various ceremonies, particularly the medicine-dance and the war bundle feast. However, in the myths she is represented as a being nowise interested in furthering the welfare of mankind. On the contrary, she is spoken of as the sister of those bad spirits who are bent on destroying the human race" (p. 286). See also pp. 440, 449, 459, 469, 536.

Reagan, Albert. "Whaling of the Olympic Peninsula Indians of Washington." *Natural History* 25 (1925):25–32. See reference to Se-kah-til rendered by Reagan as Mother Earth, pp. 27 and 31.

Smith, Erminie. "Myths of the Iroquois." *Second Annual Report of the Bureau of American Ethnology, 1880–1881.* Washington, D.C.: Government Printing Office, 1881. Smith says that under mission influence the Iroquois developed a form of trinity "consisting of the Great Spirit, the Sun, and Mother Earth" (p. 53).

Speck, Frank G. *A Study of the Delaware Indian Big House Ceremony.* Harrisburg: Publications of the Pennsylvania Historical Commission, 1931. Speck holds that the Delaware believe they "dwell upon our mother's body" (p. 81) and that "turtle holds up our mother's body" (p. 101).

Wildschut, William. "Crow Indian Medicine Bundles." In John C. Ewers, ed. *Contributions from the Museum of the American Indian, Heye Founda-*

tion, vol. 17. New York: Museum of the American Indian, Heye Foundation, 1960.

"The earth is regarded as our mother. From it is born our body and to it the body returns after death" (p. 2).

Will, George F., and George E. Hyde. *Corn Among the Indians of the Upper Missouri.* St. Louis: The William Harvey Minor Co., 1917. The authors suggest that corn "symbolizes" Mother Earth for the Sioux and Pawnee (p. 205). See also a reference to Mother Earth related to the pipe-smoking ceremony during the Arapaho Sun Dance (p. 263, n. 20).

Witherspoon, Gary. *Navajo Kinship and Marriage.* Chicago: University of Chicago Press, 1975.

"Essential parts, as well as the earth itself, are called mother. Agricultural fields are called mother, corn is called mother, and sheep are called mother. . . . motherhood is defined in terms of the source, sustenance, and reproduction of life" (p. 16). See also pp. 21 and 68.

Wyman, Leland C. *Blessingway.* Tucson: University of Arizona Press, 1970. See references to "the Earth" as female related to the male "Sky" in Frank Mitchell's version of this story, pp. 462–64.

Mother Worship and Mother Goddess Scholarship

There are a great many scholarly studies on mother goddesses, the mother goddess as a type, and mother worship. The following are a few of the most important and representative of these kinds of studies.

Alexander, Hartley Burr. *The World's Rim: Great Mysteries of the North American Indians.* Lincoln: University of Nebraska Press, 1953. Alexander makes many references to Mother Earth, including references to statements by Tecumseh and Smohalla. His model for interpreting Native American religions is essentially derived from Greek religion. See pp. 91, 92, 187.

Briffault, Robert. *The Mothers: A Study of the Origins and Sentiments and Institutions.* New York: Macmillan, 1927. See the discussion of Mother Earth, vol. 3, pp. 54–61.

Jung, Carl G. *The Archetypes and the Collective Unconscious.* 2d ed. Princeton: Princeton University Press, 1969. See Jung's discussion of the Mother Earth archetype, pp. 105–10 and 183–88.

Neumann, Erich. *The Great Mother: An Analysis of the Archetype.* Bollingen Series 47. Princeton: Princeton University Press, 1955.

Preston, James J., ed. *Mother Worship: Theme and Variations.* Chapel Hill: University of North Carolina Press, 1982.

Schmidt, Wilhelm. "The Position of Women with Regard to Property in Primitive Society." *American Anthropologist,* n.s. 37 (1935):244–56. See his discussion of Mother Earth, p. 252.

General References to Mother Earth

There are hundreds of references in general and popular literature to Mother Earth as "the goddess of the Indians." I have made no attempt to extensively collect such references, for they are so numerous, particularly in recent years, as to be nearly daily appearances in newspapers and magazines. I have collected some of the more distinctive references and those that are likely to have been more widely read and known. A selection of these follows.

Catlin, George. *George Catlin: Letters and Notes on the North American Indians*. Michael McDonald Mooney, ed. New York: Clarkson N. Potter, 1975.

> "In the 1740s the Iroquois granted control of the upper Ohio to a Virginia real estate company. 'The land is our Mother,' went the Iroquois tradition. 'How can we sell our Mother?'" (p. 51).
> "Tecumseh, Shawnee Chief in the Ohio Valley, repeated the pattern. He insisted the land was held by all tribes in common and no one tribe could sell its particular tract: 'Sell a country! Why not sell the air, the clouds, and the great sea? . . . Did not the Great Spirit make them all for the use of his children?'" (p. 54).

Collier, John. *From Every Zenith: A Memoir and Some Essays on Life and Thought*. Denver: Sage Books, 1963. Mother-Earth reference, p. 183.

Gilmore, Melvin R. *Prairie Smoke*. New York: Columbia University Press, 1929. Gilmore is strongly influenced by Greek religion. See section of stories entitled "Mother Earth," pp. 1–42.

Hughes, J. Donald. *American Indian Ecology*. El Paso: Texas Western Press, 1983. See his chapter "The Gifts of Mother Earth."

Indians of All Tribes. "Planning Grant Proposal to Develop an All-Indian University and Cultural Complex on Indian Land, Alcatraz." In *Congressional Record*, 91st Congress, 2nd Session. Quoted in *Great Documents in American Indian History*. Wayne Moguin, ed. New York: Praeger, 1973, pp. 374–79. See references to Mother Earth, pp. 374 and 375.

Josephy, Alvin M., Jr. *The Indian Heritage of America*. New York: Bantam, 1969. See reference to Mother Earth, related to Taos Pueblo, p. 26.

Leupp, Francis. *The Indian and His Problem*. New York: Charles Scribner's Sons, 1910. Leupp referes to "the earth, mother of all," on p. 275.

Matthews, John Joseph (Osage). "Planting Moon." *Nimrod* 16, no. 2 (1972):76ff. Matthews refers to "Mother Earth" on p. 76.

Morgan, Dan. "A Revolution on the Reservation: Indian Schools Stressing 'Cultural Awareness'." *Washington Post*, Monday, November 17, 1980. This article includes contemporary Indian quotations about Mother Earth.

Quetone, Allen, et al. "A Symposium on Indian Education, June, 1968." In *Can the Red Man Help the White Man?* Sylvester M. Morrey, ed. New York: G. Church, 1970. Quoted in *Great Documents in American Indian*

History. Wayne Moguin, ed. New York: Praeger, 1973. Joshua Wetsit, an Assinoboine, makes reference to Mother Earth p. 363.

Steiger, Stan. *Medicine Talk: A Guide to Walking in Balance and Surviving on the Earth Mother*. Garden City, N.Y.: Doubleday, 1975. See poem by Seneca Twylah Nitsch, pp. 42–45.

Steiner, Stan. *The New Indians*. New York: Harper & Row, 1968. This book has numerous references to Earth Mother. See for example pp. 218–19.

————. *The Vanishing White Man*. New York: Harper & Row, 1976. A Hopi, Alvin Dashee, makes a statement related to Mother Earth, p. 14.

Udall, Stewart. *The Quiet Crisis*. New York: Holt, Rinehart & Winston, 1963.

"The land and the Indians were bound together by the ties of kinship and nature, rather than by an understanding of property ownership. 'The land is our mother,' said Iroquois tradition, said the Midwest Sauk and Foxes, said the Northwest Nez Perce Chief Joseph. The corn, fruits, roots, fish, and game were to all tribes the gifts which the Earth Mother gave freely to her children" (p. 5).

Index

193